D0029946

DREAMS

from

The Collected Works of C. G. Jung

VOLUMES 4, 8, 12, 16

BOLLINGEN SERIES XX

The Dream of Nebuchadnezzar
From the "Speculum humanae salvationis," Codex Palatinus Latinus 413,
Vatican, 15th cent. (see p. 79)

DREAMS

C. G. JUNG

TRANSLATED BY R.F.C. HULL

BOLLINGEN SERIES

PRINCETON UNIVERSITY PRESS

COPYRIGHT © 1974 BY PRINCETON UNIVERSITY PRESS
PRINCETON, NEW JERSEY

All Rights Reserved

"The Analysis of Dreams" and "On the Significance of Number Dreams" extracted from Volume 4 in The Collected Works of C. G. Jung, *Freud and Psychoanalysis,* Copyright © 1961 by Bollingen Foundation, New York. "General Aspects of Dream Psychology" and "On the Nature of Dreams" extracted from Volume 8, *The Structure and Dynamics of the Psyche,* Copyright © 1960 by Bollingen Foundation, New York, N.Y.; 2nd Edn., Copyright © 1969 by Princeton University Press. "The Practical Use of Dream-Analysis" extracted from Volume 16, *The Practice of Psychotherapy,* Copyright 1954 by Bollingen Foundation Inc., New York, N.Y.; new material Copyright © 1966 by Bollingen Foundation. "Individual Dream Symbolism in Relation to Alchemy" extracted from Volume 12, *Psychology and Alchemy,* Copyright 1953 by Bollingen Foundation Inc., New York, N.Y.; new material Copyright © 1968 by Bollingen Foundation.

All the volumes comprising the *Collected Works* constitute number XX in Bollingen Series, under the editorship of Herbert Read (d. 1968), Michael Fordham, and Gerhard Adler; executive editor, William McGuire.

First Princeton/Bollingen Paperback Edition, 1974

LIBRARY OF CONGRESS CATALOGUE CARD NUMBER: 72-11949
ISBN 0-691-01792-1
PRINTED IN THE UNITED STATES OF AMERICA

EDITORIAL NOTE

"For many years I have carefully analysed about 2,000 dreams per annum, thus I have acquired a certain experience in this matter,"[1] C. G. Jung wrote in 1954, when he was seventy-nine.

Dreams are the very fabric of the analytical process, whether it is called psychoanalysis in Freud's system or analytical psychology in Jung's, and the writings of both of the great pioneers are thronged with accounts and analyses of dreams and expositions of dream theory. Jung's earliest work that we know was a report of Freud's *On Dreams* which he prepared for his colleagues at the Burghölzli Asylum in 1900. During his period of activity as a psychoanalyst, he published several papers on dreams, and two of these are included in the present selection. Each of the other papers reprinted here, first published between 1916 and 1945, is a significant statement on diverse aspects of Jung's dream psychology.

These papers by no means exhaust Jung's contributions on dreams. The index of Jung's autobiographical *Memories, Dreams, Reflections*, edited by Aniela Jaffé, lists in its index no fewer than forty-two of Jung's own dreams which he recounts as key episodes in his life course. Many others are described in his *Letters*, selected and edited by Gerhard Adler. The famous seminar on "Dream Analysis," which Jung gave to a small group of students in Zurich in 1928–29, is devoted to the discussion-in-depth of a great many dreams brought to him by patients. (Published version in preparation, edited by R.F.C. Hull.) Each volume of the *Collected Works* contains dream material, and the volume indexes catalogue, by descriptive phrases, all the dreams that Jung discusses. Finally, a valuable distillation of Jung's statements on dreams is to be found under that rubric in the anthology *Psychological Reflections* (new edition, 1970; Princeton/Bollingen Paperback no. 284), edited by Jolande Jacobi and R.F.C. Hull.

---

[1] Letter of 8 Nov. 1954 to Calvin S. Hall, *C. G. Jung: Letters*, ed. Gerhard Adler in collaboration with Aniela Jaffé, vol. 2 (1974).

*

For the paperback edition, the paragraph numbers of the *Collected Works* have been retained to facilitate reference, at well as the original figure numbers for the illustrations in "Individual Dream Symbolism in Relation to Alchemy." The index and bibliography have been reworked for this presentation.

TABLE OF CONTENTS

PART III

THE PRACTICAL USE OF DREAM-ANALYSIS

PART IV

INDIVIDUAL DREAM SYMBOLISM IN RELATION TO ALCHEMY

NOTE OF ACKNOWLEDGMENT

The illustrations are derived from:

(1) Rare books, MSS., and other works in the author's collection at Küsnacht, which have been reproduced by kind permission of Mr. Franz Jung and photographed under the supervision of Mrs. Aniela Jaffé; indicated by the initials "C.G.J."

(2) Rare books in Mr. Paul Mellon's former collection, reproduced by kind permission of him and of the Yale University Library, where the collection has been deposited under the name "Mellon Collection of the Alchemical and Occult"; photographed by Yale University Library; indicated by the initials "M.C.A.O."

(3) Photographs in private collections, in particular that of Dr. Jolande Jacobi, Zurich, and that of the C. G. Jung Institute, Zurich (indicated as "Inst.").

(4) Books, MSS., and other works in various museums, libraries, archives, etc., as indicated; photographed by the institution unless otherwise noted. Commercial photographic agencies are credited.

(5) In a few cases, the blocks used in earlier editions and kindly made available by Rascher Verlag, Zurich.

LIST OF ILLUSTRATIONS

References to documentary sources, which are somewhat shortened in the captions to the illustrations, are given more fully in this list.

xiii

xvii

I

DREAMS AND PSYCHOANALYSIS

THE ANALYSIS OF DREAMS [1]

64   In 1900, Sigmund Freud published in Vienna a voluminous
work on the analysis of dreams. Here are the principal results
of his investigations.

65   The dream, far from being the confusion of haphazard and
meaningless associations it is commonly believed to be, or a
result merely of somatic sensations during sleep as many authors
suppose, is an autonomous and meaningful product of psychic
activity, susceptible, like all other psychic functions, of a systematic analysis. The organic sensations felt during sleep are
not the cause of the dream; they play but a secondary role and
furnish only elements (the material) upon which the psyche
works. According to Freud the dream, like every complex psychic product, is a creation, a piece of work which has its motives,
its trains of antecedent associations; and like any considered
action it is the outcome of a logical process, of the competition
between various tendencies and the victory of one tendency
over another. Dreaming has a meaning, like everything else we
do.

66   It may be objected that all empirical reality is against this
theory, since the impression of incoherence and obscurity that
dreams make upon us is notorious. Freud calls this sequence of
confused images the *manifest content* of the dream; it is the
façade behind which he looks for what is essential—namely, the
dream-thought or the *latent content*. One may ask what reason
Freud has for thinking that the dream itself is only the façade
of a vast edifice, or that it really has any meaning. His supposition is not founded on a dogma, nor on an *a priori* idea, but on
empiricism alone—namely, the common experience that no
psychic (or physical) fact is accidental. It must have, then, its

1 [Written in French. Translated by Philip Mairet from "L'Analyse des rêves,"
Année psychologique (Paris), XV (1909), 160–67, and revised by R. F. C. Hull.
—Editors.]

train of causes, being always the product of a complicated combination of phenomena; for every existing mental element is the resultant of anterior psychic states and ought in theory to be capable of analysis. Freud applies to the dream the same principle that we always instinctively use when inquiring into the causes of human actions.

67   He asks himself, quite simply: why does this particular person dream this particular thing? He must have his specific reasons, otherwise there would be a breakdown in the law of causality. A child's dream is different from an adult's, just as the dream of an educated man differs from that of an illiterate. There is something individual in the dream: it is in agreement with the psychological disposition of the subject. In what does this psychological disposition consist? It is itself the result of our psychic past. Our present mental state depends upon our history. In each person's past there are elements of different value which determine the psychic "constellation." The events which do not awaken any strong emotions have little influence on our thoughts or actions, whereas those which provoke strong emotional reactions are of great importance for our subsequent psychological development. These memories with a strong feeling-tone form complexes of associations which are not only long enduring but are very powerful and closely interlinked. An object which I regard with little interest calls forth few associations and soon vanishes from my intellectual horizon. An object in which, on the contrary, I feel much interest will evoke numerous associations and preoccupy me for a long while. Every emotion produces a more or less extensive complex of associations which I have called the "feeling-toned complex of ideas." In studying an individual case history we always discover that the complex exerts the strongest "constellating" force, from which we conclude that in any analysis we shall meet with it from the start. The complexes appear as the chief components of the psychological disposition in every psychic structure. In the dream, for example, we encounter the emotional components, for it is easy to understand that all the products of psychic activity depend above all upon the strongest "constellating" influences.

68   One does not have to look far to find the complex that sets Gretchen, in *Faust,* singing:

4

> There was a king in Thule,
> True even to his grave—
> To him his dying mistress
> A golden beaker gave.

69   The hidden thought is Gretchen's doubt about Faust's fidelity. The song, unconsciously chosen by Gretchen, is what we have called the *dream-material,* which corresponds to the secret thought. One might apply this example to the dream, and suppose that Gretchen had not sung but dreamed this romance.[2] In that case the song, with its tragic story of the loves of a far-off king of old, is the "manifest content" of the dream, its "façade." Anyone who did not know of Gretchen's secret sorrow would have no idea why she dreamt of this king. But we, who know the dream-thought which is her tragic love for Faust, can understand why the dream makes use of this particular song, for it is about the "rare faithfulness" of the king. Faust is not faithful, and Gretchen would like his faithfulness to her to resemble that of the king in the story. Her dream—in reality her song—expresses in a disguised form *the ardent desire of her soul.* Here we touch upon the real nature of the feeling-toned complex; it is always a question of *a wish and resistance to it.* Our life is spent in struggles for the realization of our wishes: all our actions proceed from the wish that something should or should not come to pass.

70   It is for this that we work, for this we think. If we cannot fulfil a wish in reality, we realize it at least in fantasy. The religious and the philosophic systems of every people in every age are the best proof of this. The thought of immortality, even in philosophic guise, is no other than a wish, for which philosophy is but the façade, even as Gretchen's song is only the outward form, a beneficent veil drawn over her grief. *The dream represents her wish as fulfilled.* Freud says that *every dream represents the fulfilment of a repressed wish.*

71   Carrying our illustration further, we see that in the dream

---

2 It might be objected that such a supposition is not permissible, as there is a great deal of difference between a song and a dream. But thanks to the researches of Freud we now know that all the products of any dreaming state have something in common. First, they are all variations on the complex, and second, they are only a kind of symbolic expression of the complex. That is why I think I am justified in making this supposition.

Faust is replaced by the king. A transformation has taken place. Faust has become the far-off old king; the personality of Faust, which has a strong feeling-tone, is replaced by a neutral, legendary person. The king is an association by analogy, a *symbol* for Faust, and the "mistress" for Gretchen. We may ask what is the purpose of this arrangement, why Gretchen should dream, so to speak, indirectly about this thought, why she cannot conceive it clearly and without equivocation. This question is easily answered: Gretchen's sadness contains a thought that no one likes to dwell upon; it would be too painful. Her doubt about Faust's faithfulness is repressed and kept down. It makes its reappearance in the form of a melancholy story which, although it realizes her wish, is not accompanied by pleasant feelings. Freud says that the wishes which form the dream-thought are never desires which one openly admits to oneself, but desires that are repressed because of their painful character; and it is because they are excluded from conscious reflection in the waking state that they float up, indirectly, in dreams.

72   This reasoning is not at all surprising if we look at the lives of the saints. One can understand without difficulty the nature of the feelings repressed by St. Catherine of Siena, which reappeared indirectly in the vision of her celestial marriage, and see what are the wishes that manifest themselves more or less symbolically in the visions and temptations of the saints. As we know, there is as little difference between the somnambulistic consciousness of the hysteric and the normal dream as there is between the intellectual life of hysterics and that of normal people.

73   Naturally, if we ask someone why he had such and such a dream, what are the secret thoughts expressed in it, he cannot tell us. He will say that he had eaten too much in the evening, that he was lying on his back; that he had seen or heard this or that the day before—in short, all the things we can read in the numerous scientific books about dreams. As for the dream-thought, he does not and he cannot know it for, according to Freud, the thought is repressed because it is too disagreeable. So, if anyone solemnly assures us that he has never found in his own dreams any of the things Freud talks about, we can hardly suppress a smile; he has been straining to see things it is impossible to see directly. The dream disguises the repressed complex

to prevent it from being recognized. By changing Faust into the King of Thule, Gretchen renders the situation inoffensive. Freud calls this mechanism, which prevents the repressed thought from showing itself clearly, the *censor*. The censor is nothing but the resistance which also prevents us, in the daytime, from following a line of reasoning right to the end. The censor will not allow the thought to pass until it is so disguised that the dreamer is unable to recognize it. If we try to acquaint the dreamer with the thought behind his dream, he will always oppose to us the same resistance that he opposes to his repressed complex.

74   We can now ask ourselves a series of important questions. Above all, what must we do to get behind the façade into the inside of the house—that is, beyond the manifest content of the dream to the real, secret thought behind it?

75   Let us return to our example and suppose that Gretchen is an hysterical patient who comes to consult me about a disagreeable dream. I will suppose, moreover, that I know nothing about her. In this case I would not waste my time questioning her directly, for as a rule these intimate sorrows cannot be uncovered without arousing the most intense resistance. I would try rather to conduct what I have called an "association experiment," [3] which would reveal to me the whole of her love-affair (her secret pregnancy, etc.). The conclusion would be easy to draw, and I should be able to submit the dream-thought to her without hesitation. But one may proceed more prudently.

76   I would ask her, for instance: Who is not so faithful as the King of Thule, or who ought to be? This question would very quickly illuminate the situation. In uncomplicated cases such as this, the interpretation or analysis of a dream is limited to a few simple questions.

77   Here is an example of such a case. It concerns a man of whom I know nothing except that he lives in the colonies and happens at present to be in Europe on leave. During one of our interviews he related a dream which had made a profound impression on him. Two years before, he had dreamt that *he was in a wild and desert place, and he saw, on a rock, a man dressed in*

---

[3] See *Experimental Researches*, Coll. Works, Vol. 2.

black covering his face with both hands. Suddenly he set out towards a precipice, when a woman, likewise clothed in black, appeared and tried to restrain him. He flung himself into the abyss, dragging her with him. The dreamer awoke with a cry of anguish.

78   The question, Who was that man who put himself in a dangerous situation and dragged a woman to her doom? moved the dreamer deeply, for that man was the dreamer himself. Two years before, he had been on a journey of exploration across a rocky and desert land. His expedition was pursued relentlessly by the savage inhabitants of that country, who at night made attacks in which several of its members perished. He had undertaken this extremely perilous journey because at that time *life had no value for him.* The feeling he had when engaging in this adventure was that he was *tempting fate.* And the reason for his despair? For several years he had lived alone in a country with a very dangerous climate. When on leave in Europe two and a half years ago, he made the acquaintance of a young woman. They fell in love and the young woman wanted to marry him. He knew, however, that he would have to go back to the murderous climate of the tropics, and he had no wish to take a woman there and condemn her to almost certain death. He therefore broke off his engagement, after prolonged moral conflicts which plunged him into profound despair. It was in such a state of mind that he started on his perilous journey. The analysis of the dream does not end with this statement, for the wish-fulfilment is not yet evident. But as I am only citing this dream in order to demonstrate the discovery of the essential complex, the sequel of the analysis is without interest for us.

79   In this case the dreamer was a frank and courageous man. A little less frankness, or any feeling of unease or mistrust towards me, and the complex would not have been admitted. There are even some who would calmly have asseverated that the dream had no meaning and that my question was completely beside the point. In these cases the resistance is too great, and the complex cannot be brought up from the depths directly into ordinary consciousness. Generally the resistance is such that a direct inquiry, unless it is conducted with great experience, leads to no result. By creating the "psychoanalytic method" Freud has

given us a valuable instrument for resolving or overcoming the most tenacious resistances.

80   This method is practised in the following manner. One selects some specially striking portion of the dream, and then questions the subject about the associations that attach themselves to it. He is directed to say frankly whatever comes into his mind concerning this part of the dream, eliminating as far as possible any criticism. Criticism is nothing but the censor at work; it is the resistance against the complex, and it tends to suppress what is of the most importance.

81   The subject should, therefore, say absolutely everything that comes into his head without paying any attention to it. This is always difficult at first, especially in an introspective examination when his attention cannot be suppressed so far as to eliminate the inhibiting effect of the censor. For it is towards oneself that one has the strongest resistances. The following case demonstrates the course of an analysis against strong resistances.

82   A gentleman of whose intimate life I was ignorant told me the following dream: *"I found myself in a little room, seated at a table beside Pope Pius X, whose features were far more handsome than they are in reality, which surprised me. I saw on one side of our room a great apartment with a table sumptuously laid, and a crowd of ladies in evening-dress. Suddenly I felt a need to urinate, and I went out. On my return the need was repeated; I went out again, and this happened several times. Finally I woke up, wanting to urinate."*

83   The dreamer, a very intelligent and well-educated man, naturally explained this to himself as a dream caused by irritation of the bladder. Indeed, dreams of this class are always so explained.

84   He argued vigorously against the existence of any components of great individual significance in this dream. It is true that the façade of the dream was not very transparent, and I could not know what was hidden behind it. My first deduction was that the dreamer had a strong resistance because he put so much energy into protesting that the dream was meaningless.

85   In consequence, I did not venture to put the indiscreet question: Why did you compare yourself to the Pope? I only asked him what ideas he associated with "Pope." The analysis developed as follows:

9

Pope. "The Pope lives royally . . ." (A well-known students' song.) Note that this gentleman was thirty-one and unmarried.

Seated beside the Pope. "Just in the same way I was seated at the side of a Sheikh of a Moslem sect, whose guest I was in Arabia. The Sheikh is a sort of Pope."

86   The Pope is a celibate, the Moslem a polygamist. The idea behind the dream seems to be clear: "I am a celibate like the Pope, but I would like to have many wives like the Moslem." I kept silent about these conjectures.

The room and the apartment with the table laid. "They are apartments in my cousin's house, where I was present at a large dinner-party he gave a fortnight ago."

The ladies in evening dress. "At this dinner there were also ladies, my cousin's daughters, girls of marriageable age."

87   Here he stopped: he had no further associations. The appearance of this phenomenon, known as a mental inhibition, always justifies the conclusion that one has hit on an association which arouses strong resistance. I asked:

And these young women? "Oh, nothing; recently one of them was at F. She stayed with us for some time. When she went away I went to the station with her, along with my sister."

88   Another inhibition: I helped him out by asking:

What happened then? "Oh! I was just thinking [this thought had evidently been repressed by the censor] that I had said something to my sister that made us laugh, but I have completely forgotten what it was."

89   In spite of his sincere efforts to remember, it was at first impossible for him to recall what this was. Here we have a very common instance of forgetfulness caused by inhibition. All at once he remembered:

"On the way to the station we met a gentleman who greeted us and whom I seemed to recognize. Later, I asked my sister, Was that the gentleman who is interested in —— [the cousin's daughter]?"

90   (She is now engaged to this gentleman, and I must add that the cousin's family was very wealthy and that the dreamer was interested too, but he was too late.)

The dinner at the cousin's house. "I shall shortly have to go to the wedding of two friends of mine."

The Pope's features. "The nose was exceedingly well-formed and slightly pointed."

Who has a nose like that? (Laughing.) "A young woman I'm taking a great interest in just now."

Was there anything else noteworthy about the Pope's face? "Yes, his mouth. It was a very shapely mouth. [Laughing.] Another young woman, who also attracts me, has a mouth like that."

91   This material is sufficient to elucidate a large part of the dream. The "Pope" is a good example of what Freud would call a *condensation*. In the first place he symbolizes the dreamer (celibate life), secondly he is a transformation of the polygamous Sheikh. Then he is the person seated beside the dreamer during a dinner, that is to say, one or rather two ladies—in fact, the two ladies who interest the dreamer.

92   But how comes it that this material is associated with the need to urinate? To find the answer to this question I formulated the situation in this way:

You were taking part in a marriage ceremony and in the presence of a young lady when you felt you wanted to pass water? "True, that did happen to me once. It was very unpleasant. I had been invited to the marriage of a relative, when I was about eleven. In the church I was sitting next to a girl of my own age. The ceremony went on rather a long time, and I began to want to urinate. But I restrained myself until it was too late. I wetted my trousers."

93   The association of marriage with the desire to urinate dates from that event. I will not pursue this analysis, which does not end here, lest this paper should become too long. But what has been said is sufficient to show the technique, the procedure of analysis. Obviously it is impossible to give the reader a comprehensive survey of these new points of view. The illumination that the psychoanalytic method brings to us is very great, not only for the understanding of dreams but for that of hysteria and the most important mental illnesses.

94   The psychoanalytic method, which is in use everywhere, has already given rise to a considerable literature in German. I am persuaded that the study of this method is extremely important,

not only for psychiatrists and neurologists but also for psychologists. The following works are recommended. For normal psychology: Freud, *The Interpretation of Dreams,* and "Jokes and Their Relation to the Unconscious." For the neuroses: Breuer and Freud, *Studies on Hysteria;* Freud, "Fragment of an Analysis of a Case of Hysteria." For the psychoses: Jung, *The Psychology of Dementia Praecox.* The writings of Maeder in the *Archives de psychologie* also give an excellent summary of Freud's ideas.[4]

[4] [See the bibliography for fuller data.—EDITORS.]

ON THE SIGNIFICANCE OF NUMBER DREAMS [1]

129   The symbolism of numbers, which greatly engaged the philosophic fantasy of earlier centuries, has acquired a fresh interest from the analytical researches of Freud and his school. In the material of number dreams we no longer discover conscious speculations on the symbolic connections between numbers, but rather the unconscious roots of number symbolism. As there is nothing fundamentally new to be offered in this field since the researches of Freud, Adler, and Stekel, we must content ourselves with corroborating their experience by citing parallel cases. I have under observation a few cases of this kind which may be worth reporting for their general interest.

130   The first three examples are from a middle-aged man whose conflict of the moment was an extramarital love-affair. The dream-fragment from which I take the symbolical number is: *. . . the dreamer shows his season ticket to the conductor. The conductor protests at the high number on the ticket. It was 2477.*

131   The analysis of the dream brought out a rather ungentlemanly reckoning up of the expenses of this love-affair, which was foreign to the dreamer's generous nature. His unconscious made use of this in order to resist the affair. The most obvious interpretation would be that this number had a financial significance and origin. A rough estimate of the expenses so far involved led to a number which in fact approached 2477 francs; a more careful calculation gave 2387 francs, a number which could only arbitrarily be translated into 2477. I then left the number to the free association of the patient. It occurred to him that in the dream the number appeared divided: 24 77. Perhaps it was a telephone number. This conjecture proved incorrect. The next association was that it was the sum of various

1 [Originally published as "Ein Beitrag zur Kenntnis des Zahlentraumes," *Zentralblatt für Psychoanalyse* (Wiesbaden), I (1910/11), 567–72. Previously translated by M. D. Eder in *Collected Papers on Analytical Psychology* (London and New York, 1916; 2nd edn., 1917).—EDITORS.]

other numbers. At this point the patient remembered telling me earlier that he had just celebrated the hundredth birthday of his mother and himself, since she was sixty-five and he was thirty-five. (Their birthdays fell on the same day.) In this way he arrived at the following series of associations:

He was born on	26. II [2]
His mistress	28. VIII
His wife	1. III
His mother (his father was long dead)	26. II
His two children	29. IV
	13. VII
He was born	II. 75 [3]
His mistress	VIII. 85
He was now	36
His mistress	25

132   If this series of associations is written down in the usual figures, we get the following sum:

$$\begin{array}{r} 262 \\ 288 \\ 13 \\ 262 \\ 294 \\ 137 \\ 275 \\ 885 \\ 36 \\ 25 \\ \hline 2477 \end{array}$$

133   This series, which includes all the members of his family, thus gives the number 2477. Its composition led to a deeper layer of the dream's meaning. The patient was greatly attached to his family but on the other hand very much in love with his mistress. This caused him severe conflicts. The details of the "conductor's" appearance (omitted here for the sake of brevity) pointed to the analyst, from whom the patient both feared and wished firm control as well as sharp censure of his dependent state.

[2] [Day and month.]   [3] [Month and year.]

14

134   The dream that followed shortly afterwards ran (much abbreviated): *The analyst asked the patient what he actually did when he was with his mistress. The patient said he gambled, and always on a very high number: 152. The analyst remarked: "You are sadly cheated."*

135   Analysis once more revealed a repressed tendency to reckon up the costs of the affair. The monthly expenses amounted to close on 152 francs (actually between 148 and 158). The remark that he was being cheated alluded to the point at issue between himself and his mistress. She asserted that he deflowered her, but he was quite convinced that she was not a virgin and had already been deflowered by someone else at a time when he was seeking her favours and she was refusing him. The word "number" led to the association "size in gloves," "size of calibre." From there it was but a short step to the fact that he had noted at the first coitus a remarkable width of the opening instead of the expected resistance of the hymen. This seemed to him proof of deception. The unconscious naturally used this discovery as a most effective means of resistance against the relationship. The number 152 proved refractory at first to further analysis. But on a later occasion it led to the not so distant idea of a "house number," followed by these associations: when he first knew her the lady lived at 17 X Street, then at 129 Y Street, then at 48 Z Street.

136   Here the patient realized that he had already gone far beyond 152, for the total was 194. It then occurred to him that, for certain reasons, the lady had left 48 Z Street at his instigation, so the total must be $194 - 48 = 146$. She was now living at 6 A Street, hence it was $146 + 6 = 152$.

137   Later in the analysis he had the following dream: *He received a bill from the analyst charging him interest of 1 franc on a sum of 315 francs for delay in payment from the 3rd to the 29th September.*

138   This reproach of meanness and avariciousness levelled at the analyst covered, as analysis proved, a strong unconscious envy. There were several things in the analyst's life that might arouse the envy of the patient. One thing in particular had made an impression on him: the analyst had lately had an addition to his family. The disturbed relations between the patient and his wife unfortunately permitted no such expectation in his case.

There was therefore ample ground for invidious comparisons.

139   As before, the analysis started by dividing the number 315 into 3 1 5. The patient associated 3 with the fact that the analyst had 3 children, with the recent addition of another 1. He himself would have had 5 children if all were living, as it was he had 3 — 1 = 2, for 3 children were stillborn. But these associations were far from exhausting the number symbolism of the dream.

140   The patient remarked that the period from the 3rd to the 29th September comprised 26 days. His next thought was to add this and the remaining numbers together: 26 + 315 + 1 = 342. He then carried out the same operation on 342 as on 315, dividing it into 3 4 2. Whereas before it came out that the analyst had 3 children, with 1 in addition, and the patient would have had 5, now the meaning was: the analyst had 3 children, now has 4, but the patient only 2. He remarked that the second number sounded like a rectification of the wish-fulfilment of the first.

141   The patient, who had discovered this explanation for himself without my help, declared himself satisfied. His analyst, however, was not; to him it seemed that the above revelations did not exhaust the possibilities determining the unconscious products. In connection with the number 5, the patient had carefully noted that, of the 3 stillborn children, 1 was born in the 9th and 2 in the 7th month. He also emphasized that his wife had had 2 miscarriages, 1 in the 5th week and 1 in the 7th. If we add these figures together we get the determination of the number 26:

1 child	7 months
1 "	7 "
1 "	9 "
2 miscarriages (5 + 7 weeks) =	3 "
	26

142   It seems as if 26 were determined by the number of lost periods of pregnancy. In the dream the period of 26 days denoted a delay for which the patient was charged 1 franc interest. Owing to the lost pregnancies he did in fact suffer a delay, for during the time in which the patient knew him the analyst got

16

ahead by 1 child. 1 franc may therefore mean 1 child. We have already noted the patient's tendency to add together all his children, including the dead ones, in order to outdo his rival. The thought that his analyst had outdone him by 1 child might influence even more strongly the determination of the number 1. We shall therefore follow up this tendency of the patient and continue his number game by adding to 26 the 2 successful pregnancies of 9 months each: $26 + 18 = 44$.

143   Dividing the numbers again into integers we get $2 + 6$ and $4 + 4$, two groups of figures which have only one thing in common, that each gives 8 by addition. It is to be noted that these figures are composed entirely of the months of pregnancy accruing to the patient. If we compare them with the figures indicating the progenitive capacity of the analyst, namely 315 and 342, we observe that the latter, added crosswise, each gives a total of 9. Now $9 - 8 = 1$. Again it seems as if the thought of the difference of 1 were asserting itself. The patient had remarked earlier that 315 seemed to him a wish-fulfilment and 342 a rectification. Letting our fantasy play round them, we discover the following difference between the two numbers:

$$3 \times 1 \times 5 = 15 \qquad 3 \times 4 \times 2 = 24 \qquad 24 - 15 = 9$$

144   Once more we come upon the significant figure 9, which fits very aptly into this calculus of pregnancies and births.

145   It is difficult to say where the borderline of play begins—necessarily so, for an unconscious product is the creation of sportive fantasy, of that psychic impulse out of which play itself arises. It is repugnant to the scientific mind to indulge in this kind of playfulness, which tails off everywhere in inanity. But we should never forget that the human mind has for thousands of years amused itself with just this kind of game, so it would be no wonder if those tendencies from the distant past gained a hearing in dreams. Even in his waking life the patient gave free rein to his number-fantasies, as the fact of celebrating the 100th birthday shows. Their presence in his dreams is therefore beyond question. For a single example of unconscious determination exact proofs are lacking, only the sum of our experiences can corroborate the accuracy of the individual discoveries. In investigating the realm of free creative fantasy we have to rely,

more almost than anywhere else, on a broad empiricism; and though this enjoins on us a high degree of modesty with regard to the accuracy of individual results, it by no means obliges us to pass over in silence what has happened and been observed, simply from fear of being execrated as unscientific. There must be no parleying with the superstition-phobia of the modern mind, for this is one of the means by which the secrets of the unconscious are kept veiled.

146   It is particularly interesting to see how the problems of the patient were mirrored in the unconscious of his wife. His wife had the following dream: she dreamt—and this is the whole dream—*Luke 137*. Analysis of this number showed that she associated as follows: the analyst has got 1 more child. He had 3. If all her children (counting the miscarriages) were living, she would have 7; now she has only $3 - 1 = 2$. But she wants $1 + 3 + 7 = 11$ (a twin number, 1 and 1), which expresses her wish that her two children had been pairs of twins, for then she would have had the same number of children as the analyst. Her mother once had twins. The hope of getting a child by her husband was very precarious, and this had long since implanted in the unconscious the thought of a second marriage.

147   Other fantasies showed her as "finished" at 44, i.e., when she reached the climacteric. She was now 33, so there were only 11 more years to go till she was 44. This was a significant number, for her father died in his 44th year. Her fantasy of the 44th year thus contained the thought of her father's death. The emphasis on the death of her father corresponded to the repressed fantasy of the death of her husband, who was the obstacle to a second marriage.

148   At this point the material to "Luke 137" comes in to help solve the conflict. The dreamer, it must be emphatically remarked, was not at all well up in the Bible, she had not read it for an incredible time and was not in the least religious. It would therefore be quite hopeless to rely on associations here. Her ignorance of the Bible was so great that she did not even know that "Luke 137" could refer only to the Gospel according to St. Luke. When she turned up the New Testament she opened it instead at the Acts of the Apostles.[4] As Acts 1 has only 26

[4] [Sometimes called in German *Apostelgeschichte St Lucae*.—TRANS.]

verses, she took the 7th verse: "It is not for you to know the times or the seasons, which the Father hath put in his own power." But if we turn to Luke 1 : 37, we find the Annunciation of the Virgin:

35. The Holy Ghost shall come upon thee, and the power of the Highest shall overshadow thee: therefore also that holy thing which shall be born of thee shall be called the Son of God.

36. And, behold, thy cousin Elisabeth, she hath also conceived a son in her old age: and this is the sixth month with her, who was called barren.

37. For with God nothing shall be impossible.

149   The logical continuation of the analysis of "Luke 137" requires us also to look up Luke 13 : 7. There we read:

6. A certain man had a fig tree planted in his vineyard; and he came and sought fruit thereon, and found none.

7. Then said he unto the dresser of his vineyard, Behold, these three years I come seeking fruit on this fig tree, and find none: cut it down; why cumbereth it the ground?

150   The fig-tree, since ancient times a symbol of the male genitals, must be cut down on account of its unfruitfulness. This passage is in complete accord with the numerous sadistic fantasies of the dreamer, which were concerned with cutting off or biting off the penis. The allusion to her husband's unfruitful organ is obvious. It was understandable that the dreamer withdrew her libido from her husband, for with her he was impotent,[5] and equally understandable that she made a regression to her father (". . . which the Father hath put in his own power") and identified with her mother, who had twins. By thus advancing her age she put her husband in the role of a son or boy, of an age when impotence is normal. We can also understand her wish to get rid of her husband, as was moreover confirmed by her earlier analysis. It is therefore only a further confirmation of what has been said if, following up the material to "Luke 137," we turn to Luke 7 : 13:

12. Now when he came nigh to the gate of the city, behold, there was a dead man carried out, the only son of his mother, and she was a widow . . .

5 The husband's principal trouble was a pronounced mother complex.

13. And when the Lord saw her, he had compassion on her, and said unto her, Weep not.

14. And he came and touched the bier: and they that bare him stood still. And he said, Young man, I say unto thee, Arise.

151   In the particular psychological situation of the dreamer the allusion to the raising up of the dead man acquires a pretty significance as the curing of her husband's impotence. Then the whole problem would be solved. There is no need for me to point out in so many words the numerous wish-fulfilments contained in this material; the reader can see them for himself.

152   Since the dreamer was totally ignorant of the Bible, "Luke 137" must be regarded as a cryptomnesia. Both Flournoy [6] and myself [7] have already drawn attention to the important effects of this phenomenon. So far as one can be humanly certain, any manipulation of the material with intent to deceive is out of the question in this case. Those familiar with psychoanalysis will know that the whole nature of the material rules out any such suspicion.

153   I am aware that these observations are floating in a sea of uncertainties, but I think it would be wrong to suppress them, for luckier investigators may come after us who will be able to put them in the right perspective, as we cannot do for lack of adequate knowledge.

[6] *From India to the Planet Mars* (1900); "Nouvelles Observations sur un cas de somnambulisme avec glossolalie" (1901).

[7] Cf. *Psychiatric Studies*, pars. 139ff. and 166ff.

II

DREAMS AND PSYCHIC ENERGY

GENERAL ASPECTS OF DREAM PSYCHOLOGY [1]

443   Dreams have a psychic structure which is unlike that of other contents of consciousness because, so far as we can judge from their form and meaning, they do not show the continuity of development typical of conscious contents. They do not appear, as a rule, to be integral components of our conscious psychic life, but seem rather to be extraneous, apparently accidental occurrences. The reason for this exceptional position of dreams lies in their peculiar mode of origin: they do not arise, like other conscious contents, from any clearly discernible, logical and emotional continuity of experience, but are remnants of a peculiar psychic activity taking place during sleep. Their mode of origin is sufficient in itself to isolate dreams from the other contents of consciousness, and this is still further increased by the content of the dreams themselves, which contrasts strikingly with our conscious thinking.

444   An attentive observer, however, will have no difficulty in discovering that dreams are not entirely cut off from the

1 [First published in English: "The Psychology of Dreams," in *Collected Papers on Analytical Psychology*, edited by Constance Long (London, 1916; 2nd edn., London, 1917, and New York, 1920). The translation was by Dora Hecht from a ms., which, in much expanded form, was published as "Allgemeine Gesichtspunkte zur Psychologie des Traumes," in *Über die Energetik der Seele* (Psychologische Abhandlungen, II; Zurich, 1928). It was again expanded in *Über psychische Energetik und das Wesen der Träume* (Zurich, 1948), and this version is translated here.—EDITORS.]

continuity of consciousness, for in almost every dream certain details can be found which have their origin in the impressions, thoughts, and moods of the preceding day or days. To that extent a certain continuity does exist, though at first sight it points *backwards*. But anyone sufficiently interested in the dream problem cannot have failed to observe that dreams also have a continuity *forwards*—if such an expression be permitted—since dreams occasionally exert a remarkable influence on the conscious mental life even of persons who cannot be considered superstitious or particularly abnormal. These after-effects consist mostly in more or less distinct alterations of mood.

445   It is probably in consequence of this loose connection with the other contents of consciousness that the recollected dream is so extremely unstable. Many dreams baffle all attempts at reproduction, even immediately after waking; others can be remembered only with doubtful accuracy, and comparatively few can be called really distinct and clearly reproducible. This peculiar behaviour may be explained by considering the characteristics of the various elements combined in a dream. The combination of ideas in dreams is essentially *fantastic;* they are linked together in a sequence which is as a rule quite foreign to our "reality thinking," and in striking contrast to the logical sequence of ideas which we consider to be a special characteristic of conscious mental processes.

446   It is to this characteristic that dreams owe the vulgar epithet "meaningless." But before pronouncing this verdict we should remember that the dream and its context is something that *we* do not understand. With such a verdict, therefore, we would merely be projecting our own lack of understanding upon the object. But that would not prevent dreams from having an inherent meaning of their own.

447   Apart from the efforts that have been made for centuries to extract a prophetic meaning from dreams, Freud's discoveries are the first successful attempt in practice to find their real significance. His work merits the term "scientific" because he has evolved a technique which not only he but many other investigators assert achieves its object, namely the understanding of the meaning of the dream. This meaning is not identical with the fragmentary meanings suggested by the manifest dream-content.

448   This is not the place for a critical discussion of Freud's psychology of dreams. I shall try, rather, to give a brief summary of what may be regarded as the more or less established facts of dream psychology today.

449   The first question we must discuss is: what is our justification for attributing to dreams any other significance than the unsatisfying fragmentary meaning suggested by the manifest dream-content? One especially cogent argument in this respect is the fact that Freud discovered the hidden meaning of dreams *empirically* and *not deductively*. A further argument in favour of a possible hidden meaning is obtained by comparing dream-fantasies with other fantasies of the waking state in one and the same individual. It is not difficult to see that waking fantasies have not merely a superficial, concretistic meaning but also a deeper psychological meaning. There is a very old and widespread type of fantastic story, of which Aesop's fables are typical examples, that provides a very good illustration of what may be said about the meaning of fantasies in general. For instance, a fantastic tale is told about the doings of a lion and an ass. Taken superficially and concretely, the tale is an impossible phantasm, but the hidden moral meaning is obvious to anyone who reflects upon it. It is characteristic that children are pleased and satisfied with the exoteric meaning of the fable.

450   But by far the best argument for the existence of a hidden meaning in dreams is obtained by conscientiously applying the technical procedure for breaking down the manifest dream-content. This brings us to our second main point, the question of analytic procedure. Here again I desire neither to defend nor to criticize Freud's views and discoveries, but shall confine myself to what seem to me to be firmly established facts. If we start from the fact that a dream is a psychic product, we have not the least reason to suppose that its constitution and function obey laws and purposes other than those applicable to any other psychic product. In accordance with the maxim "Principles are not to be multiplied beyond the necessary," we have to treat the dream, analytically, just like any other psychic product until experience teaches us a better way.

451   We know that every psychic structure, regarded from the causal standpoint, is the result of antecedent psychic contents. We know, furthermore, that every psychic structure, regarded

from the final standpoint, has its own peculiar meaning and purpose in the actual psychic process. This criterion must also be applied to dreams. When, therefore, we seek a psychological explanation of a dream, we must first know what were the preceding experiences out of which it is composed. We must trace the antecedents of every element in the dream-picture. Let me give an example: someone dreams that *he is walking down a street—suddenly a child crosses in front of him and is run over by a car.*

452   We reduce the dream-picture to its antecedents with the help of the dreamer's recollections. He recognizes the street as one down which he had walked on the previous day. The child he recognizes as his brother's child, whom he had seen on the previous evening when visiting his brother. The car accident reminds him of an accident that had actually occurred a few days before, but of which he had only read in a newspaper. As we know, most people are satisfied with a reduction of this kind. "Aha," they say, "that's why I had this dream."

453   Obviously this reduction is quite unsatisfying from the scientific point of view. The dreamer had walked down many streets on the previous day; why was this particular one selected? He had read about several accidents; why did he select just this one? The discovery of a single antecedent is by no means sufficient, for a plausible determination of the dream-images results only from the competition of several causes. The collection of additional material proceeds according to the same principle of recollection, which has also been called the method of free association. The result, as can readily be understood, is an accumulation of very diverse and largely heterogeneous material, having apparently nothing in common but the fact of its evident associative connection with the dream-content, otherwise it could never have been reproduced by means of this content.

454   How far the collection of such material should go is an important question from the technical point of view. Since the entire psychic content of a life could ultimately be disclosed from any single starting point, theoretically the whole of a person's previous life-experience might be found in every dream. But we need to collect only just so much material as is absolutely necessary in order to understand the dream's meaning. The limitation of the material is obviously an arbitrary proceed-

ing, in accordance with Kant's principle that to "comprehend" a thing is to "cognize it to the extent necessary for our purpose." [2] For instance, when undertaking a survey of the causes of the French Revolution, we could, in amassing our material, include not only the history of medieval France but also that of Rome and Greece, which certainly would not be "necessary for our purpose," since we can understand the historical genesis of the Revolution just as well from much more limited material. So in collecting the material for a dream we go only so far as seems necessary to us in order to extract from it a valid meaning.

455   Except for the aforesaid arbitrary limitation, the collection of material lies outside the choice of the investigator. The material collected must now be sifted and examined according to principles which are always applied to the examination of historical or any other empirical material. The method is essentially a comparative one, which obviously does not work automatically but is largely dependent on the skill and aim of the investigator.

456   When a psychological fact has to be explained, it must be remembered that psychological data necessitate a twofold point of view, namely that of *causality* and that of *finality*. I use the word finality intentionally, in order to avoid confusion with the concept of teleology. By finality I mean merely the immanent psychological striving for a goal. Instead of "striving for a goal" one could also say "sense of purpose." All psychological phenomena have some such sense of purpose inherent in them, even merely reactive phenomena like emotional reactions. Anger over an insult has its purpose in revenge; the purpose of ostentatious mourning is to arouse the sympathy of others, and so on.

457   Applying the causal point of view to the material associated with the dream, we reduce the manifest dream-content to certain fundamental tendencies or ideas exhibited by the material. These, as one would expect, are of an elementary and general nature. For example, a young man dreams: *"I was standing in a strange garden and picked an apple from a tree. I looked about cautiously, to make sure that no one saw me."*

458   The associated dream-material is a memory of having once, when a boy, plucked a couple of pears surreptitiously from a

2 [Cf. *Introduction to Logic*, p. 55.—EDITORS.]

neighbour's garden. The feeling of bad conscience, which is a prominent feature of the dream, reminds him of a situation experienced on the previous day. He met a young lady in the street—a casual acquaintance—and exchanged a few words with her. At that moment a gentleman passed whom he knew, whereupon he was suddenly seized with a curious feeling of embarrassment, as if he were doing something wrong. He associated the apple with the scene in the Garden of Eden, and also with the fact that he had never really understood why the eating of the forbidden fruit should have had such dire consequences for our first parents. This had always made him feel angry; it seemed to him an unjust act of God, for God had made men as they were, with all their curiosity and greed.

459   Another association was that sometimes his father had punished him for certain things in a way that seemed to him incomprehensible. The worst punishment had been bestowed on him after he was caught secretly watching girls bathing. This led up to the confession that he had recently begun a love-affair with a housemaid but had not yet carried it through to its natural conclusion. On the evening before the dream he had had a rendezvous with her.

460   Reviewing this material, we can see that the dream contains a very transparent reference to the last-named incident. The associative material shows that the apple episode is obviously intended as an erotic scene. For various other reasons, too, it may be considered extremely probable that this experience of the previous day has gone on working in the dream. In the dream the young man plucks the apple of Paradise, which in reality he has not yet plucked. The remainder of the material associated with the dream is concerned with another experience of the previous day, namely the peculiar feeling of bad conscience which seized the dreamer when he was talking to his casual lady acquaintance. This, again, was associated with the fall of man in Paradise, and finally with an erotic misdemeanour of his childhood, for which his father had punished him severely. All these associations are linked together by the idea of *guilt*.

461   We shall first consider this material from the causal standpoint of Freud; in other words, we shall "interpret" the dream, to use Freud's expression. A wish has been left unfulfilled from the day before. In the dream this wish is fulfilled under the

symbol of the apple episode. But why is this fulfilment disguised and hidden under a symbolical image instead of being expressed in a clearly sexual thought? Freud would point to the unmistakable element of guilt in this material and say that the morality inculcated into the young man from childhood is bent on repressing such wishes, and to that end brands the natural craving as something painful and incompatible. The repressed painful thought can therefore express itself only "symbolically." As these thoughts are incompatible with the moral content of consciousness, a psychic authority postulated by Freud, called the censor, prevents this wish from passing undisguised into consciousness.

462   Considering a dream from the standpoint of finality, which I contrast with the causal standpoint of Freud, does not—as I would expressly like to emphasize—involve a denial of the dream's causes, but rather a different interpretation of the associative material gathered round the dream. The material facts remain the same, but the criterion by which they are judged is different. The question may be formulated simply as follows: What is the purpose of this dream? What effect is it meant to have? These questions are not arbitrary inasmuch as they can be applied to every psychic activity. Everywhere the question of the "why" and the "wherefore" may be raised, because every organic structure consists of a complicated network of purposive functions, and each of these functions can be resolved into a series of individual facts with a purposive orientation.

463   It is clear that the material added by the dream to the previous day's erotic experience chiefly emphasizes the element of guilt in the erotic act. The same association had already shown itself to be operative in another experience of the previous day, in that meeting with the casual lady acquaintance, when the feeling of a bad conscience was automatically and inexplicably aroused, as if in that instance too the young man was doing something wrong. This feeling also plays a part in the dream and is further intensified by the association of the additional material, the erotic experience of the day before being depicted by the story of the Fall, which was followed by such severe punishment.

464   I maintain that there exists in the dreamer an unconscious propensity or tendency to represent his erotic experiences as

guilt. It is characteristic that the dream is followed by the association with the Fall and that the young man had never really grasped why the punishment should have been so drastic. This association throws light on the reasons why he did not think simply: "What I am doing is not right." Obviously he does not know that he might condemn his conduct as morally wrong. This is actually the case. His conscious belief is that his conduct does not matter in the least morally, as all his friends were acting in the same way, besides which he was quite unable on other grounds to understand why such a fuss should be made about it.

465   Now whether this dream should be considered meaningful or meaningless depends on a very important question, namely, whether the standpoint of morality, handed down through the ages, is itself meaningful or meaningless. I do not wish to wander off into a philosophical discussion of this question, but would merely observe that mankind must obviously have had very strong reasons for devising this morality, for otherwise it would be truly incomprehensible why such restraints should be imposed on one of man's strongest desires. If we give this fact its due, we are bound to pronounce the dream to be meaningful, because it shows the young man the necessity of looking at his erotic conduct for once from the standpoint of morality. Primitive tribes have in some respects extremely strict laws concerning sexuality. This proves that sexual morality is a not-to-be-neglected factor in the higher functions of the psyche and deserves to be taken fully into account. In the case in question we should have to say that the young man, hypnotized by his friends' example, has somewhat thoughtlessly given way to his erotic desires, unmindful of the fact that man is a morally responsible being who, voluntarily or involuntarily, submits to the morality that he himself has created.

466   In this dream we can discern a compensating function of the unconscious whereby those thoughts, inclinations, and tendencies which in conscious life are too little valued come spontaneously into action during the sleeping state, when the conscious process is to a large extent eliminated.

467   Here the question might certainly be asked: of what use is this to the dreamer if he does not understand the dream?

468   To this I must remark that understanding is not an exclu-

sively intellectual process for, as experience shows, a man may be influenced, and indeed convinced in the most effective way, by innumerable things of which he has no intellectual understanding. I need only remind my readers of the effectiveness of religious symbols.

469 The above example might lead one to suppose that the function of dreams is a distinctly "moral" one. Such it appears to be in this case, but if we recall the formula that dreams contain the subliminal material of a given moment, we cannot speak simply of a "moral" function. For it is worth noting that the dreams of those persons whose actions are morally unassailable bring material to light that might well be described as "immoral" in the ordinary meaning of the term. Thus it is characteristic that St. Augustine was glad that God did not hold him responsible for his dreams. The unconscious is the unknown at any given moment, so it is not surprising that dreams add to the conscious psychological situation of the moment all those aspects which are essential for a totally different point of view. It is evident that this function of dreams amounts to a psychological adjustment, a compensation absolutely necessary for properly balanced action. In a conscious process of reflection it is essential that, so far as possible, we should realize all the aspects and consequences of a problem in order to find the right solution. This process is continued automatically in the more or less unconscious state of sleep, where, as experience seems to show, all those aspects occur to the dreamer (at least by way of allusion) that during the day were insufficiently appreciated or even totally ignored—in other words, were comparatively unconscious.

470 As regards the much discussed *symbolism* of dreams, its evaluation varies according to whether it is considered from the causal or from the final standpoint. The causal approach of Freud starts from a desire or craving, that is, from the repressed dream-wish. This craving is always something comparatively simple and elementary, which can hide itself under manifold disguises. Thus the young man in question could just as well have dreamt that he had to open a door with a key, that he was flying in an aeroplane, kisssing his mother, etc. From this point of view all those things could have the same meaning. Hence it is that the more rigorous adherents of the Freudian school have

come to the point of interpreting—to give a gross example—pretty well all oblong objects in dreams as phallic symbols and all round or hollow objects as feminine symbols.

471   From the standpoint of finality the images in a dream each have an intrinsic value of their own. For instance if the young man, instead of dreaming of the apple scene, had dreamt he had to open a door with a key, this dream-image would probably have furnished associative material of an essentially different character, which would have supplemented the conscious situation in a way quite different from the material connected with the apple scene. From this standpoint, the significance lies precisely in the diversity of symbolical expressions in the dream and not in their uniformity of meaning. The causal point of view tends by its very nature towards uniformity of meaning, that is, towards a fixed significance of symbols. The final point of view, on the other hand, perceives in the altered dream-image the expression of an altered psychological situation. It recognizes no fixed meaning of symbols. From this standpoint, all the dream-images are important in themselves, each one having a special significance of its own, to which, indeed, it owes its inclusion in the dream. Keeping to our previous example, we can see that from the final standpoint the symbol in the dream has more the value of a parable: it does not conceal, it teaches. The apple scene vividly recalls the sense of guilt while at the same time disguising the deed of our first parents.

472   It is clear that we reach very dissimilar interpretations of the meaning of dreams according to the point of view we adopt. The question now arises: which is the better or truer interpretation? After all, for us psychotherapists it is a practical and not merely a theoretical necessity that we should have *some* interpretation of the meaning of dreams. If we want to treat our patients we must for quite practical reasons endeavour to lay hold of any means that will enable us to educate them effectively. It should be obvious from the foregoing example that the material associated with the dream has touched on a question calculated to open the eyes of the young man to many things which till now he had heedlessly overlooked. But by disregarding these things he was really overlooking something in himself, for he has a moral standard and a moral need just like any other man. By trying to live without taking this fact into account his life was

one-sided and incomplete, as if unco-ordinated—with the same consequences for psychic life as a one-sided and incomplete diet would have for the body. In order to educate an individuality to completeness and independence we need to bring to fruition all those functions which have hitherto attained but little conscious development or none at all. And to achieve this aim we must for therapeutic reasons enter into all the unconscious aspects of the contribution made by the dream-material. This makes it abundantly clear that the standpoint of finality is of great importance as an aid to the development of the individual.

473   The causal point of view is obviously more sympathetic to the scientific spirit of our time with its strictly causalistic reasoning. Much may be said for Freud's view as a scientific explanation of dream psychology. But I must dispute its completeness, for the psyche cannot be conceived merely in causal terms but requires also a final view. Only a combination of points of view—which has not yet been achieved in a scientifically satisfactory manner, owing to the enormous difficulties, both practical and theoretical, that still remain to be overcome—can give us a more complete conception of the nature of dreams.

474   I would now like to treat briefly of some further problems of dream psychology which are contingent to a general discussion of dreams. First, as to the *classification of dreams,* I would not put too high a value either on the practical or on the theoretical importance of this question. I investigate yearly some fifteen hundred to two thousand dreams, and on the basis of this experience I can assert that typical dreams do actually exist. But they are not very frequent, and from the final point of view they lose much of the importance which the causal standpoint attaches to them on account of the fixed significance of symbols. It seems to me that the *typical motifs* in dreams are of much greater importance since they permit a comparison with the motifs of mythology. Many of those mythological motifs—in collecting which Frobenius in particular has rendered such signal service—are also found in dreams, often with precisely the same significance. Though I cannot enter into this question more fully here, I would like to emphasize that the comparison of typical dream-motifs with those of mythology suggests the idea—already put forward by Nietzsche—that dream-thinking should be regarded as a phylogenetically older mode of thought.

Instead of multiplying examples I can best show what I mean by reference to our specimen dream. It will be remembered that the dream introduced the apple scene as a typical way of representing erotic guilt. The thought abstracted from it would boil down to: "I am doing wrong by acting like this." It is characteristic that dreams never express themselves in this logical, abstract way but always in the language of parable or simile. This is also a characteristic of primitive languages, whose flowery turns of phrase are very striking. If we remember the monuments of ancient literature, we find that what nowadays is expressed by means of abstractions was then expressed mostly by similes. Even a philosopher like Plato did not disdain to express certain fundamental ideas in this way.

475 Just as the body bears the traces of its phylogenetic development, so also does the human mind. Hence there is nothing surprising about the possibility that the figurative language of dreams is a survival from an archaic mode of thought.

476 At the same time the theft of the apple is a typical dream-motif that occurs in many different variations in numerous dreams. It is also a well-known mythological motif, which is found not only in the story of the Garden of Eden but in countless myths and fairytales from all ages and climes. It is one of those universally human symbols which can reappear autochthonously in any one, at any time. Thus dream psychology opens the way to a general comparative psychology from which we may hope to gain the same understanding of the development and structure of the human psyche as comparative anatomy has given us concerning the human body.[3]

477 Dreams, then, convey to us in figurative language—that is, in sensuous, concrete imagery—thoughts, judgments, views, directives, tendencies, which were unconscious either because of repression or through mere lack of realization. Precisely because they are contents of the unconscious, and the dream is a derivative of unconscious processes, it contains a reflection of the unconscious contents. It is not a reflection of unconscious contents in general but only of certain contents, which are linked together associatively and are selected by the conscious situation of the moment. I regard this observation as a very important one in practice. If we want to interpret a dream

[3] [The original 1916 version ends at this point.—EDITORS.]

correctly, we need a thorough knowledge of the conscious situation at that moment, because the dream contains its unconscious complement, that is, the material which the conscious situation has constellated in the unconscious. Without this knowledge it is impossible to interpret a dream correctly, except by a lucky fluke. I would like to illustrate this by an example:

478   A man once came to me for a first consultation. He told me that he was engaged in all sorts of learned pursuits and was also interested in psychoanalysis from a literary point of view. He was in the best of health, he said, and was not to be considered in any sense a patient. He was merely pursuing his psycho-analytic interests. He was very comfortably off and had plenty of time to devote himself to his pursuits. He wanted to make my acquaintance in order to be inducted by me into the theoretical secrets of analysis. He admitted it must be very boring for me to have to do with a normal person, since I must certainly find "mad" people much more interesting. He had written to me a few days before to ask when I could see him. In the course of conversation we soon came to the question of dreams. I there-upon asked him whether he had had a dream the night before he visited me. He affirmed this and told me the following dream: *"I was in a bare room. A sort of nurse received me, and wanted me to sit at a table on which stood a bottle of fermented milk, which I was supposed to drink. I wanted to go to Dr. Jung, but the nurse told me that I was in a hospital and that Dr. Jung had no time to receive me."*

479   It is clear even from the manifest content of the dream that the anticipated visit to me had somehow constellated his un-conscious. He gave the following associations: Bare room: "A sort of frosty reception room, as in an official building, or the waiting-room in a hospital. I was never in a hospital as a pa-tient." Nurse: "She looked repulsive, she was cross-eyed. That reminds me of a fortune-teller and palmist whom I once visited to have my fortune told. Once I was sick and had a deaconess as a nurse." Bottle of fermented milk: "Fermented milk is nauseat-ing, I cannot drink it. My wife is always drinking it, and I make fun of her for this because she is obsessed with the idea that one must always be doing something for one's health. I remember I was once in a sanatorium—my nerves were not so good—and there I had to drink fermented milk."

480   At this point I interrupted him with the indiscreet question: had his neurosis entirely disappeared since then? He tried to worm out of it, but finally had to admit that he still had his neurosis, and that actually his wife had for a long time been urging him to consult me. But he certainly didn't feel so nervous that he had to consult me on that account, he was after all not mad, and I treated only mad people. It was merely that he was interested in learning about my psychological theories, etc.

481   From this we can see how the patient has falsified the situation. It suits his fancy to come to me in the guise of a philosopher and psychologist and to allow the fact of his neurosis to recede into the background. But the dream reminds him of it in a very disagreeable way and forces him to tell the truth. He has to swallow this bitter drink. His recollection of the fortune-teller shows us very clearly just how he had imagined my activities. As the dream informs him, he must first submit to treatment before he can get to me.

482   The dream rectifies the situation. It contributes the material that was lacking and thereby improves the patient's attitude. That is the reason we need dream-analysis in our therapy.

483   I do not wish to give the impression that all dreams are as simple as this one, or that they are all of this type. I believe it is true that all dreams are compensatory to the content of consciousness, but certainly not in all dreams is the compensatory function so clear as in this example. Though dreams contribute to the self-regulation of the psyche by automatically bringing up everything that is repressed or neglected or unknown, their compensatory significance is often not immediately apparent because we still have only a very incomplete knowledge of the nature and the needs of the human psyche. There are psychological compensations that seem to be very remote from the problem on hand. In these cases one must always remember that every man, in a sense, represents the whole of humanity and its history. What was possible in the history of mankind at large is also possible on a small scale in every individual. What mankind has needed may eventually be needed by the individual too. It is therefore not surprising that religious compensations play a great role in dreams. That this is increasingly so in our time is a natural consequence of the prevailing materialism of our outlook.

484   Lest it be thought that the compensatory significance of
dreams is a new discovery or has simply been "made up" to suit
the convenience of interpretation, I shall cite a very old and
well-known example which can be found in the fourth chapter
of the Book of Daniel (10–16, AV). When Nebuchadnezzar was
at the height of his power he had the following dream:

> . . . I saw, and behold a tree in the midst of the earth, and the
> height thereof was great.
> The tree grew, and was strong, and the height thereof reached
> unto heaven, and the sight thereof to the end of all the earth.
> The leaves thereof were fair, and the fruit thereof much, and in
> it was meat for all: the beasts of the field had shadow under it, and
> the fowls of the heaven dwelt in the boughs thereof, and all flesh
> was fed of it.
> I saw in the visions of my head upon my bed, and behold, a
> watcher and an holy one came down from heaven;
> He cried aloud, and said thus, Hew down the tree, and cut off
> his branches, shake off his leaves, and scatter his fruit: let the beasts
> get away from under it, and the fowls from his branches.
> Nevertheless leave the stump of his roots in the earth, even with
> a band of iron and brass in the tender grass of the field; and let it
> be wet with the dew of heaven, and let his portion be with the
> beasts in the grass of the earth:
> Let his heart be changed from man's, and let a beast's heart be
> given unto him; and let seven times pass over him.

485   In the second part of the dream the tree becomes personified,
so that it is easy to see that the great tree is the dreaming king
himself. Daniel interprets the dream in this sense. Its meaning is
obviously an attempt to compensate the king's megalomania
which, according to the story, developed into a real psychosis.
To interpret the dream-process as compensatory is in my view
entirely consistent with the nature of the biological process in
general. Freud's view tends in the same direction, since he too
ascribes a compensatory role to dreams in so far as they preserve
sleep. There are, as Freud has demonstrated, dreams which show
how certain external stimuli that would rob the dreamer of
sleep are distorted in such a way that they abet the wish to sleep,
or rather the desire not to be disturbed. Equally, there are
innumerable dreams in which, as Freud was able to show,
intrapsychic excitations, such as personal ideas that would be

37

likely to release powerful affective reactions, are distorted in such a way as to fit in with a dream-context which disguises the painful ideas and makes any strong affective reaction impossible.

486   As against this, we should not overlook the fact that the very dreams which disturb sleep most—and these are not uncommon —have a dramatic structure which aims logically at creating a highly affective situation, and builds it up so efficiently that the affect unquestionably wakes the dreamer. Freud explains these dreams by saying that the censor was no longer able to suppress the painful affect. It seems to me that this explanation fails to do justice to the facts. Dreams which concern themselves in a very disagreeable manner with the painful experiences and activities of daily life and expose just the most disturbing thoughts with the most painful distinctness are known to everyone. It would, in my opinion, be unjustified to speak here of the dream's sleep-preserving, affect-disguising function. One would have to stand reality on its head to see in these dreams a confirmation of Freud's view. The same is true of those cases where repressed sexual fantasies appear undisguised in the manifest dream content.

487   I have therefore come to the conclusion that Freud's view that dreams have an essentially wish-fulfilling and sleep-preserving function is too narrow, even though the basic thought of a compensatory biological function is certainly correct. This compensatory function is concerned only to a limited extent with the sleeping state; its chief significance is rather in relation to conscious life. Dreams, I maintain, are compensatory to the conscious situation of the moment. They preserve sleep whenever possible: that is to say, they function necessarily and automatically under the influence of the sleeping state; but they break through when their function demands it, that is, when the compensatory contents are so intense that they are able to counteract sleep. A compensatory content is especially intense when it has a vital significance for conscious orientation.

488   As far back as 1907 I pointed out the compensatory relation between consciousness and the split-off complexes and also emphasized their purposive character. Flournoy did the same thing independently of me.[4] From these observations the possi-

4 Cf. my "The Psychology of Dementia Praecox." Flournoy, "Automatisme téléologique antisuicide" (1908).

bility of purposive unconscious impulses became evident. It should be emphasized, however, that the final orientation of the unconscious does not run parallel with our conscious intentions. As a rule, the unconscious content contrasts strikingly with the conscious material, particularly when the conscious attitude tends too exclusively in a direction that would threaten the vital needs of the individual. The more one-sided his conscious attitude is, and the further it deviates from the optimum, the greater becomes the possibility that vivid dreams with a strongly contrasting but purposive content will appear as an expression of the self-regulation of the psyche. Just as the body reacts purposively to injuries or infections or any abnormal conditions, so the psychic functions react to unnatural or dangerous disturbances with purposive defence-mechanisms. Among these purposive reactions we must include the dream, since it furnishes the unconscious material constellated in a given conscious situation and supplies it to consciousness in symbolical form. In this material are to be found all those associations which remained unconscious because of their feeble accentuation but which still possess sufficient energy to make themselves perceptible in the sleeping state. Naturally the purposive nature of the dream-content is not immediately discernible from outside without further investigation. An analysis of the manifest dream-content is required before we can get at the really compensatory factors in the latent dream-content. Most of the physical defence-mechanisms are of this non-obvious and, so to speak, indirect nature, and their purposiveness can be recognized only after careful investigation. I need only remind you of the significance of fever or of suppuration processes in an infected wound.

489   The processes of psychic compensation are almost always of a very individual nature, and this makes the task of proving their compensatory character considerably more difficult. Because of this peculiarity, it is often very difficult, especially for the beginner, to see how far a dream-content has a compensatory significance. On the basis of the compensation theory, one would be inclined to assume, for instance, that anyone with a too pessimistic attitude to life must have very cheerful and optimistic dreams. This expectation is true only in the case of someone whose nature allows him to be stimulated and encouraged

in this way. But if he has a rather different nature, his dreams will purposively assume a much blacker character than his conscious attitude. They can then follow the principle of like curing like.

490   It is therefore not easy to lay down any special rules for the type of dream-compensation. Its character is always closely bound up with the whole nature of the individual. The possibilities of compensation are without number and inexhaustible, though with increasing experience certain basic features gradually crystallize out.

491   In putting forward a compensation theory I do not wish to assert that this is the only possible theory of dreams or that it completely explains *all* the phenomena of dream-life. The dream is an extraordinarily complicated phenomenon, just as complicated and unfathomable as the phenomena of consciousness. It would be inappropriate to try to understand all conscious phenomena from the standpoint of the wish-fulfilment theory or the theory of instinct, and it is as little likely that dream-phenomena are susceptible of so simple an explanation. Nor should we regard dream-phenomena as merely compensatory and secondary to the contents of consciousness, even though it is commonly supposed that conscious life is of far greater significance for the individual than the unconscious. This view, however, may yet have to be revised, for, as our experience deepens, it will be realized that the function of the unconscious in the life of the psyche has an importance of which we perhaps have still too low an estimate. It is analytical experience, above all, which has discovered to an increasing degree the influences of the unconscious on our conscious psychic life—influences whose existence and significance had till then been overlooked. In my view, which is based on many years of experience and on extensive research, the significance of the unconscious in the total performance of the psyche is probably just as great as that of consciousness. Should this view prove correct, then not only should the function of the unconscious be regarded as compensatory and relative to the content of consciousness, but the content of consciousness would have to be regarded as relative to the momentarily constellated unconscious content. In this case active orientation towards goals and purposes would not be the privilege of consciousness alone but would also be true

of the unconscious, so that it too would be just as capable of taking a finally oriented lead. The dream, accordingly, would then have the value of a positive, guiding idea or of an aim whose vital meaning would be greatly superior to that of the momentarily constellated conscious content. This possibility meets with the approval of the *consensus gentium,* since in the superstitions of all times and races the dream has been regarded as a truth-telling oracle. Making allowances for exaggeration and prejudice, there is always a grain of truth in such widely disseminated views. Maeder has laid energetic stress on the prospective-final significance of dreams as a purposive unconscious function which paves the way for the solution of real conflicts and problems and seeks to portray it with the help of gropingly chosen symbols.[5]

492   I should like to distinguish between the *prospective* function of dreams and their *compensatory* function. The latter means that the unconscious, considered as relative to consciousness, adds to the conscious situation all those elements from the previous day which remained subliminal because of repression or because they were simply too feeble to reach consciousness. This compensation, in the sense of being a self-regulation of the psychic organism, must be called purposive.

493   The prospective function, on the other hand, is an anticipation in the unconscious of future conscious achievements, something like a preliminary exercise or sketch, or a plan roughed out in advance. Its symbolic content sometimes outlines the solution of a conflict, excellent examples of this being given in Maeder. The occurrence of prospective dreams cannot be denied. It would be wrong to call them prophetic, because at bottom they are no more prophetic than a medical diagnosis or a weather forecast. They are merely an anticipatory combination of probabilities which may coincide with the actual behaviour of things but need not necessarily agree in every detail. Only in the latter case can we speak of "prophecy." That the prospective function of dreams is sometimes greatly superior to the combinations we can consciously foresee is not surprising, since a dream results from the fusion of subliminal elements and is thus a combination of all the perceptions, thoughts, and

[5] "Sur le mouvement psychanalytique"; "Über die Funktion des Traumes"; *The Dream Problem.*

feelings which consciousness has not registered because of their feeble accentuation. In addition, dreams can rely on subliminal memory traces that are no longer able to influence consciousness effectively. With regard to prognosis, therefore, dreams are often in a much more favourable position than consciousness.

494 Although the prospective function is, in my view, an essential characteristic of dreams, one would do well not to overestimate this function, for one might easily be led to suppose that the dream is a kind of psychopomp which, because of its superior knowledge, infallibly guides life in the right direction. However much people underestimate the psychological significance of dreams, there is an equally great danger that anyone who is constantly preoccupied with dream-analysis will overestimate the significance of the unconscious for real life. But, judging from all previous experience, we do have a right to assume that the importance of the unconscious is about equal to that of consciousness. Undoubtedly there are conscious attitudes which are surpassed by the unconscious—attitudes so badly adapted to the individual as a whole that the unconscious attitude or constellation is a far better expression of his essential nature. But this is by no means always the case. Very often the dreams contribute only the merest fragments to the conscious attitude, because the latter is on the one hand sufficiently well adapted to reality and on the other satisfies fairly well the nature of the individual. A more or less exclu ve regard for the dream standpoint without considering the conscious situation would be inappropriate in this case and would serve only to confuse and disrupt the conscious performance. Only if there is an obviously unsatisfactory and defective conscious attitude have we a right to allow the unconscious a higher value. The criteria necessary for such a judgment constitute, of course, a delicate problem. It goes without saying that the value of a conscious attitude can never be judged from an exclusively collective standpoint. For this a thorough investigation of the individuality in question is needed, and only from an accurate knowledge of the individual character can it be decided in what respect the conscious attitude is unsatisfactory. When I lay stress on knowledge of individual character I do not mean that the demands of the collective standpoint should be entirely neglected. As we know, the individual is not conditioned by

himself alone but just as much by his collective relationships. When, therefore, the conscious attitude is more or less adequate, the meaning of the dream will be confined simply to its compensatory function. This is the general rule for the normal individual living under normal inner and outer conditions. For these reasons it seems to me that the compensation theory provides the right formula and fits the facts by giving dreams a compensatory function in the self-regulation of the psychic organism.

495   But when the individual deviates from the norm in the sense that his conscious attitude is unadapted both objectively and subjectively, the—under normal conditions—merely compensatory function of the unconscious becomes a guiding, prospective function capable of leading the conscious attitude in a quite different direction which is much better than the previous one, as Maeder has successfully shown in the books I have mentioned. Into this category come dreams of the Nebuchadnezzar type. It is obvious that dreams of this sort are found chiefly in people who are not living on their true level. It is equally obvious that this lack of proportion is very frequent. Hence we have frequent occasion to consider dreams from the standpoint of their prospective value.

496   There is yet another side of dreams to be considered, and one that should certainly not be overlooked. There are many people whose conscious attitude is defective not as regards adaptation to environment but as regards expression of their own character. These are people whose conscious attitude and adaptive performance exceed their capacities as individuals; that is to say, they appear to be better and more valuable than they really are. Their outward success is naturally never paid for out of their individual resources alone, but very largely out of the dynamic reserves generated by collective suggestion. Such people climb above their natural level thanks to the influence of a collective ideal or the lure of some social advantage, or the support offered by society. They have not grown inwardly to the level of their outward eminence, for which reason the unconscious in all these cases has a *negatively compensating, or reductive,* function. It is clear that in these circumstances a reduction or devaluation is just as much a compensatory effort at self-regulation as in other cases, and also that

this function may be eminently prospective (witness Nebuchad-nezzar's dream). We like to associate "prospective" with the idea of construction, preparation, synthesis. But in order to under-stand these reductive dreams we must entirely divorce the term "prospective" from any such idea, for reductive dreams have an effect that is the very reverse of constructive, preparatory, or synthetic—it tends rather to disintegrate, to dissolve, to devalue, even to destroy and demolish. This is naturally not to say that the assimilation of a reductive content must have an altogether destructive effect on the individual as a whole; on the contrary, the effect is often very salutary, in so far as it affects merely his attitude and not the entire personality. But this secondary effect does not alter the essential character of such dreams, which bear a thoroughly reductive and retrospective stamp and for this reason cannot properly be called prospective. For purposes of exact qualification it would be better to call them reductive dreams and the corresponding function a reductive function of the unconscious although, at bottom, it is still the same com-pensatory function. We must accustom ourselves to the fact that the unconscious does not always present the same aspect any more than the conscious attitude does. It alters its appearance and its function just as much as the latter—which is another reason why it is so extremely difficult to form any concrete idea of the nature of the unconscious.

497   Our knowledge of the reductive function of the unconscious we owe mainly to the researches of Freud. His dream-interpreta-tion limits itself in essentials to the repressed personal back-ground of the individual and its infantile-sexual aspects. Subsequent researches then established the bridge to the archaic elements, to the suprapersonal, historical, phylogenetic func-tional residues in the unconscious. Today we can safely assert that the reductive function of dreams constellates material which consists in the main of repressed infantile-sexual wishes (Freud), infantile claims to power (Adler), and suprapersonal, archaic elements of thought, feeling, and instinct. The reproduction of such elements, with their thoroughly retrospective character, does more than anything else to undermine effectively a posi-tion that is too high, and to reduce the individual to his human nullity and to his dependence on physiological, historical, and phylogenetic conditions. Every appearance of false grandeur and

44

importance melts away before the reductive imagery of the dream, which analyses his conscious attitude with pitiless criticism and brings up devastating material containing a complete inventory of all his most painful weaknesses. One is precluded at the outset from calling such a dream prospective, for everything in it, down to the last detail, is retrospective and can be traced back to a past which the dreamer imagined long since buried. This naturally does not prevent the dream-content from being compensatory to the conscious content and finally oriented, since the reductive tendency may sometimes be of the utmost importance for adaptation. Patients can often feel, quite spontaneously, how the dream-content is related to their conscious situation, and it is felt to be prospective, reductive, or compensatory in accordance with this sensed knowledge. Yet this is not always so, by a long way, and it must be emphasized that in general, particularly at the beginning of an analysis, the patient has an insuperable tendency to interpret the results of the analytical investigation of his material obstinately in terms of his pathogenic attitude.

498   Such cases need the help of the analyst in order to interpret their dreams correctly. This makes it exceedingly important how the analyst judges the conscious psychology of his patient. For dream-analysis is not just the practical application of a method that can be learnt mechanically; it presupposes a familiarity with the whole analytical point of view, and this can only be acquired if the analyst has been analysed himself. The greatest mistake an analyst can make is to assume that his patient has a psychology similar to his own. This projection may hit the mark once, but mostly it remains a mere projection. Everything that is unconscious is projected, and for this reason the analyst should be conscious of at least the most important contents of his unconscious, lest unconscious projections cloud his judgment. Everyone who analyses the dreams of others should constantly bear in mind that there is no simple and generally known theory of psychic phenomena, neither with regard to their nature, nor to their causes, nor to their purpose. We therefore possess no general criterion of judgment. We know that there are all kinds of psychic phenomena, but we know nothing certain about their essential nature. We know only that, though the observation of the psyche from any one isolated standpoint

45

can yield very valuable results, it can never produce a satisfactory theory from which one could make deductions. The sexual theory and the wish theory, like the power theory, are valuable points of view without, however, doing anything like justice to the profundity and richness of the human psyche. Had we a theory that did, we could then content ourselves with learning a method mechanically. It would then be simply a matter of reading certain signs that stood for fixed contents, and for this it would only be necessary to learn a few semiotic rules by heart. Knowledge and correct assessment of the conscious situation would then be as superfluous as in the performance of a lumbar puncture. The overworked practitioner of our day has learnt to his sorrow that the psyche remains completely refractory to all methods that approach it from a single exclusive standpoint. At present the only thing we know about the contents of the unconscious, apart from the fact that they are subliminal, is that they stand in a compensatory relationship to consciousness and are therefore essentially relative. It is for this reason that knowledge of the conscious situation is necessary if we want to understand dreams.

499   Reductive, prospective, or simply compensatory dreams do not exhaust the possibilities of interpretation. There is a type of dream which could be called simply a *reaction-dream*. One would be inclined to class in this category all those dreams which seem to be nothing more than the reproduction of an experience charged with affect, did not the analysis of such dreams disclose the deeper reason why these experiences are reproduced so faithfully. It turns out that these experiences also have a symbolical side which escaped the dreamer, and only because of this side is the experience reproduced in the dream. These dreams, however, do not belong to the reaction type, but only those in respect of which certain objective events have caused a trauma that is not merely psychic but at the same time a physical lesion of the nervous system. Such cases of severe shock were produced in abundance by the war, and here we may expect a large number of pure reaction-dreams in which the trauma is the determining factor.

500   Although it is certainly very important for the over-all functioning of the psyche that the traumatic content gradually loses its autonomy by frequent repetition and in this way takes

its place again in the psychic hierarchy, a dream of this kind, which is essentially only a reproduction of the trauma, can hardly be called compensatory. Apparently it brings back a split-off, autonomous part of the psyche, but it soon proves that conscious assimilation of the fragment reproduced by the dream does not by any means put an end to the disturbance which determined the dream. The dream calmly goes on "reproducing": that is to say, the content of the trauma, now become autonomous, goes on working and will continue to do so until the traumatic stimulus has exhausted itself. Until that happens, conscious "realization" is useless.

501   In practice it is not easy to decide whether a dream is essentially reactive or is merely reproducing a traumatic situation symbolically. But analysis can decide the question, because in the latter case the reproduction of the traumatic scene ceases at once if the interpretation is correct, whereas reactive reproduction is left undisturbed by dream-analysis.

502   We find similar reactive dreams in pathological physical conditions where, for instance, severe pain influences the course of the dream. But, in my view, it is only in exceptional cases that somatic stimuli are the determining factor. Usually they coalesce completely with the symbolical expression of the unconscious dream-content; in other words, they are used as a means of expression. Not infrequently the dreams show that there is a remarkable inner symbolical connection between an undoubted physical illness and a definite psychic problem, so that the physical disorder appears as a direct mimetic expression of the psychic situation. I mention this curious fact more for the sake of completeness than to lay any particular stress on this problematic phenomenon. It seems to me, however, that a definite connection does exist between physical and psychic disturbances and that its significance is generally underrated, though on the other hand it is boundlessly exaggerated owing to certain tendencies to regard physical disturbances merely as an expression of psychic disturbances, as is particularly the case with Christian Science. Dreams throw very interesting sidelights on the inter-functioning of body and psyche, which is why I raise this question here.

503   Another dream-determinant that deserves mention is telepathy. The authenticity of this phenomenon can no longer be disputed today. It is, of course, very simple to deny its existence

without examining the evidence, but that is an unscientific procedure which is unworthy of notice. I have found by experience that telepathy does in fact influence dreams, as has been asserted since ancient times. Certain people are particularly sensitive in this respect and often have telepathically influenced dreams. But in acknowledging the phenomenon of telepathy I am not giving unqualified assent to the popular theory of action at a distance. The phenomenon undoubtedly exists, but the theory of it does not seem to me so simple. In every case one must consider the possibilities of concordance of associations, of parallel psychic processes [6] which have been shown to play a very great role especially in families, and which also manifest themselves in an identity or far-reaching similarity of attitude. Equally one must take into account the possibility of cryptomnesia, on which special emphasis has been laid by Flournoy.[7] It sometimes causes the most astounding phenomena. Since any kind of subliminal material shows up in dreams, it is not at all surprising that cryptomnesia sometimes appears as a determining factor. I have had frequent occasion to analyse telepathic dreams, among them several whose telepathic significance was still unknown at the moment of analysis. The analysis yielded subjective material, like any other dream-analysis, in consequence of which the dream had a significance that bore on the situation of the dreamer at the moment. It yielded nothing that could have shown that the dream was telepathic. So far I have found no dream in which the telepathic content lay beyond a doubt in the associative material brought up by analysis (i.e., in the latent dream-content). It invariably lay in the manifest dream-content.

504   Usually in the literature of telepathic dreams only those are mentioned where a powerfully affective event is anticipated "telepathically" in space or time, that is to say when the human importance of the event, such as a death, would help to explain the premonition of it or its perception at a distance or at least make it more intelligible. The telepathic dreams I have observed were mostly of this type. A few of them, however, were distinguished by the remarkable fact that the manifest dream-content contained a telepathic statement about something com-

---

6 Fürst, "Statistical Investigations . . . on Familial Agreement," pp. 407ff.
7 *From India to the Planet Mars* and "Nouvelles observations sur un cas de somnambulisme avec glossolalie."

pletely unimportant, for instance the face of an unknown and quite commonplace individual, or a certain arrangement of furniture in indifferent surroundings, or the arrival of an unimportant letter, etc. Naturally when I say "unimportant" I mean only that neither by the usual questioning nor by analysis could I discover any content whose importance would have "justified" the telepathic phenomenon. In such cases one is inclined, more so than in those first mentioned, to think of "chance." But it seems to me, unfortunately, that the hypothesis of chance is always an *asylum ignorantiae*. Certainly no one will deny that very strange chance events do occur, but the fact that one can count with some probability on their repetition excludes their chance nature. I would not, of course, assert that the law behind them is anything "supernatural," but merely something which we cannot get at with our present knowledge. Thus even questionable telepathic contents possess a reality character that mocks all expectations of probability. Although I would not presume to a theoretical opinion on these matters, I nevertheless consider it right to recognize and emphasize their reality. This standpoint brings an enrichment to dream-analysis.[8]

505 As against Freud's view that the dream is essentially a wish-fulfilment, I hold with my friend and collaborator Alphonse Maeder that the dream is a *spontaneous self-portrayal, in symbolic form, of the actual situation in the unconscious.* Our view coincides at this point with the conclusions of Silberer.[9] The agreement with Silberer is the more gratifying in that it came about as the result of mutually independent work.

506 Now this view contradicts Freud's formula only in so far as it declines to make a definite statement about the meaning of dreams. Our formula merely says that the dream is a symbolical representation of an unconscious content. It leaves the question open whether these contents are always wish-fulfilments. Further researches, expressly referred to by Maeder, have shown that the sexual language of dreams is not always to be interpreted in a concretistic way [10]—that it is, in fact, an archaic language which naturally uses all the analogies readiest to hand without their necessarily coinciding with a real sexual content. It is

8 On the question of telepathy see Rhine, *New Frontiers of the Mind.*
9 Cf. Silberer's works on "symbol-formation": "Über die Symbolbildung."
10 At this point we meet with agreement from Adler.

49

therefore unjustifiable to take the sexual language of dreams literally under all circumstances, while other contents are explained as symbolical. But as soon as you take the sexual metaphors as symbols for something unknown, your conception of the nature of dreams at once deepens. Maeder has demonstrated this from a practical example given by Freud.[11] So long as the sexual language of dreams is understood concretistically, there can be only a direct, outward, and concrete solution, or else nothing is done at all—one resigns oneself opportunistically to one's inveterate cowardice or laziness. There is no real conception of, and no attitude to, the problem. But that immediately becomes possible when the concretistic misconception is dropped, that is, when the patient stops taking the unconscious sexual language of the dream literally and interpreting the dream-figures as real persons.

507   Just as we tend to assume that the world is as we see it, we naïvely suppose that people are as we imagine them to be. In this latter case, unfortunately, there is no scientific test that would prove the discrepancy between perception and reality. Although the possibility of gross deception is infinitely greater here than in our perception of the physical world, we still go on naïvely projecting our own psychology into our fellow human beings. In this way everyone creates for himself a series of more or less imaginary relationships based essentially on projection. Among neurotics there are even cases where fantasy projections provide the sole means of human relationship. A person whom I perceive mainly through my projections is an *imago* or, alternatively, a *carrier* of imagos or symbols. All the contents of our unconscious are constantly being projected into our surroundings, and it is only by recognizing certain properties of the objects as projections or imagos that we are able to distinguish them from the real properties of the objects. But if we are not aware that a property of the object is a projection, we cannot do anything else but be naïvely convinced that it really does belong to the object. All human relationships swarm with these projections; anyone who cannot see this in his personal life need only have his attention drawn to the psychology of the press in wartime. *Cum grano salis,* we always see our own

11 Maeder, *The Dream Problem,* pp. 31ff.

unavowed mistakes in our opponent. Excellent examples of this are to be found in all personal quarrels. Unless we are possessed of an unusual degree of self-awareness we shall never see through our projections but must always succumb to them, because the mind in its natural state presupposes the existence of such projections. It is the natural and given thing for unconscious contents to be projected. In a comparatively primitive person this creates that characteristic relationship to the object which Lévy-Bruhl has fittingly called "mystic identity" or "participation mystique." [12] Thus every normal person of our time, who is not reflective beyond the average, is bound to his environment by a whole system of projections. So long as all goes well, he is totally unaware of the compulsive, i.e., "magical" or "mystical," character of these relationships. But if a paranoid disturbance sets in, then these unconscious relationships turn into so many compulsive ties, decked out, as a rule, with the same unconscious material that formed the content of these projections during the normal state. So long as the libido can use these projections as agreeable and convenient bridges to the world, they will alleviate life in a positive way. But as soon as the libido wants to strike out on another path, and for this purpose begins running back along the previous bridges of projection, they will work as the greatest hindrances it is possible to imagine, for they effectively prevent any real detachment from the former object. We then witness the characteristic phenomenon of a person trying to devalue the former object as much as possible in order to detach his libido from it. But as the previous identity is due to the projection of subjective contents, complete and final detachment can only take place when the imago that mirrored itself in the object is restored, together with its meaning, to the subject. This restoration is achieved through conscious recognition of the projected content, that is, by acknowledging the "symbolic value" of the object.

508 The frequency of such projections is as certain as the fact that they are never seen through. That being so, it is hardly

12 *How Natives Think*, p. 129. It is to be regretted that Lévy-Bruhl expunged this exceedingly apt term from later editions of his books. Probably he succumbed to the attacks of those stupid persons who imagine that "mystic" means their own nonsensical conception of it. [Cf. the original edn., *Les Fonctions mentales*, p. 140.—EDITORS.]

surprising that the naïve person takes it as self-evident from the start that when he dreams of Mr. X this dream-image is identical with the real Mr. X. It is an assumption that is entirely in accord with his ordinary, uncritical conscious attitude, which makes no distinction between the object as such and the idea one has of it. But there is no denying that, looked at critically, the dream-image has only an outward and very limited connection with the object. In reality it is a complex of psychic factors that *has fashioned itself*—albeit under the influence of certain external stimuli—and therefore consists mainly of subjective factors that are peculiar to the subject and often have very little to do with the real object. We understand another person in the same way as we understand, or seek to understand, ourselves. What we do not understand in ourselves we do not understand in the other person either. So there is plenty to ensure that his image will be for the most part subjective. As we know, even an intimate friendship is no guarantee of objective knowledge.

509 Now if one begins, as the Freudian school does, by taking the manifest content of the dream as "unreal" or "symbolical," and explains that though the dream speaks of a church-spire it really means a phallus, then it is only a step to saying that the dream often speaks of sexuality but does not always mean it, and equally, that the dream often speaks of the father but really means the dreamer himself. Our imagos are constituents of our minds, and if our dreams reproduce certain ideas these ideas are primarily *our* ideas, in the structure of which our whole being is interwoven. They are subjective factors, grouping themselves as they do in the dream, and expressing this or that meaning, not for extraneous reasons but from the most intimate promptings of our psyche. The whole dream-work is essentially subjective, and a dream is a theatre in which the dreamer is himself the scene, the player, the prompter, the producer, the author, the public, and the critic. This simple truth forms the basis for a conception of the dream's meaning which I have called *interpretation on the subjective level.* Such an interpretation, as the term implies, conceives all the figures in the dream as personified features of the dreamer's own personality.[13]

13 Several examples of interpretation on the subjective level have been furnished by Maeder. The two kinds of interpretation are discussed in detail in *Two Essays on Analytical Psychology,* pars. 128ff.

510   This view has aroused a considerable amount of resistance. One line of argument appeals to the naïve assumption we have just mentioned, concerning Mr. X. Another argument is based on the question of principle: which is the more important, the "objective level" or the "subjective level"? I can really think of no valid objection to the theoretical probability of a subjective level. But the second problem is considerably more difficult. For just as the image of an object is composed subjectively on the one side, it is conditioned objectively on the other side. When I reproduce it in myself, I am producing something that is determined as much subjectively as objectively. In order to decide which side predominates in any given case, it must first be shown whether the image is reproduced for its subjective or for its objective significance. If, therefore, I dream of a person with whom I am connected by a vital interest, the interpretation on the objective level will certainly be nearer to the truth than the other. But if I dream of a person who is not important to me in reality, then interpretation on the subjective level will be nearer the truth. It is, however, possible—and this happens very frequently in practice—that the dreamer will at once associate this unimportant person with someone with whom he is connected by a strong emotion or affect. Formerly one would have said: the unimportant figure has been thrust forward in the dream intentionally, in order to cover up the painfulness of the other figure. In that case I would follow the path of nature and say: in the dream that highly emotional reminiscence has obviously been replaced by the unimportant figure of Mr. X, hence interpretation on the subjective level would be nearer the truth. To be sure, the substitution achieved by the dream amounts to a repression of the painful reminiscence. But if this reminiscence can be thrust aside so easily it cannot be all that important. The substitution shows that this personal affect allows itself to be depersonalized. I can therefore rise above it and shall not get myself back into the personal, emotional situation again by devaluing the depersonalization achieved by the dream as a mere "repression." I think I am acting more correctly if I regard the replacement of the painful figure by an unimportant one as a depersonalization of the previously personal affect. In this way the affect, or the corresponding sum of libido, has become impersonal, freed from its personal attachment to the object, and

53

I can now shift the previous real conflict on to the subjective plane and try to understand to what extent it is an exclusively subjective conflict. I would like, for clarity's sake, to illustrate this by a short example:

511   I once had a personal conflict with a Mr. A, in the course of which I gradually came to the conclusion that the fault was more on his side than on mine. About this time I had the following dream: *I consulted a lawyer on a certain matter, and to my boundless astonishment he demanded a fee of no less than five thousand francs for the consultation—which I strenuously resisted.*

512   The lawyer was an unimportant reminiscence from my student days. But the student period was important because at that time I got into many arguments and disputes. With a surge of affect, I associated the brusque manner of the lawyer with the personality of Mr. A and also with the continuing conflict. I could now proceed on the objective level and say: Mr. A is hiding behind the lawyer, therefore Mr. A is asking too much of me. He is in the wrong. Shortly before this dream a poor student approached me for a loan of five thousand francs. Thus (by association) Mr. A is a poor student, in need of help and incompetent, because he is at the beginning of his studies. Such a person has no right to make any demands or have any opinions. That, then, would be the wish-fulfilment: my opponent would be gently devalued and pushed aside, and my peace of mind would be preserved. But in reality I woke up at this point with the liveliest affect, furious with the lawyer for his presumption. So I was not in the least calmed by the "wish-fulfilment."

513   Sure enough, behind the lawyer is the unpleasant affair with Mr. A. But it is significant that the dream should dig up that unimportant jurist from my student days. I associate "lawyer" with lawsuit, being in the right, self-righteousness, and hence with that memory from my student days when, right or wrong, I often defended my thesis tenaciously, obstinately, self-righteously, in order at least to win for myself the appearance of superiority by fighting for it. All this, so I feel, has played its part in the dispute with Mr. A. Then I know that he is really myself, that part of me which is unadapted to the present and demands too much, just as I used to do—in other words, squeezes

54

too much libido out of me. I know then that the dispute with Mr. A. cannot die because the self-righteous disputant in me would still like to see it brought to a "rightful" conclusion.

514   This interpretation led to what seemed to me a meaningful result, whereas interpretation on the objective level was unproductive, since I am not in the least interested in proving that dreams are wish-fulfilments. If a dream shows me what sort of mistake I am making, it gives me an opportunity to correct my attitude, which is always an advantage. Naturally such a result can only be achieved through interpretation on the subjective level.

515   Enlightening as interpretation on the subjective level may be in such a case, it may be entirely worthless when a vitally important relationship is the content and cause of the conflict. Here the dream-figure must be related to the real object. The criterion can always be discovered from the conscious material, except in cases where the transference enters into the problem. The transference can easily cause falsifications of judgment, so that the analyst may sometimes appear as the absolutely indispensable *deus ex machina* or as an equally indispensable prop for reality. So far as the patient is concerned he actually is so. It must be left to the analyst to decide how far he himself is the patient's real problem. As soon as the objective level of interpretation starts getting monotonous and unproductive, it is time to regard the figure of the analyst as a symbol for projected contents that belong to the patient. If the analyst does not do that, he has only two alternatives: either he can devalue, and consequently destroy, the transference by reducing it to infantile wishes, or he can accept its reality and sacrifice himself for the patient, sometimes in the teeth of the latter's unconscious resistance. This is to the advantage of neither party, and the analyst invariably comes off worst. But if it is possible to shift the figure of the analyst on to the subjective level, all the projected contents can be restored to the patient with their original value. An example of the withdrawal of projections can be found in my *Two Essays on Analytical Psychology*.[14]

516   It is clear to me that anyone who is not a practising analyst himself will see no particular point in discussing the relative

14 Pars. 206ff. Concerning projections in the transference, see "Psychology of the Transference," index, *s.v.* "transference," "projection."

merits of the "subjective level" and the "objective level." But the more deeply we penetrate into the problem of dreams, the more the technical aspects of practical treatment have to be taken into account. In this regard necessity is indeed the mother of invention, for the analyst must constantly strive to develop his techniques in such a way that they can be of help even in the most difficult cases. We owe it to the difficulties presented by the daily treatment of the sick that we were driven to formulate views which shake the foundations of our everyday beliefs. Although it is a truism to say that an imago is subjective, this statement nevertheless has a somewhat philosophical ring that sounds unpleasant to certain ears. Why this should be so is immediately apparent from what was said above, that the naïve mind at once identifies the imago with the object. Anything that disturbs this assumption has an irritating effect on this class of people. The idea of a subjective level is equally repugnant to them because it disturbs the naïve assumption that conscious contents are identical with objects. As events in wartime [15] have clearly shown, our mentality is distinguished by the shameless naïveté with which we judge our enemy, and in the judgment we pronounce upon him we unwittingly reveal our own defects: we simply accuse our enemy of our own unadmitted faults. We see everything in the other, we criticize and condemn the other, we even want to improve and educate the other. There is no need for me to adduce case material to prove this proposition; the most convincing proof can be found in every newspaper. But it is quite obvious that what happens on a large scale can also happen on a small scale in the individual. Our mentality is still so primitive that only certain functions and areas have outgrown the primary mystic identity with the object. Primitive man has a minimum of self-awareness combined with a maximum of attachment to the object; hence the object can exercise a direct magical compulsion upon him. All primitive magic and religion are based on these magical attachments, which simply consist in the projection of unconscious contents into the object. Self-awareness gradually developed out of this initial state of identity and went hand in hand with the differentiation of subject and object. This differentiation was fol-

15 The first World War.

lowed by the realization that certain qualities which, formerly, were naïvely attributed to the object are in reality subjective contents. Although the men of antiquity no longer believed that they were red cockatoos or brothers to the crocodile, they were still enveloped in magical fantasies. In this respect, it was not until the Age of Enlightenment that any essential advance was made. But as everyone knows, our self-awareness is still a long way behind our actual knowledge. When we allow ourselves to be irritated out of our wits by something, let us not assume that the cause of our irritation lies simply and solely outside us, in the irritating thing or person. In that way we endow them with the power to put us into the state of irritation, and possibly even one of insomnia or indigestion. We then turn round and unhesitatingly condemn the object of offence, while all the time we are raging against an unconscious part of ourselves which is projected into the exasperating object.

517   Such projections are legion. Some of them are favourable, serving as bridges for easing off the libido, some of them are unfavourable, but in practice these are never regarded as obstacles because the unfavourable projections usually settle outside our circle of intimate relationships. To this the neurotic is an exception: consciously or unconsciously, he has such an intensive relationship to his immediate surroundings that he cannot prevent even the unfavourable projections from flowing into the objects closest to him and arousing conflicts. He is therefore compelled—if he wants to be cured—to gain insight into his primitive projections to a far higher degree than the normal person does. It is true that the normal person makes the same projections, but they are better distributed: for the favourable ones the object is close at hand, for the unfavourable ones it is at a distance. It is the same for the primitive: anything strange is hostile and evil. This line of division serves a purpose, which is why the normal person feels under no obligation to make these projections conscious, although they are dangerously illusory. War psychology has made this abundantly clear: everything my country does is good, everything the others do is bad. The centre of all iniquity is invariably found to lie a few miles behind the enemy lines. Because the individual has this same primitive psychology, every attempt to bring these age-old projections to consciousness is felt as irritating. Naturally

57

one would like to have better relations with one's fellows, but only on the condition that *they* live up to *our* expectations—in other words, that they become willing carriers of our projections. Yet if we make ourselves conscious of these projections, it may easily act as an impediment to our relations with others, for there is then no bridge of illusion across which love and hate can stream off so relievingly, and no way of disposing so simply and satisfactorily of all those alleged virtues that are intended to edify and improve others. In consequence of this obstruction there is a damming up of libido, as a result of which the negative projections become increasingly conscious. The individual is then faced with the task of putting down to his own account all the iniquity, devilry, etc. which he has blandly attributed to others and about which he has been indignant all his life. The irritating thing about this procedure is the conviction, on the one hand, that if everybody acted in this way life would be so much more endurable, and a violent resistance, on the other hand, against applying this principle seriously to oneself. If everybody else did it, how much better the world would be; but to do it oneself—how intolerable!

518   The neurotic is *forced* by his neurosis to take this step, but the normal person is not. Instead, he acts out his psychic disturbances socially and politically, in the form of mass psychoses like wars and revolutions. The real existence of an enemy upon whom one can foist off everything evil is an enormous relief to one's conscience. You can then at least say, without hesitation, who the devil is; you are quite certain that the cause of your misfortune is outside, and not in your own attitude. Once you have accepted the somewhat disagreeable consequences of interpretation on the subjective level, however, the misgiving forces itself on you that it is surely impossible that *all* the bad qualities which irritate you in others should belong to you. By that token the great moralist, the fanatical educationist and world-improver, would be the worst of all. Much could be said about the close proximity of good and evil, and even more about the direct relations between pairs of opposites, but that would lead us too far from our theme.

519   The interpretation on the subjective level should not, of course, be carried to extremes. It is simply a question of a rather more critical examination of what is pertinent and what is not.

Something that strikes me about the object may very well be a real property of that object. But the more subjective and emotional this impression is, the more likely it is that the property will be a projection. Yet here we must make a not unimportant distinction: between the quality actually present in the object, without which a projection could not take place, and the value, significance, or energy of this quality. It is not impossible for a quality to be projected upon the object of which the object shows barely any trace in reality (for instance, the primitive projection of magical qualities into inanimate objects). But it is different with the ordinary projection of traits of character or momentary attitudes. Here it frequently happens that the object offers a hook to the projection, and even lures it out. This is generally the case when the object himself (or herself) is not conscious of the quality in question: in that way it works directly upon the unconscious of the projicient. *For all projections provoke counter-projections* when the object is unconscious of the quality projected upon it by the subject, in the same way that a transference is answered by a counter-transference from the analyst when it projects a content of which he is unconscious but which nevertheless exists in him.[16] The counter-transference is then just as useful and meaningful, or as much of a hindrance, as the transference of the patient, according to whether or not it seeks to establish that better rapport which is essential for the realization of certain unconscious contents. Like the transference, the counter-transference is compulsive, a forcible tie, because it creates a "mystical" or unconscious identity with the object. Against these unconscious ties there are always resistances—conscious resistances if the subject's attitude allows him to give his libido only voluntarily, but not to have it coaxed or forced out of him; unconscious resistances if he likes nothing better than having his libido taken away from him. Thus transference and counter-transference, if their contents remain unconscious, create abnormal and untenable relationships which aim at their own destruction.

520   But even supposing some trace of the projected quality can be found in the object, the projection still has a purely subjective significance in practice and recoils upon the subject, because

16 Cf. "The Psychology of the Transference," pars. 364ff., 383f.

it gives an exaggerated value to whatever trace of that quality was present in the object.

521   When the projection corresponds to a quality actually present in the object, the projected content is nevertheless present in the subject too, where it forms a part of the object-imago. The object-imago itself is a psychological entity that is distinct from the actual perception of the object; it is an image existing independently of, and yet based on, all perception,[17] and the relative autonomy of this image remains unconscious so long as it coincides with the actual behaviour of the object. The autonomy of the imago is therefore not recognized by the conscious mind and is unconsciously projected on the object—in other words, it is contaminated with the autonomy of the object. This naturally endows the object with a compelling reality in relation to the subject and gives it an exaggerated value. This value springs from the projection of the imago on the object, from its *a priori* identity with it, with the result that the outer object becomes at the same time an inner one. In this way the outer object can exert, via the unconscious, a direct psychic influence on the subject, since, by virtue of its identity with the imago, it has so to speak a direct hand in the psychic mechanism of the subject. Consequently the object can gain "magical" power over the subject. Excellent examples of this can be found among primitives, who treat their children or any other objects with "souls" exactly as they treat their own psyches. They dare not do anything to them for fear of offending the soul of the child or object. That is why the children are given as little education as possible until the age of puberty, when suddenly a belated education is thrust upon them, often a rather gruesome one (initiation).

522   I have just said that the autonomy of the imago remains unconscious because it is identified with that of the object. The death of the object would, accordingly, be bound to produce remarkable psychological effects, since the object does not disappear completely but goes on existing in intangible form. This is indeed the case. The unconscious imago, which no longer has an object to correspond to it, becomes a ghost and now exerts

[17] For the sake of completeness I should mention that no imago comes exclusively from outside. Its specific form is due just as much to the *a priori* psychic disposition, namely the archetype.

influences on the subject which cannot be distinguished in principle from psychic phenomena. The subject's unconscious projections, which canalized unconscious contents into the imago and identified it with the object, outlive the actual loss of the object and play an important part in the life of primitives as well as of all civilized peoples past and present. These phenomena offer striking proof of the autonomous existence of the object-imagos in the unconscious. They are evidently in the unconscious because they have never been consciously differentiated from the object.

523   Every advance, every conceptual achievement of mankind, has been connected with an advance in self-awareness: man differentiated himself from the object and faced Nature as something distinct from her. Any reorientation of psychological attitude will have to follow the same road: it is evident that the identity of the object with the subjective imago gives it a significance which does not properly belong to it but which it has possessed from time immemorial. This identity is the original state of things. For the subject, however, it is a primitive condition, which can last only so long as it does not lead to serious inconvenience. Overvaluation of the object is one of the things most liable to prejudice the development of the subject. An over-accentuated, "magical" object orients the subject's consciousness in the direction of the object and thwarts any attempt at individual differentiation, which would obviously have to set in with the detachment of the imago from the object. The direction of his individual differentiation cannot possibly be maintained if external factors "magically" interfere with the psychic mechanism. The detachment of the imagos that give the objects their exaggerated significance restores to the subject that split-off energy which he urgently needs for his own development.

524   To interpret the dream-imagos on the subjective level has therefore the same meaning for modern man as taking away his ancestral figures and fetishes would have for primitive man, and trying to convince him that his "medicine" is a spiritual force which dwells not in the object but in the human psyche. The primitive feels a legitimate resistance against this heretical assumption, and in the same way modern man feels that it is disagreeable, perhaps even somehow dangerous, to dissolve the

61

time-honoured and sacrosanct identity between imago and object. The consequences for our psychology, too, can scarcely be imagined: we would no longer have anybody to rail against, nobody whom we could make responsible, nobody to instruct, improve, and punish! On the contrary we would have to begin, in all things, with ourselves; we would have to demand of ourselves, and of no one else, all the things which we habitually demand of others. That being so, it is understandable why the interpretation of dream-imagos on the subjective level is no light step, particularly as it leads to one-sidednesses and exaggerations in one direction or the other.

525   Apart from this purely moral difficulty there are a number of intellectual obstacles as well. It has often been objected that interpretation on the subjective level is a philosophical problem and that the application of this principle verges on a *Weltanschauung* and therefore ceases to be scientific. It does not surprise me that psychology debouches into philosophy, for the thinking that underlies philosophy is after all a psychic activity which, as such, is the proper study of psychology. I always think of psychology as encompassing the whole of the psyche, and that includes philosophy and theology and many other things besides. For underlying all philosophies and all religions are the facts of the human soul, which may ultimately be the arbiters of truth and error.

526   It does not matter greatly to our psychology whether our problems touch on the one sphere or on the other. We have to do first and foremost with practical necessities. If the patient's view of the world becomes a psychological problem, we have to treat it regardless of whether philosophy pertains to psychology or not. Similarly, religious questions are primarily psychological questions so far as we are concerned. It is a regrettable defect that present-day medical psychology should, in general, hold aloof from these problems, and nowhere is this more apparent than in the treatment of the psychogenic neuroses, which often have a better chance of cure anywhere rather than in academic medicine. Although I am a doctor myself, and, on the principle that dog does not eat dog, would have every reason not to criticize the medical profession, I must nevertheless confess that doctors are not always the best guardians of the psychiatric art. I have often found that the medical psychologists

try to practise their art in the routine manner inculcated into them by the peculiar nature of their studies. The study of medicine consists on the one hand in storing up in the mind an enormous number of facts, which are simply memorized without any real knowledge of their foundations, and on the other hand in learning practical skills, which have to be acquired on the principle "Don't think, act!" Thus it is that, of all the professionals, the medical man has the least opportunity of developing the function of *thinking*. So it is no wonder that even psychologically trained doctors have the greatest difficulty in following my reflections, if they follow them at all. They have habituated themselves to handing out prescriptions and mechanically applying methods which they have not thought out themselves. This tendency is the most unsuitable that can be imagined for the practice of medical psychology, for it clings to the skirts of authoritarian theories and techniques and hinders the development of independent thought. I have found that even elementary distinctions, such as those between subjective level and objective level, ego and self, sign and symbol, causality and finality, etc., which are of the utmost importance in practical treatment, overtax their thinking capacities. This may explain their obstinate adherence to views that are out of date and have long been in need of revision. That this is not merely my own subjective opinion is evident from the fanatical one-sidedness and sectarian exclusiveness of certain psychoanalytical groups. Everyone knows that this attitude is a symptom of over-compensated doubt. But then, who applies psychological criteria to himself?

527   The interpretation of dreams as infantile wish-fulfilments or as finalistic "arrangements" subserving an infantile striving for power is much too narrow and fails to do justice to the essential nature of dreams. A dream, like every element in the psychic structure, is a product of the total psyche. Hence we may expect to find in dreams everything that has ever been of significance in the life of humanity. Just as human life is not limited to this or that fundamental instinct, but builds itself up from a multiplicity of instincts, needs, desires, and physical and psychic conditions, etc., so the dream cannot be explained by this or that element in it, however beguilingly simple such an explanation may appear to be. We can be certain that it is incorrect, because

63

no simple theory of instinct will ever be capable of grasping the human psyche, that mighty and mysterious thing, nor, consequently, its exponent, the dream. In order to do anything like justice to dreams, we need an interpretive equipment that must be laboriously fitted together from all branches of the humane sciences.

528   Critics have sometimes accused me outright of "philosophical" or even "theological" tendencies, in the belief that I want to explain everything "philosophically" and that my psychological views are "metaphysical." [18] But I use certain philosophical, religious, and historical material for the exclusive purpose of *illustrating* the psychological facts. If, for instance, I make use of a God-concept or an equally metaphysical concept of energy, I do so because they are images which have been found in the human psyche from the beginning. I find I must emphasize over and over again that neither the moral order, nor the idea of God, nor any religion has dropped into man's lap from outside, straight down from heaven, as it were, but that he contains all this *in nuce* within himself, and for this reason can produce it all out of himself. It is therefore idle to think that nothing but enlightenment is needed to dispel these phantoms. The ideas of the moral order and of God belong to the ineradicable substrate of the human soul. That is why any honest psychology, which is not blinded by the garish conceits of enlightenment, must come to terms with these facts. They cannot be explained away and killed with irony. In physics we can do without a God-image, but in psychology it is a definite fact that has got to be reckoned with, just as we have to reckon with "affect," "instinct," "mother," etc. It is the fault of the everlasting contamination of object and imago that people can make no conceptual distinction between "God" and "God-image," and therefore think that when one speaks of the "God-image" one is speaking of God and offering "theological" explanations. It is not for psychology, as a science, to demand a hypostatization of the God-image. But, the facts being what they are, it does have to reckon with the existence of a God-image. In the same way it reckons with instinct but does not deem itself competent to say what "instinct" really is. The psychological factor thereby

18 By this they mean the theory of archetypes. But is the biological concept of the "pattern of behaviour" also "metaphysical"?

denoted is clear to everyone, just as it is far from clear what that factor is in itself. It is equally clear that the God-image corresponds to a definite complex of psychological facts, and is thus a quantity which we can operate with; but what God is in himself remains a question outside the competence of all psychology. I regret having to repeat such elementary truths.

529   Herewith I have said pretty well all I have to say about the general aspects of dream psychology.[19] I have purposely refrained from going into details; this must be reserved for studies of case material. Our discussion of the general aspects has led us to wider problems which are unavoidable in speaking of dreams. Naturally very much more could be said about the aims of dream-analysis, but since dream-analysis is instrumental to analytical treatment in general, this could only be done if I were to embark on the whole question of therapy. But a thorough-going description of the therapy would require a number of preliminary studies that tackled the problem from different sides. This question is an exceedingly complex one, despite the fact that certain authors outdo one another in simplifications and try to make us believe that the known "roots" of the illness can be extracted with the utmost simplicity. I must warn against all such frivolous undertakings. I would rather see serious minds settling down to discuss, thoroughly and conscientiously, the great problems which analysis has brought in its train. It is really high time academic psychologists came down to earth and wanted to hear about the human psyche as it really is and not merely about laboratory experiments. It is insufferable that professors should forbid their students to have anything to do with analytical psychology, that they should prohibit the use of analytical concepts and accuse our psychology of taking account, in an unscientific manner, of "everyday experiences." I know that psychology in general could derive the greatest benefit from a serious study of the dream problem once it could rid itself of the unjustified lay prejudice that dreams are caused solely by somatic stimuli. This overrating of the somatic factor in psychiatry is one of the basic reasons why psychopathology has made no advances unless directly fertilized by analytical procedures. The dogma that "mental diseases are diseases of the brain" is a hangover from the materialism of the 1870's. It has

19 A few additions will be found in the next paper, written very much later.

become a prejudice which hinders all progress, with nothing to justify it. Even if it were true that all mental diseases are diseases of the brain, that would still be no reason for not investigating the psychic side of the disease. But the prejudice is used to discredit at the outset all attempts in this direction and to strike them dead. Yet the proof that all mental diseases are diseases of the brain has never been furnished and never can be furnished, any more than it can be proved that man thinks or acts as he does because this or that protein has broken down or formed itself in this or that cell. Such a view leads straight to the materialistic gospel: "Man *is* what he eats." Those who think in this way conceive our mental life as anabolic and catabolic processes in the brain-cells. These processes are necessarily thought of merely as laboratory processes of synthesis and disintegration—for to think of them as living processes is totally impossible so long as we cannot think in terms of the life-process itself. But that is how we would have to think of the cell-processes if validity were to be claimed for the materialistic view. In that case we would already have passed beyond materialism, for life can never be thought of as a function of matter, but only as a process existing in and for itself, to which energy and matter are subordinate. Life as a function of matter postulates spontaneous generation, and for proof of that we shall have a very long time to wait. We have no more justification for understanding the psyche as a brain-process than we have for understanding life in general from a one-sided, arbitrarily materialistic point of view that can never be proved, quite apart from the fact that the very attempt to imagine such a thing is crazy in itself and has always engendered craziness whenever it was taken seriously. We have, on the contrary, to consider the psychic process as psychic and not as an organic cell-process. However indignant people may get about "metaphysical phantoms" when cell-processes are explained vitalistically, they nevertheless continue to regard the physical hypothesis as "scientific," although it is no less fantastic. But it fits in with the materialistic prejudice, and therefore every bit of nonsense, provided only that it turns the psychic into the physical, becomes scientifically sacrosanct. Let us hope that the time is not far off when this antiquated relic of ingrained and thoughtless materialism will be eradicated from the minds of our scientists.

ON THE NATURE OF DREAMS [1]

530   Medical psychology differs from all other scientific disci-
plines in that it has to deal with the most complex problems
without being able to rely on tested rules of procedure, on a
series of verifiable experiments and logically explicable facts.
On the contrary, it is confronted with a mass of shifting irrational happenings, for the psyche is perhaps the most baffling
and unapproachable phenomenon with which the scientific
mind has ever had to deal. Although we must assume that all
psychic phenomena are somehow, in the broadest sense, causally
dependent, it is advisable to remember at this point that causality is in the last analysis no more than a statistical truth.
Therefore we should perhaps do well in certain cases to make
allowance for absolute irrationality even if, on heuristic grounds,
we approach each particular case by inquiring into its causality.
Even then, it is advisable to bear in mind at least one of the
classical distinctions, namely that between *causa efficiens* and
causa finalis. In psychological matters, the question "Why does
it happen?" is not necessarily more productive of results than
the other question "To what purpose does it happen?"

531   Among the many puzzles of medical psychology there is one

1 [First published as "Vom Wesen der Träume," *Ciba-Zeitschrift* (Basel), IX : 99
(July, 1945). Revised and expanded in *Über psychische Energetik und das Wesen
der Träume* (Psychologische Abhandlungen, II; Zurich, 1948).—EDITORS.]

problem-child, the dream. It would be an interesting, as well as difficult, task to examine the dream exclusively in its medical aspects, that is, with regard to the diagnosis and prognosis of pathological conditions. The dream does in fact concern itself with both health and sickness, and since, by virtue of its source in the unconscious, it draws upon a wealth of subliminal perceptions, it can sometimes produce things that are very well worth knowing. This has often proved helpful to me in cases where the differential diagnosis between organic and psychogenic symptoms presented difficulties. For prognosis, too, certain dreams are important.[2] In this field, however, the necessary preliminary studies, such as careful records of case histories and the like, are still lacking. Doctors with psychological training do not as yet make a practice of recording dreams systematically, so as to preserve material which would have a bearing on a subsequent outbreak of severe illness or a lethal issue—in other words, on events which could not be foreseen at the beginning of the record. The investigation of dreams in general is a life-work in itself, and their detailed study requires the co-operation of many workers. I have therefore preferred, in this short review, to deal with the fundamental aspects of dream psychology and interpretation in such a way that those who have no experience in this field can at least get some idea of the problem and the method of inquiry. Anyone who is familiar with the material will probably agree with me that a knowledge of fundamentals is more important than an accumulation of case histories, which still cannot make up for lack of experience.

532   The dream is a fragment of involuntary psychic activity, just conscious enough to be reproducible in the waking state. Of all psychic phenomena the dream presents perhaps the largest number of "irrational" factors. It seems to possess a minimum of that logical coherence and that hierarchy of values shown by the other contents of consciousness, and is therefore less transparent and understandable. Dreams that form logically, morally, or aesthetically satisfying wholes are exceptional. Usually a dream is a strange and disconcerting product distinguished by many "bad qualities," such as lack of logic, questionable morality, uncouth form, and apparent absurdity or nonsense. People are

[2] Cf. "The Practical Use of Dream-Analysis," pars. 343ff.

therefore only too glad to dismiss it as stupid, meaningless, and worthless.

533   Every interpretation of a dream is a psychological statement about certain of its contents. This is not without danger, as the dreamer, like most people, usually displays an astonishing sensitiveness to critical remarks, not only if they are wrong, but even more if they are right. Since it is not possible, except under very special conditions, to work out the meaning of a dream without the collaboration of the dreamer, an extraordinary amount of tact is required not to violate his self-respect unnecessarily. For instance, what is one to say when a patient tells a number of indecent dreams and then asks: "Why should *I* have such disgusting dreams?" To this sort of question it is better to give no answer, since an answer is difficult for several reasons, especially for the beginner, and one is very apt under such circumstances to say something clumsy, above all when one thinks one knows what the answer is. So difficult is it to understand a dream that for a long time I have made it a rule, when someone tells me a dream and asks for my opinion, to say first of all to myself: "I have no idea what this dream means." After that I can begin to examine the dream.

534   Here the reader will certainly ask: "Is it worth while in any individual case to look for the meaning of a dream—supposing that dreams have any meaning at all and that this meaning can be proved?"

535   It is easy to prove that an animal is a vertebrate by laying bare the spine. But how does one proceed to lay bare the inner, meaningful structure of a dream? Apparently the dream follows no clearly determined laws or regular modes of behaviour, apart from the well-known "typical" dreams, such as nightmares. Anxiety dreams are not unusual but they are by no means the rule. Also, there are typical dream-motifs known to the layman, such as of flying, climbing stairs or mountains, going about with insufficient clothing, losing your teeth, crowds of people, hotels, railway stations, trains, aeroplanes, automobiles, frightening animals (snakes), etc. These motifs are very common but by no means sufficient to confirm the existence of any system in the organization of a dream.

536   Some people have recurrent dreams. This happens particularly in youth, but the recurrence may continue over several

decades. These are often very impressive dreams which convince one that they "must surely have a meaning." This feeling is justified in so far as one cannot, even taking the most cautious view, avoid the assumption that a definite psychic situation does arise from time to time which causes the dream. But a "psychic situation" is something that, if it can be formulated, is identical with a definite *meaning*—provided, of course, that one does not stubbornly hold to the hypothesis (certainly not proven) that all dreams can be traced back to stomach trouble or sleeping on one's back or the like. Such dreams do indeed tempt one to conjecture some kind of cause. The same is true of so-called typical motifs which repeat themselves frequently in longer series of dreams. Here again it is hard to escape the impression that they mean something.

537   But how do we arrive at a plausible meaning and how can we confirm the rightness of the interpretation? One method—which, however, is not scientific—would be to predict future happenings from the dreams by means of a dream-book and to verify the interpretation by subsequent events, assuming of course that the meaning of dreams lies in their anticipation of the future.

538   Another way to get at the meaning of the dream directly might be to turn to the past and reconstruct former experiences from the occurrence of certain motifs in the dreams. While this is possible to a limited extent, it would have a decisive value only if we could discover in this way something which, though it had actually taken place, had remained unconscious to the dreamer, or at any rate something he would not like to divulge under any circumstances. If neither is the case, then we are dealing simply with memory-images whose appearance in the dream is (a) not denied by anyone, and (b) completely irrelevant so far as a meaningful dream function is concerned, since the dreamer could just as well have supplied the information consciously. This unfortunately exhausts the possible ways of proving the meaning of a dream directly.

539   It is Freud's great achievement to have put dream-interpretation on the right track. Above all, he recognized that no interpretation can be undertaken without the dreamer. The words composing a dream-narrative have not just *one* meaning, but many meanings. If, for instance, someone dreams of a table, we

are still far from knowing what the "table" of the dreamer signifies, although the word "table" sounds unambiguous enough. For the thing we do not know is that this "table" is the very one at which his father sat when he refused the dreamer all further financial help and threw him out of the house as a good-for-nothing. The polished surface of this table stares at him as a symbol of his lamentable worthlessness in his daytime consciousness as well as in his dreams at night. This is what our dreamer understands by "table." Therefore we need the dreamer's help in order to limit the multiple meanings of words to those that are essential and convincing. That the "table" stands as a mortifying landmark in the dreamer's life may be doubted by anyone who was not present. But the dreamer does not doubt it, nor do I. Clearly, dream-interpretation is in the first place an experience which has immediate validity for only two persons.

540   If, therefore, we establish that the "table" in the dream means just that fatal table, with all that this implies, then, although we have not explained the dream, we have at least interpreted one important motif of it; that is, we have recognized the subjective context in which the word "table" is embedded.

541   We arrived at this conclusion by a methodical questioning of the dreamer's own associations. The further procedures to which Freud subjects the dream-contents I have had to reject, for they are too much influenced by the preconceived opinion that dreams are the fulfilment of "repressed wishes." Although there are such dreams, this is far from proving that all dreams are wish-fulfilments, any more than are the thoughts of our conscious psychic life. There is no ground for the assumption that the unconscious processes underlying the dream are more limited and one-sided, in form and content, than conscious processes. One would rather expect that the latter could be limited to known categories, since they usually reflect the regularity or even monotony of the conscious way of life.

542   On the basis of these conclusions and for the purpose of ascertaining the meaning of the dream, I have developed a procedure which I call "taking up the context." This consists in making sure that every shade of meaning which each salient feature of the dream has for the dreamer is determined by the

associations of the dreamer himself. I therefore proceed in the same way as I would in deciphering a difficult text. This method does not always produce an immediately understandable result; often the only thing that emerges, at first, is a hint that looks significant. To give an example: I was working once with a young man who mentioned in his anamnesis that he was happily engaged, and to a girl of "good" family. In his dreams she frequently appeared in very unflattering guise. The context showed that the dreamer's unconscious connected the figure of his bride with all kinds of scandalous stories from quite another source—which was incomprehensible to him and naturally also to me. But, from the constant repetition of such combinations, I had to conclude that, despite his conscious resistance, there existed in him an unconscious tendency to show his bride in this ambiguous light. He told me that if such a thing were true it would be a catastrophe. His acute neurosis had set in a short time after his engagement. Although it was something he could not bear to think about, this suspicion of his bride seemed to me a point of such capital importance that I advised him to instigate some inquiries. These showed the suspicion to be well founded, and the shock of the unpleasant discovery did not kill the patient but, on the contrary, cured him of his neurosis and also of his bride. Thus, although the taking up of the context resulted in an "unthinkable" meaning and hence in an apparently nonsensical interpretation, it proved correct in the light of facts which were subsequently disclosed. This case is of exemplary simplicity, and it is superfluous to point out that only rarely do dreams have so simple a solution.

543   The examination of the context is, to be sure, a simple, almost mechanical piece of work which has only a preparatory significance. But the subsequent production of a readable text, i.e., the actual interpretation of the dream, is as a rule a very exacting task. It needs psychological empathy, ability to coordinate, intuition, knowledge of the world and of men, and above all a special "canniness" which depends on wide understanding as well as on a certain "intelligence du cœur." All these presupposed qualifications, including even the last, are valuable for the art of medical diagnosis in general. No sixth sense is needed to understand dreams. But more is required than routine recipes such as are found in vulgar little dream-

books, or which invariably develop under the influence of preconceived notions. Stereotyped interpretation of dream-motifs
is to be avoided; the only justifiable interpretations are those
reached through a painstaking examination of the context. Even
if one has great experience in these matters, one is again and
again obliged, before each dream, to admit one's ignorance and,
renouncing all preconceived ideas, to prepare for something
entirely unexpected.

544   Even though dreams refer to a definite attitude of consciousness and a definite psychic situation, their roots lie deep in the
unfathomably dark recesses of the conscious mind. For want of
a more descriptive term we call this unknown background the
unconscious. We do not know its nature in and for itself, but
we observe certain effects from whose qualities we venture certain conclusions in regard to the nature of the unconscious
psyche. Because dreams are the most common and most normal
expression of the unconscious psyche, they provide the bulk of
the material for its investigation.

545   Since the meaning of most dreams is *not* in accord with the
tendencies of the conscious mind but shows peculiar deviations,
we must assume that the unconscious, the matrix of dreams, has
an independent function. This is what I call the autonomy of
the unconscious. The dream not only fails to obey our will but
very often stands in flagrant opposition to our conscious intentions. The opposition need not always be so marked; sometimes
the dream deviates only a little from the conscious attitude and
introduces only slight modifications; occasionally it may even
coincide with conscious contents and tendencies. When I attempted to express this behaviour in a formula, the concept of
compensation seemed to me the only adequate one, for it alone
is capable of summing up all the various ways in which a dream
behaves. Compensation must be strictly distinguished from *com-
plementation*. The concept of a complement is too narrow and
too restricting; it does not suffice to explain the function of
dreams, because it designates a relationship in which two things
supplement one another more or less mechanically.[3] Compensation, on the other hand, as the term implies, means balancing

[3] This is not to deny the principle of *complementarity*. "Compensation" is simply
a psychological refinement of this concept.

and comparing different data or points of view so as to produce an adjustment or a rectification.

546   In this regard there are three possibilities. If the conscious attitude to the life situation is in large degree one-sided, then the dream takes the opposite side. If the conscious has a position fairly near the "middle," the dream is satisfied with variations. If the conscious attitude is "correct" (adequate), then the dream coincides with and emphasizes this tendency, though without forfeiting its peculiar autonomy. As one never knows with certainty how to evaluate the conscious situation of a patient, dream-interpretation is naturally impossible without questioning the dreamer. But even if we know the conscious situation we know nothing of the attitude of the unconscious. As the unconscious is the matrix not only of dreams but also of psychogenic symptoms, the question of the attitude of the unconscious is of great practical importance. The unconscious, not caring whether I and those about me feel my attitude to be right, may—so to speak—be of "another mind." This, especially in the case of a neurosis, is not a matter of indifference, as the unconscious is quite capable of bringing about all kinds of unwelcome disturbances "by mistake," often with serious consequences, or of provoking neurotic symptoms. These disturbances are due to lack of harmony between conscious and unconscious. "Normally," as we say, such harmony should be present. The fact is, however, that very frequently it is simply not there, and this is the reason for a vast number of psychogenic misfortunes ranging from severe accidents and illness to harmless slips of the tongue. We owe our knowledge of these relationships to the work of Freud.[4]

547   Although in the great majority of cases compensation aims at establishing a normal psychological balance and thus appears as a kind of self-regulation of the psychic system, one must not forget that under certain circumstances and in certain cases (for instance, in latent psychoses) compensation may lead to a fatal outcome owing to the preponderance of destructive tendencies. The result is suicide or some other abnormal action, apparently preordained in the life-pattern of certain hereditarily tainted individuals.

[4] *The Psychopathology of Everyday Life.*

548   In the treatment of neurosis, the task before us is to re-establish an approximate harmony between conscious and unconscious. This, as we know, can be achieved in a variety of ways: from "living a natural life," persuasive reasoning, strengthening the will, to analysis of the unconscious.

549   Because the simpler methods so often fail and the doctor does not know how to go on treating the patient, the compensatory function of dreams offers welcome assistance. I do not mean that the dreams of modern people indicate the appropriate method of healing, as was reported of the incubation-dreams dreamt in the temples of Aesculapius.[5] They do, however, illuminate the patient's situation in a way that can be exceedingly beneficial to health. They bring him memories, insights, experiences, awaken dormant qualities in the personality, and reveal the unconscious element in his relationships. So it seldom happens that anyone who has taken the trouble to work over his dreams with qualified assistance for a longer period of time remains without enrichment and a broadening of his mental horizon. Just because of their compensatory behaviour, a methodical analysis of dreams discloses new points of view and new ways of getting over the dreaded impasse.

550   The term "compensation" naturally gives us only a very general idea of the function of dreams. But if, as happens in long and difficult treatments, the analyst observes a series of dreams often running into hundreds, there gradually forces itself upon him a phenomenon which, in an isolated dream, would remain hidden behind the compensation of the moment. This phenomenon is a kind of developmental process in the personality itself. At first it seems that each compensation is a momentary adjustment of one-sidedness or an equalization of disturbed balance. But with deeper insight and experience, these apparently separate acts of compensation arrange themselves into a kind of plan. They seem to hang together and in the deepest sense to be subordinated to a common goal, so that a long dream-series no longer appears as a senseless string of incoherent and isolated happenings, but resembles the successive steps in a planned and orderly process of development. I have called this unconscious process spontaneously expressing

5 [Cf. Meier, *Ancient Incubation and Modern Psychotherapy.*—EDITORS.]

itself in the symbolism of a long dream-series the individuation process.

551   Here, more than anywhere else in a discussion of dream psychology, illustrative examples would be desirable. Unfortunately, this is quite impossible for technical reasons. I must therefore refer the reader to my book *Psychology and Alchemy*, which contains an investigation into the structure of a dream-series with special reference to the individuation process.

552   The question whether a long series of dreams recorded outside the analytical procedure would likewise reveal a development aiming at individuation is one that cannot be answered at present for lack of the necessary material. The analytical procedure, especially when it includes a systematic dream-analysis, is a "process of quickened maturation," as Stanley Hall once aptly remarked. It is therefore possible that the motifs accompanying the individuation process appear chiefly and predominantly in dream-series recorded under analysis, whereas in "extra-analytical" dream-series they occur only at much greater intervals of time.

553   I have mentioned before that dream-interpretation requires, among other things, specialized knowledge. While I am quite ready to believe that an intelligent layman with some psychological knowledge and experience of life could, with practice, diagnose dream-compensation correctly, I consider it impossible for anyone without knowledge of mythology and folklore and without some understanding of the psychology of primitives and of comparative religion to grasp the essence of the individuation process, which, according to all we know, lies at the base of psychological compensation.

554   Not all dreams are of equal importance. Even primitives distinguish between "little" and "big" dreams, or, as we might say, "insignificant" and "significant" dreams. Looked at more closely, "little" dreams are the nightly fragments of fantasy coming from the subjective and personal sphere, and their meaning is limited to the affairs of everyday. That is why such dreams are easily forgotten, just because their validity is restricted to the day-to-day fluctuations of the psychic balance. Significant dreams, on the other hand, are often remembered for a lifetime, and not infrequently prove to be the richest jewel in the treasure-house of psychic experience. How many people have I

encountered who at the first meeting could not refrain from saying: "I once had a dream!" Sometimes it was the first dream they could ever remember, and one that occurred between the ages of three and five. I have examined many such dreams, and often found in them a peculiarity which distinguishes them from other dreams: they contain symbolical images which we also come across in the mental history of mankind. It is worth noting that the dreamer does not need to have any inkling of the existence of such parallels. This peculiarity is characteristic of dreams of the individuation process, where we find the mythological motifs or mythologems I have designated as archetypes. These are to be understood as specific forms and groups of images which occur not only at all times and in all places but also in individual dreams, fantasies, visions, and delusional ideas. Their frequent appearance in individual case material, as well as their universal distribution, prove that the human psyche is unique and subjective or personal only in part, and for the rest is collective and objective.[6]

555   Thus we speak on the one hand of a *personal* and on the other of a *collective* unconscious, which lies at a deeper level and is further removed from consciousness than the personal unconscious. The "big" or "meaningful" dreams come from this deeper level. They reveal their significance—quite apart from the subjective impression they make—by their plastic form, which often has a poetic force and beauty. Such dreams occur mostly during the critical phases of life, in early youth, puberty, at the onset of middle age (thirty-six to forty), and within sight of death. Their interpretation often involves considerable difficulties, because the material which the dreamer is able to contribute is too meagre. For these archetypal products are no longer concerned with personal experiences but with general ideas, whose chief significance lies in their intrinsic meaning and not in any personal experience and its associations. For example, a young man dreamed of *a great snake that guarded a golden bowl in an underground vault*. To be sure, he had once seen a huge snake in a zoo, but otherwise he could suggest nothing that might have prompted such a dream, except perhaps the reminiscence of fairytales. Judging by this unsatisfactory

---

[6] Cf. *Two Essays on Analytical Psychology*, I, chs. V–VII.

context the dream, which actually produced a very powerful effect, would have hardly any meaning. But that would not explain its decided emotionality. In such a case we have to go back to mythology, where the combination of snake or dragon with treasure and cave represents an ordeal in the life of the hero. Then it becomes clear that we are dealing with a collective emotion, a typical situation full of affect, which is not primarily a personal experience but becomes one only secondarily. Primarily it is a universally human problem which, because it has been overlooked subjectively, forces itself objectively upon the dreamer's consciousness.[7]

556 A man in middle life still feels young, and age and death lie far ahead of him. At about thirty-six he passes the zenith of life, without being conscious of the meaning of this fact. If he is a man whose whole make-up and nature do not tolerate excessive unconsciousness, then the import of this moment will be forced upon him, perhaps in the form of an archetypal dream. It would be in vain for him to try to understand the dream with the help of a carefully worked out context, for it expresses itself in strange mythological forms that are not familiar to him. The dream uses collective figures because it has to express an eternal human problem that repeats itself endlessly, and not just a disturbance of personal balance.

557 All these moments in the individual's life, when the universal laws of human fate break in upon the purposes, expectations, and opinions of the personal consciousness, are stations along the road of the individuation process. This process is, in effect, the spontaneous realization of the whole man. The ego-conscious personality is only a part of the whole man, and its life does not yet represent his total life. The more he is merely "I," the more he splits himself off from the collective man, of whom he is also a part, and may even find himself in opposition to him. But since everything living strives for wholeness, the inevitable one-sidedness of our conscious life is continually being corrected and compensated by the universal human being in us, whose goal is the ultimate integration of conscious and unconscious, or better, the assimilation of the ego to a wider personality.

[7] Cf. my and C. Kerényi's *Essays on* (or *Introduction to*) *a Science of Mythology*. [Also, *Symbols of Transformation*, pars. 572ff., 577ff.]

558   Such reflections are unavoidable if one wants to understand the meaning of "big" dreams. They employ numerous mythological motifs that characterize the life of the hero, of that greater man who is semi-divine by nature. Here we find the dangerous adventures and ordeals such as occur in initiations. We meet dragons, helpful animals, and demons; also the Wise Old Man, the animal-man, the wishing tree, the hidden treasure, the well, the cave, the walled garden, the transformative processes and substances of alchemy, and so forth—all things which in no way touch the banalities of everyday. The reason for this is that they have to do with the realization of a part of the personality which has not yet come into existence but is still in the process of becoming.

559   How such mythologems get "condensed" in dreams, and how they modify one another, is shown by the picture of the Dream of Nebuchadnezzar (Daniel 4 : 7ff.) [*frontispiece*]. Although purporting to be no more than a representation of that dream, it has, so to speak, been dreamed over again by the artist, as is immediately apparent if one examines the details more closely. The tree is growing (in a quite unbiblical manner) out of the king's navel: it is therefore the genealogical tree of Christ's ancestors, that grows from the navel of Adam, the tribal father.[8] For this reason it bears in its branches the pelican, who nourishes its young with its blood—a well-known allegory of Christ. Apart from that the pelican, together with the four birds that take the place of the four symbols of the evangelists, form a quincunx, and this quincunx reappears lower down in the stag, another symbol of Christ,[9] with the four animals looking

---

[8] The tree is also an alchemical symbol. Cf. *Psychology and Alchemy*, index, *s.v.* "tree"; and "The Philosophical Tree."

[9] The stag is an allegory of Christ because legend attributes to it the capacity for self-renewal. Thus Honorius of Autun writes in his *Speculum de Mysteriis Ecclesiae* (Migne, *P.L.*, vol. 172, col. 847): "They say that the deer, after he has swallowed a serpent, hastens to the water, that by a draught of water he may eject the poison, and then cast his horns and his hair and so take new." In the *Saint-Graal* (III, pp. 219 and 224), it is related that Christ sometimes appeared to the disciples as a white stag with four lions (= four evangelists). In alchemy, Mercurius is allegorized as the stag (Manget, *Bibl. chem.*, Tab. IX, fig. XIII, and elsewhere) because the stag can renew itself. "Les os du cuer du serf vault moult pour conforter le cuer humain" (Delatte, *Textes latins et vieux français relatifs aux Cyranides*, p. 346).

expectantly upwards. These two quaternities have the closest connections with alchemical ideas: above the *volatilia,* below the *terrena,* the former traditionally represented as birds, the latter as quadrupeds. Thus not only has the Christian conception of the genealogical tree and of the evangelical quaternity insinuated itself into the picture, but also the alchemical idea of the double quaternity ("superius est sicut quod inferius"). This contamination shows in the most vivid way how individual dreams make use of archetypes. The archetypes are condensed, interwoven, and blended not only with one another (as here), but also with unique individual elements.

560   But if dreams produce such essential compensations, why are they not understandable? I have often been asked this question. The answer must be that the dream is a natural occurrence, and that nature shows no inclination to offer her fruits gratis or according to human expectations. It is often objected that the compensation must be ineffective unless the dream is understood. This is not so certain, however, for many things can be effective without being understood. But there is no doubt that we can enhance its effect considerably by understanding the dream, and this is often necessary because the voice of the unconscious so easily goes unheard. "What nature leaves imperfect is perfected by the art," says an alchemical dictum.

561   Coming now to the form of dreams, we find everything from lightning impressions to endlessly spun out dream-narrative. Nevertheless there are a great many "average" dreams in which a definite structure can be perceived, not unlike that of a drama. For instance, the dream begins with a STATEMENT OF PLACE, such as, *"I was in a street, it was an avenue"* (1), or, *"I was in a large building like a hotel"* (2). Next comes a statement about the PROTAGONISTS, for instance, *"I was walking with my friend X in a city park. At a crossing we suddenly ran into Mrs. Y"* (3), or, *"I was sitting with Father and Mother in a train compartment"* (4), or, *"I was in uniform with many of my comrades"* (5). Statements of time are rarer. I call this phase of the dream the EXPOSITION. It indicates the scene of action, the people involved, and often the initial situation of the dreamer.

562   In the second phase comes the DEVELOPMENT of the plot. For instance: *"I was in a street, it was an avenue. In the distance a car appeared, which approached rapidly. It was being driven*

very unsteadily, and I thought the driver must be drunk" (1). Or: *"Mrs. Y seemed to be very excited and wanted to whisper something to me hurriedly, which my friend X was obviously not intended to hear"* (3). The situation is somehow becoming complicated, and a definite tension develops because one does not know what will happen.

563   The third phase brings the CULMINATION or *peripeteia*. Here something decisive happens or something changes completely: *"Suddenly I was in the car and seemed to be myself this drunken driver. Only I was not drunk, but strangely insecure and as if without a steering-wheel. I could no longer control the fast moving car, and crashed into a wall"* (1). Or: *"Suddenly Mrs. Y turned deathly pale and fell to the ground"* (3).

564   The fourth and last phase is the *lysis*, the SOLUTION or RESULT produced by the dream-work. (There are certain dreams in which the fourth phase is lacking, and this can present a special problem, not to be discussed here.) Examples: *"I saw that the front part of the car was smashed. It was a strange car that I did not know. I myself was unhurt. I thought with some uneasiness of my responsibility"* (1). *"We thought Mrs. Y was dead, but it was evidently only a faint. My friend X cried out: 'I must fetch a doctor'"* (3). The last phase shows the final situation, which is at the same time the solution "sought" by the dreamer. In dream 1 a new reflectiveness has supervened after a kind of rudderless confusion, or rather, should supervene, since the dream is compensatory. The upshot of dream 3 is the thought that the help of a competent third person is indicated.

565   The first dreamer was a man who had rather lost his head in difficult family circumstances and did not want to let matters go to extremes. The other dreamer wondered whether he ought to obtain the help of a psychiatrist for his neurosis. Naturally these statements are not an interpretation of the dream, they merely outline the initial situation. This division into four phases can be applied without much difficulty to the majority of dreams met with in practice—an indication that dreams generally have a "dramatic" structure.

566   The essential content of the dream-action, as I have shown above, is a sort of finely attuned compensation of the one-sidedness, errors, deviations, or other shortcomings of the conscious attitude. An hysterical patient of mine, an aristocratic lady who

seemed to herself no end distinguished, met in her dreams a whole series of dirty fishwives and drunken prostitutes. In extreme cases the compensation becomes so menacing that the fear of it results in sleeplessness.

567   Thus the dream may either repudiate the dreamer in a most painful way, or bolster him up morally. The first is likely to happen to people who, like the last-mentioned patient, have too good an opinion of themselves; the second to those whose self-valuation is too low. Occasionally, however, the arrogant person is not simply humiliated in the dream, but is raised to an altogether improbable and absurd eminence, while the all-too-humble individual is just as improbably degraded, in order to "rub it in," as the English say.

568   Many people who know something, but not enough, about dreams and their meaning, and who are impressed by their subtle and apparently intentional compensation, are liable to succumb to the prejudice that the dream actually has a moral purpose, that it warns, rebukes, comforts, foretells the future, etc. If one believes that the unconscious always knows best, one can easily be betrayed into leaving the dreams to take the necessary decisions, and is then disappointed when the dreams become more and more trivial and meaningless. Experience has shown me that a slight knowledge of dream psychology is apt to lead to an overrating of the unconscious which impairs the power of conscious decision. The unconscious functions satisfactorily only when the conscious mind fulfils its tasks to the very limit. A dream may perhaps supply what is then lacking, or it may help us forward where our best efforts have failed. If the unconscious really were superior to consciousness it would be difficult to see wherein the advantage of consciousness lay, or why it should ever have come into being as a necessary element in the scheme of evolution. If it were nothing but a *lusus naturae*, the fact of our conscious awareness of the world and of our own existence would be without meaning. The idea that consciousness is a freak of nature is somehow difficult to digest, and for psychological reasons we should avoid emphasizing it, even if it were correct—which, by the way, we shall luckily never be in a position to prove (any more than we can prove the contrary). It is a question that belongs to the realm of metaphysics, where no criterion of truth exists. However, this is in

no way to underestimate the fact that metaphysical views are of the utmost importance for the well-being of the human psyche.

569   In the study of dream psychology we encounter far-reaching philosophical and even religious problems to the understanding of which the phenomenon of dreams has already made decisive contributions. But we cannot boast that we are, at present, in possession of a generally satisfying theory or explanation of this complicated phenomenon. We still know far too little about the nature of the unconscious psyche for that. In this field there is still an infinite amount of patient and unprejudiced work to be done, which no one will begrudge. For the purpose of research is not to imagine that one possesses the theory which alone is right, but, doubting all theories, to approach gradually nearer to the truth.

III

THE PRACTICAL USE OF
DREAM-ANALYSIS

THE PRACTICAL USE OF DREAM-ANALYSIS [1]

294   The use of dream-analysis in psychotherapy is still a much debated question. Many practitioners find it indispensable in the treatment of neuroses, and consider that the dream is a function whose psychic importance is equal to that of the conscious mind itself. Others, on the contrary, dispute the value of dream-analysis and regard dreams as a negligible by-product of the psyche. Obviously, if a person holds the view that the unconscious plays a decisive part in the aetiology of neuroses, he will attribute a high practical importance to dreams as direct expressions of the unconscious. Equally obviously, if he denies the unconscious or at least thinks it aetiologically insignificant, he will minimize the importance of dream-analysis. It might be considered regrettable that in this year of grace 1931, more than half a century after Carus formulated the concept of the unconscious, more than a century after Kant spoke of the "illimitable field of obscure ideas," and nearly two hundred years after Leibniz postulated an unconscious psychic activity, not to mention the achievements of Janet, Flournoy, Freud, and many more—that after all this, the actuality of the unconscious should still be a matter for controversy. But, since it is my intention to deal exclusively with practical questions, I will not advance in this place an apology for the unconscious, although our special problem of dream-analysis stands or falls with such an hypothesis. Without it, the dream is a mere freak of nature, a meaningless conglomeration of fragments left over from the day. Were that really so, there would be no excuse for the present discussion. We cannot treat our theme at all unless we recognize the unconscious, for the avowed aim of dream-analysis is not only to exercise our wits, but to uncover and realize those

1 [* Delivered as a lecture, "Die praktische Verwendbarkeit der Traumanalyse," at the 6th General Medical Congress for Psychotherapy, Dresden, April 1931, and published in the *Bericht* of the Congress; republished in *Wirklichkeit der Seele* (Zurich, 1934), pp. 68–103. Trans. from the *Bericht* by Cary F. Baynes and W. S. Dell in *Modern Man in Search of a Soul* (New York and London, 1933).—EDITORS.]

hitherto unconscious contents which are considered to be of importance in the elucidation or treatment of a neurosis. Anyone who finds this hypothesis unacceptable must simply rule out the question of the applicability of dream-analysis.

295   But since, according to our hypothesis, the unconscious possesses an aetiological significance, and since dreams are the direct expression of unconscious psychic activity, the attempt to analyse and interpret dreams is theoretically justified from a scientific standpoint. If successful, we may expect this attempt to give us scientific insight into the structure of psychic causality, quite apart from any therapeutic results that may be gained. The practitioner, however, tends to consider scientific discoveries as, at most, a gratifying by-product of his therapeutic work, so he is hardly likely to take the bare possibility of theoretical insight into the aetiological background as a sufficient reason for, much less an indication of, the practical use of dream-analysis. He may believe, of course, that the explanatory insight so gained is of therapeutic value, in which case he will elevate dream-analysis to a professional duty. It is well known that the Freudian school is of the firm opinion that very valuable therapeutic results are achieved by throwing light upon the unconscious causal factors—that is, by explaining them to the patient and thus making him fully conscious of the sources of his trouble.

296   Assuming for the moment that this expectation is justified by the facts, then the only question that remains is whether dream-analysis can or cannot be used, alone or in conjunction with other methods, to discover the unconscious aetiology. The Freudian answer to this question is, I may assume, common knowledge. I can confirm this answer inasmuch as dreams, particularly the initial dreams which appear at the very outset of the treatment, often bring to light the essential aetiological factor in the most unmistakable way. The following example may serve as an illustration:

297   I was consulted by a man who held a prominent position in the world. He was afflicted with a sense of anxiety and insecurity, and complained of dizziness sometimes resulting in nausea, heaviness in the head, and constriction of breath—a state that might easily be confused with mountain sickness. He had had an extraordinarily successful career, and had risen,

by dint of ambition, industry, and native talent, from his humble origins as the son of a poor peasant. Step by step he had climbed, attaining at last a leading position which held every prospect of further social advancement. He had now in fact reached the spring-board from which he could have commenced his flight into the empyrean, had not his neurosis suddenly intervened. At this point in his story the patient could not refrain from that familiar exclamation which begins with the stereotyped words: "And just now, when. . . ." The fact that he had all the symptoms of mountain sickness seemed highly appropriate as a drastic illustration of his peculiar impasse. He had also brought to the consultation two dreams from the preceding night. The first dream was as follows: *"I am back again in the small village where I was born. Some peasant lads who went to school with me are standing together in the street. I walk past, pretending not to know them. Then I hear one of them say, pointing at me: 'He doesn't often come back to our village.'"*

298   It requires no feat of interpretation to see in this dream a reference to the humble beginnings of the dreamer's career and to understand what this reference means. The dream says quite clearly: "You forgot how far down you began."

299   Here is the second dream: *"I am in a great hurry because I want to go on a journey. I keep on looking for things to pack, but can find nothing. Time flies, and the train will soon be leaving. Having finally succeeded in getting all my things together, I hurry along the street, only to discover that I have forgotten a brief-case containing important papers. I dash back all out of breath, find it at last, then race to the station, but I make hardly any headway. With a final effort I rush on to the platform only to see the train just steaming out of the station yard. It is very long, and it runs in a curious S-shaped curve, and it occurs to me that if the engine-driver does not look out, and puts on steam when he comes into the straight, the rear coaches will still be on the curve and will be thrown off the rails by the gathering speed. And this is just what happens: the engine-driver puts on steam, I try to cry out, the rear coaches give a frightful lurch and are thrown off the rails. There is a terrible catastrophe. I wake up in terror."*

300   Here again no effort is needed to understand the message of the dream. It describes the patient's frantic haste to advance

himself still further. But since the engine-driver in front steams relentlessly ahead, the neurosis happens at the back: the coaches rock and the train is derailed.

301   It is obvious that, at the present phase of his life, the patient has reached the highest point of his career; the strain of the long ascent from his lowly origin has exhausted his strength. He should have rested content with his achievements, but instead of that his ambition drives him on and on, and up and up into an atmosphere that is too thin for him and to which he is not accustomed. Therefore his neurosis comes upon him as a warning.

302   Circumstances prevented me from treating the patient further, nor did my view of the case satisfy him. The upshot was that the fate depicted in the dream ran its course. He tried to exploit the professional openings that tempted his ambition, and ran so violently off the rails that the catastrophe was realized in actual life.

303   Thus, what could only be inferred from the conscious anamnesis—namely that the mountain sickness was a symbolical representation of the patient's inability to climb any further—was confirmed by the dreams as a fact.

304   Here we come upon something of the utmost importance for the applicability of dream-analysis: the dream describes the inner situation of the dreamer, but the conscious mind denies its truth and reality, or admits it only grudgingly. Consciously the dreamer could not see the slightest reason why he should not go steadily forward; on the contrary, he continued his ambitious climbing and refused to admit his own inability which subsequent events made all too plain. So long as we move in the conscious sphere, we are always unsure in such cases. The anamnesis can be interpreted in various ways. After all, the common soldier carries the marshal's baton in his knapsack, and many a son of poor parents has achieved the highest success. Why should it not be the case here? Since my judgment is fallible, why should my conjecture be better than his? At this point the dream comes in as the expression of an involuntary, unconscious psychic process beyond the control of the conscious mind. It shows the inner truth and reality of the patient as it really is: not as I conjecture it to be, and not as he would like it to be, but *as it is*. I have therefore made it a rule to re-

gard dreams as I regard physiological facts: if sugar appears in the urine, then the urine contains sugar, and not albumen or urobilin or something else that might fit in better with my expectations. That is to say, I take dreams as diagnostically valuable facts.

305   As is the way of all dreams, my little dream example gives us rather more than we expected. It gives us not only the aetiology of the neurosis but a prognosis as well. What is more, we even know exactly where the treatment should begin: we must prevent the patient from going full steam ahead. This is just what he tells himself in the dream.

306   Let us for the time being content ourselves with this hint and return to our consideration of whether dreams enable us to throw light on the aetiology of a neurosis. The dreams I have cited actually do this. But I could equally well cite any number of initial dreams where there is no trace of an aetiological factor, although they are perfectly transparent. I do not wish for the present to consider dreams which call for searching analysis and interpretation.

307   The point is this: there are neuroses whose real aetiology becomes clear only right at the end of an analysis, and other neuroses whose aetiology is relatively unimportant. This brings me back to the hypothesis from which we started, that for the purposes of therapy it is absolutely necessary to make the patient conscious of the aetiological factor. This hypothesis is little more than a hang-over from the old trauma theory. I do not of course deny that many neuroses are traumatic in origin; I simply contest the notion that all neuroses are of this nature and arise without exception from some crucial experience in childhood. Such a view necessarily results in the causalistic approach. The doctor must give his whole attention to the patient's past; he must always ask "Why?" and ignore the equally pertinent question "What for?" Often this has a most deleterious effect on the patient, who is thereby compelled to go searching about in his memory—perhaps for years—for some hypothetical event in his childhood, while things of immediate importance are grossly neglected. The purely causalistic approach is too narrow and fails to do justice to the true significance either of the dream or of the neurosis. Hence an approach that uses dreams for the sole purpose of discovering the aetio-

logical factor is biased and overlooks the main point of the dream. Our example indeed shows the aetiology clearly enough, but it also offers a prognosis or anticipation of the future as well as a suggestion about the treatment. There are in addition large numbers of initial dreams which do not touch the aetiology at all, but deal with quite other matters, such as the patient's attitude to the doctor. As an example of this I would like to tell you three dreams, all from the same patient, and each dreamt at the beginning of a course of treatment under three different analysts. Here is the first: *"I have to cross the frontier into another country, but cannot find the frontier and nobody can tell me where it is."*

308   The ensuing treatment proved unsuccessful and was broken off after a short time. The second dream is as follows: *"I have to cross the frontier, but the night is pitch-black and I cannot find the customs-house. After a long search I see a tiny light far off in the distance, and assume that the frontier is over there. But in order to get there, I have to pass through a valley and a dark wood in which I lose my way. Then I notice that someone is near me. Suddenly he clings to me like a madman and I awake in terror."*

309   This treatment, too, was broken off after a few weeks because the analyst unconsciously identified himself with the patient and the result was complete loss of orientation on both sides.

310   The third dream took place under my treatment: *"I have to cross a frontier, or rather, I have already crossed it and find myself in a Swiss customs-house. I have only a handbag with me and think I have nothing to declare. But the customs official dives into my bag and, to my astonishment, pulls out a pair of twin beds."*

311   The patient had got married while under my treatment, and at first she developed the most violent resistance to her marriage. The aetiology of the neurotic resistance came to light only many months afterwards and there is not a word about it in the dreams. They are without exception anticipations of the difficulties she is to have with the doctors concerned.

312   These examples, like many others of the kind, may suffice to show that dreams are often anticipatory and would lose their specific meaning completely on a purely causalistic view.

They afford unmistakable information about the analytical situation, the correct understanding of which is of the greatest therapeutic importance. Doctor A understood the situation correctly and handed the patient over to Doctor B. Under him she drew her own conclusions from the dream and decided to leave. My interpretation of the third dream was a disappointment to her, but the fact that the dream showed the frontier as already crossed encouraged her to go on in spite of all difficulties.

313   Initial dreams are often amazingly lucid and clear-cut. But as the work of analysis progresses, the dreams tend to lose their clarity. If, by way of exception, they keep it we can be sure that the analysis has not yet touched on some important layer of the personality. As a rule, dreams get more and more opaque and blurred soon after the beginning of the treatment, and this makes the interpretation increasingly difficult. A further difficulty is that a point may soon be reached where, if the truth be told, the doctor no longer understands the situation as a whole. That he does not understand is proved by the fact that the dreams become increasingly obscure, for we all know that their "obscurity" is a purely subjective opinion of the doctor. To the understanding nothing is obscure; it is only when we do not understand that things appear unintelligible and muddled. In themselves dreams are naturally clear; that is, they are just what they must be under the given circumstances. If, from a later stage of treatment or from a distance of some years, we look back at these unintelligible dreams, we are often astounded at our own blindness. Thus when, as the analysis proceeds, we come upon dreams that are strikingly obscure in comparison with the illuminating initial dreams, the doctor should not be too ready to accuse the dreams of confusion or the patient of deliberate resistance; he would do better to take these findings as a sign of his own growing inability to understand—just as the psychiatrist who calls his patient "confused" should recognize that this is a projection and should rather call himself confused, because in reality it is he whose wits are confused by the patient's peculiar behaviour. Moreover it is therapeutically very important for the doctor to admit his lack of understanding in time, for nothing is more unbearable to the patient than to be always understood. He relies far too much anyway on the mysterious powers of the doctor and, by appealing to

his professional vanity, lays a dangerous trap for him. By taking refuge in the doctor's self-confidence and "profound" understanding, the patient loses all sense of reality, falls into a stubborn transference, and retards the cure.

314   Understanding is clearly a very subjective process. It can be extremely one-sided, in that the doctor understands but not the patient. In such a case the doctor conceives it to be his duty to convince the patient, and if the latter will not allow himself to be convinced, the doctor accuses him of resistance. When the understanding is all on my side, I say quite calmly that I do not understand, for in the end it makes very little difference whether the doctor understands or not, but it makes all the difference whether the patient understands. Understanding should therefore be understanding in the sense of an agreement which is the fruit of joint reflection. The danger of a one-sided understanding is that the doctor may judge the dream from the standpoint of a preconceived opinion. His judgment may be in line with orthodox theory, it may even be fundamentally correct, but it will not win the patient's assent, he will not come to an understanding with him, and that is in the practical sense incorrect—incorrect because it anticipates and thus cripples the patient's development. The patient, that is to say, does not need to have a truth inculcated into him—if we do that, we only reach his head; he needs far more to grow up to this truth, and in that way we reach his heart, and the appeal goes deeper and works more powerfully.

315   When the doctor's one-sided interpretation is based on mere agreement as to theory or on some other preconceived opinion, his chances of convincing the patient or of achieving any therapeutic results depend chiefly upon *suggestion*. Let no one deceive himself about this. In itself, suggestion is not to be despised, but it has serious limitations, not to speak of the subsidiary effects upon the patient's independence of character which, in the long run, we could very well do without. A practising analyst may be supposed to believe implicitly in the significance and value of conscious realization, whereby hitherto unconscious parts of the personality are brought to light and subjected to conscious discrimination and criticism. It is a process that requires the patient to face his problems and that taxes his powers of conscious judgment and decision. It is nothing less

than a direct challenge to his ethical sense, a call to arms that must be answered by the whole personality. As regards the maturation of personality, therefore, the analytical approach is of a higher order than suggestion, which is a species of magic that works in the dark and makes no ethical demands upon the personality. Methods of treatment based on suggestion are deceptive makeshifts; they are incompatible with the principles of analytical therapy and should be avoided if at all possible. Naturally suggestion can only be avoided if the doctor is conscious of its possibility. There is at the best of times always enough—and more than enough—unconscious suggestion.

316   The analyst who wishes to rule out conscious suggestion must therefore consider every dream interpretation invalid until such time as a formula is found which wins the assent of the patient.

317   The observance of this rule seems to me imperative when dealing with those dreams whose obscurity is evidence of the lack of understanding of both doctor and patient. The doctor should regard every such dream as something new, as a source of information about conditions whose nature is unknown to him, concerning which he has as much to learn as the patient. It goes without saying that he should give up all his theoretical assumptions and should in every single case be ready to construct a totally new theory of dreams. There are still boundless opportunities for pioneer work in this field. The view that dreams are merely the imaginary fulfilments of repressed wishes is hopelessly out of date. There are, it is true, dreams which manifestly represent wishes or fears, but what about all the other things? Dreams may contain ineluctable truths, philosophical pronouncements, illusions, wild fantasies, memories, plans, anticipations, irrational experiences, even telepathic visions, and heaven knows what besides. One thing we ought never to forget: almost half our life is passed in a more or less unconscious state. The dream is specifically the utterance of the unconscious. Just as the psyche has a diurnal side which we call consciousness, so also it has a nocturnal side: the unconscious psychic activity which we apprehend as dreamlike fantasy. It is certain that the conscious mind consists not only of wishes and fears, but of vastly more besides; and it is highly probable that our dream psyche possesses a wealth of contents and living forms

equal to or even greater than those of the conscious mind, which is characterized by concentration, limitation, and exclusion.

318   This being so, it is imperative that we should not pare down the meaning of the dream to fit some narrow doctrine. We must remember that there are not a few patients who imitate the technical or theoretical jargon of the doctor, and do this even in their dreams, in accordance with the old tag, *Canis panem somniat, piscator pisces.* This is not to say that the fishes of which the fisherman dreams are fishes and nothing more. There is no language that cannot be misused. As may easily be imagined, the misuse often turns the tables on us; it even seems as if the unconscious had a way of strangling the doctor in the coils of his own theory. Therefore I leave theory aside as much as possible when analysing dreams—not entirely, of course, for we always need some theory to make things intelligible. It is on the basis of theory, for instance, that I expect dreams to have a meaning. I cannot prove in every case that this is so, for there are dreams which the doctor and the patient simply do not understand. But I have to make such an hypothesis in order to find courage to deal with dreams at all. To say that dreams add something important to our conscious knowledge, and that a dream which fails to do so has not been properly interpreted —that, too, is a theory. But I must make this hypothesis as well in order to explain to myself why I analyse dreams in the first place. All other hypotheses, however, about the function and the structure of dreams are merely rules of thumb and must be subjected to constant modification. In dream-analysis we must never forget, even for a moment, that we move on treacherous ground where nothing is certain but uncertainty. If it were not so paradoxical, one would almost like to call out to the dream interpreter: "Do anything you like, only don't try to understand!"

319   When we take up an obscure dream, our first task is not to understand and interpret, but to establish the context with minute care. By this I do *not* mean unlimited "free association" starting from any and every image in the dream, but a careful and conscious illumination of the interconnected associations objectively grouped round particular images. Many patients have first to be educated to this, for they resemble the

doctor in their insuperable desire to understand and interpret offhand, especially when they have been primed by ill-digested reading or by a previous analysis that went wrong. They begin by associating in accordance with a theory, that is, they try to understand and interpret, and they nearly always get stuck. Like the doctor, they want to get behind the dream at once in the false belief that the dream is a mere façade concealing the true meaning. But the so-called façade of most houses is by no means a fake or a deceptive distortion; on the contrary, it follows the plan of the building and often betrays the interior arrangement. The "manifest" dream-picture is the dream itself and contains the whole meaning of the dream. When I find sugar in the urine, it is sugar and not just a façade for albumen. What Freud calls the "dream-façade" is the dream's obscurity, and this is really only a projection of our own lack of understanding. We say that the dream has a false front only because we fail to see into it. We would do better to say that we are dealing with something like a text that is unintelligible not because it has a façade—a text has no façade—but simply because we cannot read it. We do not have to get behind such a text, but must first learn to read it.

320   The best way to do this, as I have already remarked, is to establish the context. Free association will get me nowhere, any more than it would help me to decipher a Hittite inscription. It will of course help me to uncover all my own complexes, but for this purpose I have no need of a dream—I could just as well take a public notice or a sentence in a newspaper. Free association will bring out all my complexes, but hardly ever the meaning of a dream. To understand the dream's meaning I must stick as close as possible to the dream images. When somebody dreams of a "deal table," it is not enough for him to associate it with his writing-desk which does not happen to be made of deal. Supposing that nothing more occurs to the dreamer, this blocking has an objective meaning, for it indicates that a particular darkness reigns in the immediate neighbourhood of the dream-image, and that is suspicious. We would expect him to have dozens of associations to a deal table, and the fact that there is apparently nothing is itself significant. In such cases I keep on returning to the image, and I usually say to my patient, "Suppose I had no idea what the words 'deal table' mean. De-

97

scribe this object and give me its history in such a way that I cannot fail to understand what sort of a thing it is."

321   In this way we manage to establish almost the whole context of the dream-image. When we have done this for all the images in the dream we are ready for the venture of interpretation.

322   Every interpretation is an hypothesis, an attempt to read an unknown text. An obscure dream, taken in isolation, can hardly ever be interpreted with any certainty. For this reason I attach little importance to the interpretation of single dreams. A relative degree of certainty is reached only in the interpretation of a series of dreams, where the later dreams correct the mistakes we have made in handling those that went before. Also, the basic ideas and themes can be recognized much better in a dream-series, and I therefore urge my patients to keep a careful record of their dreams and of the interpretations given. I also show them how to work out their dreams in the manner described, so that they can bring the dream and its context with them in writing to the consultation. At a later stage I get them to work out the interpretation as well. In this way the patient learns how to deal correctly with his unconscious without the doctor's help.

323   Were dreams nothing more than sources of information about factors of aetiological importance, the whole work of dream-interpretation could safely be left to the doctor. Again, if their only use was to provide the doctor with a collection of useful hints and psychological tips, my own procedure would be entirely superfluous. But since, as my examples have shown, dreams contain something more than practical helps for the doctor, dream-analysis deserves very special attention. Sometimes, indeed, it is a matter of life and death. Among many instances of this sort, there is one that has remained particularly impressive. It concerns a colleague of mine, a man somewhat older than myself, whom I used to see from time to time and who always teased me about my dream-interpretations. Well, I met him one day in the street and he called out to me, "How are things going? Still interpreting dreams? By the way, I've had another idiotic dream. Does that mean something too?" This is what he had dreamed: *"I am climbing a high mountain, over steep snow-covered slopes. I climb higher and higher, and it is marvellous weather. The higher I climb the better I*

*feel. I think, 'If only I could go on climbing like this for ever!'
When I reach the summit my happiness and elation are so
great that I feel I could mount right up into space. And I discover that I can actually do so: I mount upwards on empty air,
and awake in sheer ecstasy."*

324   After some discussion, I said, "My dear fellow, I know you
can't give up mountaineering, but let me implore you not to
go alone from now on. When you go, take two guides, and
promise on your word of honour to follow them absolutely."
"Incorrigible!" he replied, laughing, and waved good-bye. I
never saw him again. Two months later the first blow fell.
When out alone, he was buried by an avalanche, but was dug
out in the nick of time by a military patrol that happened to be
passing. Three months afterwards the end came. He went on a
climb with a younger friend, but without guides. A guide
standing below saw him literally step out into the air while descending a rock face. He fell on the head of his friend, who was
waiting lower down, and both were dashed to pieces far below.
That was *ecstasis* with a vengeance! [2]

325   No amount of scepticism and criticism has yet enabled me
to regard dreams as negligible occurrences. Often enough they
appear senseless, but it is obviously we who lack the sense and
ingenuity to read the enigmatic message from the nocturnal
realm of the psyche. Seeing that at least half our psychic existence is passed in that realm, and that consciousness acts upon
our nightly life just as much as the unconscious overshadows
our daily life, it would seem all the more incumbent on medical psychology to sharpen its senses by a systematic study of
dreams. Nobody doubts the importance of conscious experience; why then should we doubt the significance of unconscious
happenings? They also are part of our life, and sometimes more
truly a part of it for weal or woe than any happenings of the
day.

326   Since dreams provide information about the hidden inner
life and reveal to the patient those components of his personality which, in his daily behaviour, appear merely as neurotic symptoms, it follows that we cannot effectively treat him
from the side of consciousness alone, but must bring about a
change in and through the unconscious. In the light of our

[2] [This dream is discussed at greater length in "Child Development and Education," pars. 117ff.—EDITORS.]

present knowledge this can be achieved only by the thorough and conscious assimilation of unconscious contents.

327 "Assimilation" in this sense means mutual penetration of conscious and unconscious, and not—as is commonly thought and practised—a one-sided evaluation, interpretation, and deformation of unconscious contents by the conscious mind. As to the value and significance of unconscious contents in general, very mistaken views are current. It is well known that the Freudian school presents the unconscious in a thoroughly negative light, much as it regards primitive man as little better than a monster. Its nursery-tales about the terrible old man of the tribe and its teachings about the "infantile-perverse-criminal" unconscious have led people to make a dangerous ogre out of something perfectly natural. As if all that is good, reasonable, worth while, and beautiful had taken up its abode in the conscious mind! Have the horrors of the World War done nothing to open our eyes, so that we still cannot see that the conscious mind is even more devilish and perverse than the naturalness of the unconscious?

328 The charge has recently been laid at my door that my teaching about the assimilation of the unconscious would undermine civilization and deliver up our highest values to sheer primitivity. Such an opinion can only be based on the totally erroneous supposition that the unconscious is a monster. It is a view that springs from fear of nature and the realities of life. Freud invented the idea of sublimation to save us from the imaginary claws of the unconscious. But what is real, what actually exists, cannot be alchemically sublimated, and if anything is apparently sublimated it never was what a false interpretation took it to be.

329 The unconscious is not a demoniacal monster, but a natural entity which, as far as moral sense, aesthetic taste, and intellectual judgment go, is completely neutral. It only becomes dangerous when our conscious attitude to it is hopelessly wrong. To the degree that we repress it, its danger increases. But the moment the patient begins to assimilate contents that were previously unconscious, its danger diminishes. The dissociation of personality, the anxious division of the day-time and the night-time sides of the psyche, cease with progressive assimilation. What my critic feared—the overwhelming of the conscious mind

by the unconscious—is far more likely to ensue when the unconscious is excluded from life by being repressed, falsely interpreted, and depreciated.

330   The fundamental mistake regarding the nature of the unconscious is probably this: it is commonly supposed that its contents have only one meaning and are marked with an unalterable plus or minus sign. In my humble opinion, this view is too naïve. The psyche is a self-regulating system that maintains its equilibrium just as the body does. Every process that goes too far immediately and inevitably calls forth compensations, and without these there would be neither a normal metabolism nor a normal psyche. In this sense we can take the theory of compensation as a basic law of psychic behaviour. Too little on one side results in too much on the other. Similarly, the relation between conscious and unconscious is compensatory. This is one of the best-proven rules of dream interpretation. When we set out to interpret a dream, it is always helpful to ask: What conscious attitude does it compensate?

331   Compensation is not as a rule merely an illusory wish-fulfilment, but an actual fact that becomes still more actual the more we repress it. We do not stop feeling thirsty by repressing our thirst. In the same way, the dream-content is to be regarded with due seriousness as an actuality that has to be fitted into the conscious attitude as a codetermining factor. If we fail to do this, we merely persist in that eccentric frame of mind which evoked the unconscious compensation in the first place. It is then difficult to see how we can ever arrive at a sane judgment of ourselves or at a balanced way of living.

332   If it should occur to anyone to replace the conscious content by an unconscious one—and this is the prospect which my critics find so alarming—he would only succeed in repressing it, and it would then reappear as an unconscious compensation. The unconscious would thus have changed its face completely: it would now be timidly reasonable, in striking contrast to its former tone. It is not generally believed that the unconscious operates in this way, yet such reversals constantly take place and constitute its proper function. That is why every dream is an organ of information and control, and why dreams are our most effective aid in building up the personality.

333   The unconscious does not harbour in itself any explosive materials unless an overweening or cowardly conscious attitude has secretly laid up stores of explosives there. All the more reason, then, for watching our step.

334   From all this it should now be clear why I make it an heuristic rule, in interpreting a dream, to ask myself: What conscious attitude does it compensate? By so doing, I relate the dream as closely as possible to the conscious situation; indeed, I would even assert that without knowledge of the conscious situation the dream can never be interpreted with any degree of certainty. Only in the light of this knowledge is it possible to make out whether the unconscious content carries a plus or a minus sign. The dream is not an isolated event completely cut off from daily life and lacking its character. If it seems so to us, that is only the result of our lack of understanding, a subjective illusion. In reality the relation between the conscious mind and the dream is strictly causal, and they interact in the subtlest of ways.

335   I should like to show by means of an example how important it is to evaluate the unconscious contents correctly. A young man brought me the following dream: *"My father is driving away from the house in his new car. He drives very clumsily, and I get very annoyed over his apparent stupidity. He goes this way and that, forwards and backwards, and manoeuvres the car into a dangerous position. Finally he runs into a wall and damages the car badly. I shout at him in a perfect fury that he ought to behave himself. My father only laughs, and then I see that he is dead drunk."* This dream has no foundation in fact. The dreamer is convinced that his father would never behave like that, even when drunk. As a motorist he himself is very careful and extremely moderate in the use of alcohol, especially when he has to drive. Bad driving, and even slight damage to the car, irritate him greatly. His relation to his father is positive. He admires him for being an unusually successful man. We can say, without any great feat of interpretation, that the dream presents a most unfavourable picture of the father. What, then, should we take its meaning to be for the son? Is his relation to his father good only on the surface, and does it really consist in over-compensated resistances? If so, we should have to give the dream-content a positive sign; we should have to tell the young man:

"That is your real relation to your father." But since I could find nothing neurotically ambivalent in the son's real relation to his father, I had no warrant for upsetting the young man's feelings with such a destructive pronouncement. To do so would have been a bad therapeutic blunder.

336   But, if his relation to his father is in fact good, why must the dream manufacture such an improbable story in order to discredit the father? In the dreamer's unconscious there must be some tendency to produce such a dream. Is that because he has resistances after all, perhaps fed by envy or some other inferior motive? Before we go out of our way to burden his conscience—and with sensitive young people this is always rather a dangerous proceeding—we would do better to inquire not *why* he had this dream, but what its purpose is. The answer in this case would be that his unconscious is obviously trying to take the father down a peg. If we regard this as a compensation, we are forced to the conclusion that his relation to his father is not only good, but actually too good. In fact he deserves the French soubriquet of *fils à papa*. His father is still too much the guarantor of his existence, and the dreamer is still living what I would call a provisional life. His particular danger is that he. cannot see his own reality on account of his father; therefore the unconscious resorts to a kind of artificial blasphemy so as to lower the father and elevate the son. "An immoral business," we may be tempted to say. An unintelligent father would probably take umbrage, but the compensation is entirely to the point, since it forces the son to contrast himself with his father, which is the only way he could become conscious of himself.

337   The interpretation just outlined was apparently the correct one, for it struck home. It won the spontaneous assent of the dreamer, and no real values were damaged, either for the father or for the son. But this interpretation was only possible when the whole conscious phenomenology of the father-son relationship had been carefully studied. Without a knowledge of the conscious situation the real meaning of the dream would have remained in doubt.

338   For dream-contents to be assimilated, it is of overriding importance that no real values of the conscious personality

should be damaged, much less destroyed, otherwise there is no one left to do the assimilating. The recognition of the unconscious is not a Bolshevist experiment which puts the lowest on top and thus re-establishes the very situation it intended to correct. We must see to it that the values of the conscious personality remain intact, for unconscious compensation is only effective when it co-operates with an integral consciousness. Assimilation is never a question of "this *or* that," but always of "this *and* that."

339   Just as the interpretation of dreams requires exact knowledge of the conscious status quo, so the treatment of dream symbolism demands that we take into account the dreamer's philosophical, religious, and moral convictions. It is far wiser in practice not to regard dream-symbols semiotically, i.e., as signs or symptoms of a fixed character, but as true symbols, i.e., as expressions of a content not yet consciously recognized or conceptually formulated. In addition, they must be considered in relation to the dreamer's immediate state of consciousness. I say that this procedure is advisable *in practice* because in theory relatively fixed symbols do exist whose meaning must on no account be referred to anything known and formulable as a concept. If there were no such relatively fixed symbols it would be impossible to determine the structure of the unconscious, for there would be nothing that could in any way be laid hold of or described.

340   It may seem strange that I should attribute an as it were indefinite content to these relatively fixed symbols. Yet if their content were not indefinite, they would not be symbols at all, but signs or symptoms. We all know how the Freudian school operates with hard-and-fast sexual "symbols"—which in this case I would call "signs"—and endows them with an apparently definitive content, namely sexuality. Unfortunately Freud's idea of sexuality is incredibly elastic and so vague that it can be made to include almost anything. The word sounds familiar enough, but what it denotes is no more than an indeterminable x that ranges from the physiological activity of the glands at one extreme to the sublime reaches of the spirit at the other. Instead of yielding to a dogmatic conviction based on the illusion that we know something because we have a familiar word for it, I prefer to regard the symbol as an unknown quantity,

hard to recognize and, in the last resort, never quite determinable. Take, for instance, the so-called phallic symbols which are supposed to stand for the *membrum virile* and nothing more. Psychologically speaking, the *membrum* is itself—as Kranefeldt points out in a recent work [3]—an emblem of something whose wider content is not at all easy to determine. But primitive people, who, like the ancients, make the freest use of phallic symbols, would never dream of confusing the phallus, as a ritualistic symbol, with the penis. The phallus always means the creative mana, the power of healing and fertility, the "extraordinarily potent," to use Lehmann's expression, whose equivalents in mythology and in dreams are the bull, the ass, the pomegranate, the yoni, the he-goat, the lightning, the horse's hoof, the dance, the magical cohabitation in the furrow, and the menstrual fluid, to mention only a few of the thousand other analogies. That which underlies all the analogies, and sexuality itself, is an archetypal image whose character is hard to define, but whose nearest psychological equivalent is perhaps the primitive mana-symbol.

341   All these symbols are relatively fixed, but in no single case can we have the *a priori* certainty that in practice the symbol must be interpreted in that way.

342   Practical necessity may call for something quite different. Of course, if we had to give an exhaustive scientific interpretation of a dream, in accordance with a theory, we should have to refer every such symbol to an archetype. But in practice that can be a positive mistake, for the patient's psychological state at the moment may require anything but a digression into dream theory. It is therefore advisable to consider first and foremost the meaning of the symbol in relation to the conscious situation—in other words, to treat the symbol as if it were not fixed. This is as much as to say that we must renounce all preconceived opinions, however knowing they make us feel, and try to discover what things mean for the patient. In so doing, we shall obviously not get very far towards a theoretical interpretation; indeed we shall probably get stuck at the very beginning. But if the practitioner operates too much with fixed symbols, there is a danger of his falling into mere routine and pernicious dogmatism, and thus failing his patient. Unfor-

3 "Komplex und Mythos."

tunately I must refrain from illustrating this point, for I should have to go into greater detail than space here permits. Moreover I have published sufficient material elsewhere in support of my statements.

343   It frequently happens at the very beginning of the treatment that a dream will reveal to the doctor, in broad perspective, the whole programme of the unconscious. But for practical reasons it may be quite impossible to make clear to the patient the deeper meaning of the dream. In this respect, too, we are limited by practical considerations. Such insight is rendered possible by the doctor's knowledge of relatively fixed symbols. It can be of the greatest value in diagnosis as well as in prognosis. I was once consulted about a seventeen-year-old girl. One specialist had conjectured that she might be in the first stages of progressive muscular atrophy, while another thought that it was a case of hysteria. In view of the second opinion, I was called in. The clinical picture made me suspect an organic disease, but there were signs of hysteria as well. I asked for dreams. The patient answered at once: "Yes, I have terrible dreams. Only recently I dreamt *I was coming home at night. Everything is as quiet as death. The door into the living-room is half open, and I see my mother hanging from the chandelier, swinging to and fro in the cold wind that blows in through the open windows.* Another time I dreamt that *a terrible noise broke out in the house at night. I get up and discover that a frightened horse is tearing through the rooms. At last it finds the door into the hall, and jumps through the hall window from the fourth floor into the street below. I was terrified when I saw it lying there, all mangled.*"

344   The gruesome character of the dreams is alone sufficient to make one pause. All the same, other people have anxiety dreams now and then. We must therefore look more closely into the meaning of the two main symbols, "mother" and "horse." They must be equivalents, for they both do the same thing: they commit suicide. "Mother" is an archetype and refers to the place of origin, to nature, to that which passively creates, hence to substance and matter, to materiality, the womb, the vegetative functions. It also means the unconscious, our natural and instinctive life, the physiological realm, the body in which we dwell or are contained; for the "mother" is also the matrix, the

hollow form, the vessel that carries and nourishes, and it thus stands psychologically for the foundations of consciousness. Being inside or contained in something also suggests darkness, something nocturnal and fearful, hemming one in. These allusions give the idea of the mother in many of its mythological and etymological variants; they also represent an important part of the Yin idea in Chinese philosophy. This is no individual acquisition of a seventeen-year-old girl; it is a collective inheritance, alive and recorded in language, inherited along with the structure of the psyche and therefore to be found at all times and among all peoples.

345 The word "mother," which sounds so familiar, apparently refers to the best-known, the individual mother—to "my mother." But the mother-symbol points to a darker background which eludes conceptual formulation and can only be vaguely apprehended as the hidden, nature-bound life of the body. Yet even this is too narrow and excludes too many vital subsidiary meanings. The underlying, primary psychic reality is so inconceivably complex that it can be grasped only at the farthest reach of intuition, and then but very dimly. That is why it needs symbols.

346 If we apply our findings to the dream, its interpretation will be: The unconscious life is destroying itself. That is the dream's message to the conscious mind of the dreamer and to anybody who has ears to hear.

347 "Horse" is an archetype that is widely current in mythology and folklore. As an animal it represents the non-human psyche, the subhuman, animal side, the unconscious. That is why horses in folklore sometimes see visions, hear voices, and speak. As a beast of burden it is closely related to the mother-archetype (witness the Valkyries that bear the dead hero to Valhalla, the Trojan horse, etc.). As an animal lower than man it represents the lower part of the body and the animal impulses that rise from there. The horse is dynamic and vehicular power: it carries one away like a surge of instinct. It is subject to panics like all instinctive creatures who lack higher consciousness. Also it has to do with sorcery and magical spells—especially the black night-horses which herald death.

348 It is evident, then, that "horse" is an equivalent of "mother" with a slight shift of meaning. The mother stands for life at its

origin, the horse for the merely animal life of the body. If we apply this meaning to the text of our dream, its interpretation will be: The animal life is destroying itself.

349   The two dreams make nearly identical statements, but, as is usually the case, the second is more specific. Note the peculiar subtlety of the dream: there is no mention of the death of the individual. It is notorious that one often dreams of one's own death, but that is no serious matter. When it is really a question of death, the dream speaks another language.

350   Both dreams point to a grave organic disease with a fatal outcome. This prognosis was soon confirmed.

351   As for the relatively fixed symbols, this example gives a fair idea of their general nature. There are a great many of them, and all are individually marked by subtle shifts of meaning. It is only through comparative studies in mythology, folklore, religion, and philology that we can evaluate their nature scientifically. The evolutionary stratification of the psyche is more clearly discernible in the dream than in the conscious mind. In the dream, the psyche speaks in images, and gives expression to instincts, which derive from the most primitive levels of nature. Therefore, through the assimilation of unconscious contents, the momentary life of consciousness can once more be brought into harmony with the law of nature from which it all too easily departs, and the patient can be led back to the natural law of his own being.

352   I have not been able, in so short a space, to deal with anything but the elements of the subject. I could not put together before your eyes, stone by stone, the edifice that is reared in every analysis from the materials of the unconscious and finally reaches completion in the restoration of the total personality. The way of successive assimilations goes far beyond the curative results that specifically concern the doctor. It leads in the end to that distant goal which may perhaps have been the first urge to life: the complete actualization of the whole human being, that is, individuation. We physicians may well be the first conscious observers of this dark process of nature. As a rule we see only the pathological phase of development, and we lose sight of the patient as soon as he is cured. Yet it is only after the cure that we would really be in a position to study the normal process, which may extend over years and decades. Had

we but a little knowledge of the ends toward which the unconscious development is tending, and were the doctor's psychological insight not drawn exclusively from the pathological phase, we should have a less confused idea of the processes mediated to the conscious mind by dreams and a clearer recognition of what the symbols point to. In my opinion, every doctor should understand that every procedure in psychotherapy, and particularly the analytical procedure, breaks into a purposeful and continuous process of development, now at this point and now at that, and thus singles out separate phases which seem to follow opposing courses. Each individual analysis by itself shows only one part or one aspect of the deeper process, and for this reason nothing but hopeless confusion can result from comparative case histories. For this reason, too, I have preferred to confine myself to the rudiments of the subject and to practical considerations; for only in closest contact with the everyday facts can we come to anything like a satisfactory understanding.

compensation
nature ʒ unconscious
archetypes
symbols – multiple meaning?
individuation + assimilation
wisdom within + context

IV

INDIVIDUAL DREAM SYMBOLISM
IN RELATION TO ALCHEMY

[Originally a lecture, "Traumsymbole des Individuationsprozesses," *Eranos-Jahrbuch 1935* (Zurich, 1936); translated as "Dream Symbols of the Process of Individuation" by Stanley Dell, in *The Integration of the Personality* (New York, 1939; London, 1940). Jung revised and augmented the essay and published it, with other material and many illustrations, in *Psychologie und Alchemie* (Zurich, 1944; 2nd edn., revised, 1952). This was translated by R.F.C. Hull and published as vol. 12 of the Collected Works in 1953; 2nd edn., completely revised and reset, 1968. It is the latter version that is published here.]

> . . . *facilis descensus Averno;*
> *noctes atque dies patet atri ianua Ditis;*
> *sed revocare gradum superasque evadere ad auras,*
> *hoc opus, hic labor est. . . .*
>
> VIRGIL, Aeneid, VI, 126–29

> . . . easy is the descent to Avernus: night and day
> the door of gloomy Dis stands open; but to recall
> thy steps and pass out to the upper air, this is the
> task, this the toil!
>
> —Trans. by H. R. Fairclough

5. Seven virgins being transformed.—Béroalde de Verville, *Le Songe de Poliphile* (1600)

1. INTRODUCTION

I. THE MATERIAL

44   The symbols of the process of individuation that appear in dreams are images of an archetypal nature which depict the centralizing process or the production of a new centre of personality. A general idea of this process may be got from my essay, "The Relations between the Ego and the Unconscious." For certain reasons mentioned there I call this centre the "self," which should be understood as the totality of the psyche. The self is not only the centre, but also the whole circumference which embraces both conscious and unconscious; it is the centre of this totality, just as the ego is the centre of consciousness.

45   The symbols now under consideration are not concerned with the manifold stages and transformations of the individuation process, but with the images that refer directly and exclusively to the new centre as it comes into consciousness. These images belong to a definite category which I call mandala symbolism.

In *The Secret of the Golden Flower,* published in collaboration with Richard Wilhelm, I have described this symbolism in some detail. In the present study I should like to put before you an individual series of such symbols in chronological order. The material consists of over a thousand dreams and visual impressions coming from a young man of excellent scientific education.[1] For the purposes of this study I have worked on the first four hundred dreams and visions, which covered a period of nearly ten months. In order to avoid all personal influence I asked one of my pupils, a woman doctor, who was then a beginner, to undertake the observation of the process. This went on for five months. The dreamer then continued his observations alone for three months. Except for a short interview at the very beginning, before the commencement of the observation, I did not see the dreamer at all during the first eight months. Thus it happened that 355 of the dreams were dreamed away from any personal contact with myself. Only the last forty-five occurred under my observation. No interpretations worth mentioning were then attempted because the dreamer, owing to his excellent scientific training and ability, did not require any assistance. Hence conditions were really ideal for unprejudiced observation and recording.

46   First of all, then, I shall present extracts from the twenty-two initial dreams in order to show how the mandala symbolism makes a very early appearance and is embedded in the rest of the dream material. Later on I shall pick out in chronological order the dreams that refer specifically to the mandala.[2]

47   With few exceptions all the dreams have been abbreviated, either by extracting the part that carries the main thought or by condensing the whole text to essentials. This simplifying procedure has not only curtailed their length but has also removed personal allusions and complications, as was necessary for reasons of discretion. Despite this somewhat doubtful interference I have, to the best of my knowledge and scrupulosity, avoided any

[1] I must emphasize that this education was not historical, philological, archaeological, or ethnological. Any references to material derived from these fields came unconsciously to the dreamer.

[2] "Mandala" (Sanskrit) means "circle," also "magic circle." Its symbolism includes—to mention only the most important forms—all concentrically arranged figures, round or square patterns with a centre, and radial or spherical arrangements.

arbitrary distortion of meaning. The same considerations had also to apply to my own interpretation, so that certain passages in the dreams may appear to have been overlooked. Had I not made this sacrifice and kept the material absolutely complete, I should not have been in a position to publish this series, which in my opinion could hardly be surpassed in intelligence, clarity, and consistency. It therefore gives me great pleasure to express my sincere gratitude here and now to the "author" for the service he has rendered to science.

II. THE METHOD

48   In my writings and lectures I have always insisted that we must give up all preconceived opinions when it comes to the analysis and interpretation of the objective psyche,[3] in other words the "unconscious." We do not yet possess a general theory of dreams that would enable us to use a deductive method with impunity, any more than we possess a general theory of consciousness from which we can draw deductive conclusions. The manifestations of the subjective psyche, or consciousness, can be predicted to only the smallest degree, and there is no theoretical argument to prove beyond doubt that any causal connection necessarily exists between them. On the contrary, we have to reckon with a high percentage of arbitrariness and "chance" in the complex actions and reactions of the conscious mind. Similarly there is no empirical, still less a theoretical, reason to assume that the same does not apply to the manifestations of the unconscious. The latter are just as manifold, unpredictable, and arbitrary as the former and must therefore be subjected to as many different ways of approach. In the case of conscious utterances we are in the fortunate position of being directly addressed and presented with a content whose purpose we can recognize; but with "unconscious" manifestations there is no directed or adapted language in our sense of the word—there is merely a psychic phenomenon that would appear to have only the loosest connections with conscious contents. If the expres-

[3] For this concept see Jung, "Basic Postulates of Analytical Psychology," and Wolff, "Einführung in die Grundlagen der komplexen Psychologie," pp. 34ff.

sions of the conscious mind are incomprehensible we can always ask what they mean. But the objective psyche is something alien even to the conscious mind through which it expresses itself. We are therefore obliged to adopt the method we would use in deciphering a fragmentary text or one containing unknown words: we examine the context. The meaning of the unknown word may become evident when we compare a series of passages in which it occurs. The psychological context of dream-contents consists in the web of associations in which the dream is naturally embedded. Theoretically we can never know anything in advance about this web, but in practice it is sometimes possible, granted long enough experience. Even so, careful analysis will never rely too much on technical rules; the danger of deception and suggestion is too great. In the analysis of isolated dreams above all, this kind of knowing in advance and making assumptions on the grounds of practical expectation or general probability is positively wrong. It should therefore be an absolute rule to assume that every dream, and every part of a dream, is unknown at the outset, and to attempt an interpretation only after carefully taking up the context. We can then apply the meaning we have thus discovered to the text of the dream itself and see whether this yields a fluent reading, or rather whether a satisfying meaning emerges. But in no circumstances may we anticipate that this meaning will fit in with any of our subjective expectations; for quite possibly, indeed very frequently, the dream is saying something surprisingly different from what we would expect. As a matter of fact, if the meaning we find in the dream happens to coincide with our expectations, that is a reason for suspicion; for as a rule the standpoint of the unconscious is complementary or compensatory[4] to consciousness and thus unexpectedly "different." I would not deny the possibility of *parallel* dreams, i.e., dreams whose meaning coincides with or supports the conscious attitude, but, in my experience at least, these are rather rare.

49   Now, the method I adopt in the present study seems to run directly counter to this basic principle of dream interpretation. It looks as if the dreams were being interpreted without the least regard for the context. And in fact I have not taken up the con-

4 I intentionally omit an analysis of the words "complementary" and "compensatory," as it would lead us too far afield.

6. A maternal figure presiding over the goddesses of fate.—Thenaud, "Traité de la cabale" (MS., 16th cent.)

text at all, seeing that the dreams in this series were not dreamed (as mentioned above) under my observation. I proceed rather as if I had had the dreams myself and were therefore in a position to supply the context.

50   This procedure, if applied to *isolated* dreams of someone unknown to me personally, would indeed be a gross technical blunder. But here we are not dealing with isolated dreams; they form a coherent series in the course of which the meaning gradually unfolds more or less of its own accord. *The series is*

the context which the dreamer himself supplies. It is as if not one text but many lay before us, throwing light from all sides on the unknown terms, so that a reading of all the texts is sufficient to elucidate the difficult passages in each individual one. Moreover, in the third chapter we are concerned with a definite archetype—the mandala—that has long been known to us from other sources, and this considerably facilitates the interpretation. Of course the interpretation of each individual passage is bound to be largely conjecture, but the series as a whole gives us all the clues we need to correct any possible errors in the preceding passages.

51   It goes without saying that while the dreamer was under the observation of my pupil he knew nothing of these interpretations and was therefore quite unprejudiced by anybody else's opinion. Moreover I hold the view, based on wide experience, that the possibility and danger of prejudgment are exaggerated. Experience shows that the objective psyche is independent in the highest degree. Were it not so, it could not carry out its most characteristic function: the compensation of the conscious mind. The conscious mind allows itself to be trained like a parrot, but the unconscious does not—which is why St. Augustine thanked God for not making him responsible for his dreams. The unconscious is an autonomous psychic entity; any efforts to drill it are only apparently successful, and moreover are harmful to consciousness. It is and remains beyond the reach of subjective arbitrary control, in a realm where nature and her secrets can be neither improved upon nor perverted, where we can listen but may not meddle.

7. The Uroboros as symbol of the aeon.—
Horapollo, *Selecta hieroglyphica* (1597)

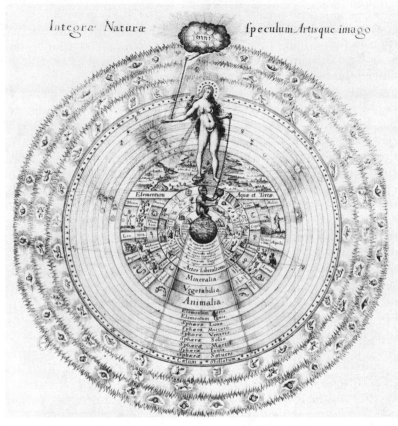

3. The *anima mundi*, guide of mankind, herself guided by God.—Engraving by J.-T. de Bry, from Fludd, *Utriusque cosmi* (1617)

2. THE INITIAL DREAMS

1. DREAM:

52   *The dreamer is at a social gathering. On leaving, he puts on a stranger's hat instead of his own.*

53   The hat, as a covering for the head, has the general sense of something that epitomizes the head. Just as in summing up we bring ideas "under one head" (*unter einen Hut*), so the hat, as a sort of leading idea, covers the whole personality and imparts its own significance to it. Coronation endows the ruler

121

with the divine nature of the sun, the doctor's hood bestows the dignity of a scholar, and a stranger's hat imparts a strange personality. Meyrink uses this theme in his novel *The Golem*, where the hero puts on the hat of Athanasius Pernath and, as a result, becomes involved in a strange experience. It is clear enough in *The Golem* that it is the unconscious which entangles the hero in fantastic adventures. Let us stress at once the significance of the *Golem* parallel and assume that the hat in the dream is the hat of an Athanasius, an immortal, a being beyond time, the universal and everlasting man as distinct from the ephemeral and "accidental" mortal man. Encircling the head, the hat is round like the sun-disc of a crown and therefore contains the first allusion to the mandala. We shall find the attribute of eternal duration confirmed in the ninth mandala dream (par. 134), while the mandala character of the hat comes out in the thirty-fifth mandala dream (par. 254). As a general result of the exchange of hats we may expect a development similar to that in *The Golem:* an emergence of the unconscious. The unconscious with its figures is already standing like a shadow behind the dreamer and pushing its way into consciousness.

2. DREAM:

54   *The dreamer is going on a railway journey, and by standing in front of the window, he blocks the view for his fellow passengers. He must get out of their way.*

55   The process is beginning to move, and the dreamer discovers that he is keeping the light from those who stand *behind* him, namely the unconscious components of his personality. We have no eyes behind us; consequently "behind" is the region of the unseen, the unconscious. If the dreamer will only stop blocking the window (consciousness), the unconscious content will become conscious.

3. HYPNAGOGIC VISUAL IMPRESSION:

56   *By the sea shore. The sea breaks into the land, flooding everything. Then the dreamer is sitting on a lonely island.*

57   The sea is the symbol of the collective unconscious, because unfathomed depths lie concealed beneath its reflecting surface.[1]

---

[1] The sea is a favourite place for the birth of visions (i.e., invasions by unconscious contents). Thus the great vision of the eagle in II Esdras 11 : 1 rises out

Those who stand behind, the shadowy personifications of the unconscious, have burst into the *terra firma* of consciousness like a flood. Such invasions have something uncanny about them because they are irrational and incomprehensible to the person concerned. They bring about a momentous alteration of his personality since they immediately constitute a painful personal secret which alienates and isolates him from his surroundings. It is something that we "cannot tell anybody." We are afraid of being accused of mental abnormality—not without reason, for much the same thing happens to lunatics. Even so, it is a far cry from the intuitive perception of such an invasion to being inundated by it pathologically, though the layman does not realize this. Isolation by a secret results as a rule in an animation of the psychic atmosphere, as a substitute for loss of contact with other people. It causes an activation of the unconscious, and this produces something similar to the illusions and hallucinations that beset lonely wanderers in the desert, seafarers, and saints. The mechanism of these phenomena can best be explained in terms of energy. Our normal relations to objects in the world at large are maintained by a certain expenditure of energy. If the relation to the object is cut off there is a "retention" of energy, which then creates an equivalent substitute. For instance, just as persecution mania comes from a relationship poisoned by mistrust, so, as a substitute for the normal animation of the environment, an illusory reality rises up in which weird ghostly shadows flit about in place of people. That is why primitive man has always believed that lonely and desolate places are haunted by "devils" and suchlike apparitions.

4. DREAM:

58   *The dreamer is surrounded by a throng of vague female forms* (cf. fig. 33). *A voice within him says, "First I must get away from Father."*

59   Here the psychic atmosphere has been animated by what the Middle Ages would call succubi. We are reminded of the visions of St. Anthony in Egypt, so eruditely described by Flau-

---

of the sea, and the vision of "Man"—ἄνθρωπος—in 13 : 3, 25, and 51 comes up "from the midst of the sea." Cf. also 13 : 52: "Like as thou canst neither seek out nor know the things that are in the deep of the sea: even so can no man upon earth see my Son. . . ."

bert in *La Tentation de Saint-Antoine*. The element of hallucination shows itself in the fact that the thought is spoken aloud. The words "first I must get away" call for a concluding sentence which would begin with "in order to." Presumably it would run "in order to follow the unconscious, i.e., the alluring female forms" (fig. 9). The father, the embodiment of the traditional spirit as expressed in religion or a general philosophy of life, is standing in his way. He imprisons the dreamer in the world of the conscious mind and its values. The traditional masculine world with its intellectualism and rationalism is felt to be an impediment, from which we must conclude that the unconscious, now approaching him, stands in direct opposition to the tendencies of the conscious mind and that the dreamer, despite this opposition, is already favourably disposed towards the unconscious. For this reason the latter should not be subordinated to the rationalistic judgments of consciousness; it ought rather to be an experience *sui generis*. Naturally it is not easy for the intellect to accept this, because it involves at least a partial, if not a total, *sacrificium intellectus*. Furthermore, the problem thus raised is very difficult for modern man to grasp; for to begin with he can only understand the unconscious as an inessential and unreal appendage of the conscious mind, and not as a special sphere of experience with laws of its own. In the course of the later dreams this conflict will appear again and again, until finally the right formula is found for the correlation of conscious and unconscious, and the personality is assigned its correct position between the two. Moreover, such a conflict cannot be solved by understanding, but only by experience. Every stage of the experience must be lived through. There is no feat of interpretation or any other trick by which to circumvent this difficulty, for the union of conscious and unconscious can only be achieved step by step.

60   The resistance of the conscious mind to the unconscious and the depreciation of the latter were historical necessities in the development of the human psyche, for otherwise the conscious mind would never have been able to differentiate itself at all. But modern man's consciousness has strayed rather too far from the fact of the unconscious. We have even forgotten that the psyche is by no means of our design, but is for the most part autonomous and unconscious. Consequently the approach of

9. The awakening of the sleeping king depicted as a judgment of Paris, with Hermes as psychopomp.—Thomas Aquinas (pseud.), "De alchimia" (MS., 16th cent.)

10, 11, 12. Melusina; two-headed Melusina; mermaid with mask.—Eleazar,
Uraltes chymisches Werk (1760)

the unconscious induces a panic fear in civilized people, not least
on account of the menacing analogy with insanity. The intellect
has no objection to "analysing" the unconscious as a passive
object; on the contrary such an activity would coincide with our
rational expectations. But to let the unconscious go its own way
and to experience it as a reality is something that exceeds the
courage and capacity of the average European. He prefers simply not to understand this problem. For the spiritually weak-
kneed this is the better course, since the thing is not without its
dangers.

61   The experience of the unconscious is a personal secret com-
municable only to very few, and that with difficulty; hence the
isolating effect we noted above. But isolation brings about a
compensatory animation of the psychic atmosphere which strikes
us as uncanny. The figures that appear in the dream are feminine, thus pointing to the feminine nature of the unconscious.
They are fairies or fascinating sirens and lamias (figs. 10, 11, 12;
cf. also fig. 157), who infatuate the lonely wanderer and lead
him astray. Likewise seductive maidens appear at the begin-

126

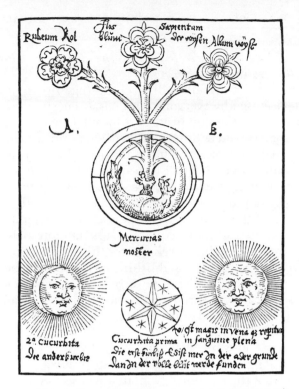

13. The "tail-eater" (Uroboros) as the *prima materia* of the alchemical process, with the red-and-white rose, the *flos sapientum*. Below, *coniunctio solis et lunae*, with the *lapis philosophorum* as the son.—Reusner, *Pandora* (1588)

ning of the *nekyia*[2] of Poliphilo[3] (fig. 33), and the Melusina of Paracelsus[4] is another such figure.

[2] Νεκνία from νέκυς (corpse), the title of the eleventh book of the Odyssey, is the sacrifice to the dead for conjuring up the departed from Hades. *Nekyia* is therefore an apt designation for the "journey to Hades," the descent into the land of the dead, and was used by Dieterich in this sense in his commentary on the Codex of Akhmim, which contains an apocalyptic fragment from the Gospel of Peter (*Nekyia: Beiträge zur Erklärung der neuentdeckten Petrusapokalypse*). Typical examples are the *Divine Comedy*, the classical *Walpurgisnacht* in *Faust*, the apocryphal accounts of Christ's descent into hell, etc.

[3] Cf. the French edition of *Hypnerotomachia*, called *Le Tableau des riches inventions* or *Songe de Poliphile* (1600), trans. Béroalde de Verville. (See fig. 4.) [The original Italian edn. appeared in 1499.]

[4] For details see Jung, "Paracelsus as a Spiritual Phenomenon," pars. 179f., 214ff.

5. VISUAL IMPRESSION:

62   *A snake describes a circle round the dreamer, who stands rooted to the ground like a tree.*

63   The drawing of a spellbinding circle (fig. 13) is an ancient magical device used by everyone who has a special or secret purpose in mind. He thereby protects himself from the "perils of the soul" that threaten him from without and attack anyone who is isolated by a secret. The same procedure has also been used since olden times to set a place apart as holy and inviolable; in founding a city, for instance, they first drew the *sulcus primigenius* or original furrow[5] (cf. fig. 31). The fact that the dreamer stands rooted to the centre is a compensation of his almost insuperable desire to run away from the unconscious. He experienced an agreeable feeling of relief after this vision—and rightly, since he has succeeded in establishing a protected *temenos*,[6] a taboo area where he will be able to meet the unconscious. His isolation, so uncanny before, is now endowed with meaning and purpose, and thus robbed of its terrors.

6. VISUAL IMPRESSION, DIRECTLY FOLLOWING UPON 5:

64   *The veiled figure of a woman seated on a stair.*

65   The motif of the unknown woman—whose technical name is the "anima" [7]—appears here for the first time. Like the throng of vague female forms in dream 4, she is a personification of the animated psychic atmosphere. From now on the figure of the unknown woman reappears in a great many of the dreams. Personification always indicates an autonomous activity of the unconscious. If some personal figure appears we may be sure that the unconscious is beginning to grow active. The activity of such figures very often has an anticipatory character: something that the dreamer himself will do later is now being done in advance. In this case the allusion is to a stair, thus indicating an ascent or a descent (fig. 14).

66   Since the process running through dreams of this kind has an historical analogy in the rites of initiation, it may not be

---

[5] Knuchel, *Die Umwandlung in Kult, Magie und Rechtsbrauch.*

[6] A piece of land, often a grove, set apart and dedicated to a god.

[7] For the concept of the "anima," see Jung, "The Relations between the Ego and the Unconscious," pars. 296ff.

14. Jacob's dream.—Watercolour by William Blake

superfluous to draw attention to the important part which the Stairway of the Seven Planets played in these rites, as we know from Apuleius, among others. The initiations of late classical syncretism, already saturated with alchemy (cf. the visions of Zosimos[8]), were particularly concerned with the theme of ascent,

8 Zosimos lived c. A.D. 300. Cf. Reitzenstein, *Poimandres,* pp. 9ff.; Berthelot, *Collection des anciens alchimistes grecs,* III, i, 2.

15. The *scala lapidis*, representing the stages of the alchemical process.—
"Emblematical Figures of the Philosophers' Stone" (MS., 17th cent.)

i.e., sublimation. The ascent was often represented by a ladder (fig. 15); hence the burial gift in Egypt of a small ladder for the *ka* of the dead.[9] The idea of an ascent through the seven spheres of the planets symbolizes the return of the soul to the sun-god from whom it originated, as we know for instance from Firmicus Maternus.[10] Thus the Isis mystery described by Apuleius[11] culminated in what early medieval alchemy, going back to Alexandrian tradition as transmitted by the Arabs,[12] called the *solificatio,* where the initiand was crowned as Helios.

7. VISUAL IMPRESSION:

67

The veiled woman uncovers her face. It shines like the sun.

68

The *solificatio* is consummated on the person of the anima. The process would seem to correspond to the *illuminatio,* or enlightenment. This "mystical" idea contrasts strongly with the rational attitude of the conscious mind, which recognizes only intellectual enlightenment as the highest form of understanding and insight. Naturally this attitude never reckons with the fact that scientific knowledge only satisfies the little tip of personality that is contemporaneous with ourselves, not the collective psyche[13] that reaches back into the grey mists of antiquity and always requires a special rite if it is to be united with present-day consciousness. It is clear, therefore, that a "lighting up" of the unconscious is being prepared, which has far more the character of an *illuminatio* than of rational "elucidation." The *solificatio* is infinitely far removed from the conscious mind and seems to it almost chimerical.

8. VISUAL IMPRESSION:

69

A rainbow is to be used as a bridge. But one must go under it and not over it. Whoever goes over it will fall and be killed.

70

Only the gods can walk rainbow bridges in safety; mere mortals fall and meet their death, for the rainbow is only a lovely semblance that spans the sky, and not a highway for

---

9 The ladder motif is confirmed in dreams 12 and 13 (pars. 78 and 82). Cf. also Jacob's ladder (fig. 14).

10 *De errore profanarum religionum:* "Animo descensus per orbem solis tribuitur" (It is said [by the pagans] that the soul descends through the circle of the sun).

11 *The Golden Ass.*   12 Cf. Ruska, *Turba.*

13 Cf. "collective unconscious" in Jung, *Psychological Types,* Def. 56.

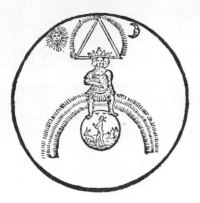

16. *Mercurius tricephalus* as Anthropos.
Below, blindfolded man led by an animal.
—Kelley, *Tractatus de Lapide philoso-*
phorum (1676)

human beings with bodies. These must pass "under it" (fig. 16).
But water flows under bridges too, following its own gradient
and seeking the lowest place. This hint will be confirmed later.

9. DREAM:

71   *A green land where many sheep are pastured. It is the "land*
of sheep."

72   This curious fragment, inscrutable at first glance, may derive from childhood impressions and particularly from those of
a religious nature, which would not be far to seek in this connection—e.g., "He maketh me to lie down in green pastures," or the
early Christian allegories of sheep and shepherd [14] (fig. 18). The
next vision points in the same direction.

10. VISUAL IMPRESSION:

73   *The unknown woman stands in the land of sheep and points*
the way.

74   The anima, having already anticipated the *solificatio,* now
appears as the psychopomp, the one who shows the way[15] (fig.
19). The way begins in the children's land, i.e., at a time when
rational present-day consciousness was not yet separated from
the historical psyche, the collective unconscious. The separation
is indeed inevitable, but it leads to such an alienation from that

[14] The direct source of the Christian sheep symbolism is to be found in the
visions of the Book of Enoch 89 : 1off. (Charles, *Apocrypha and Pseudepigrapha,*
II, p. 252). The Apocalypse of Enoch was written about the beginning of the
1st cent. B.C.
[15] In the vision of Enoch, the leader and prince appears first as a sheep or ram:
Book of Enoch 89 : 48 (Charles, II, p. 254).

17. The artifex (or Hermes) as shepherd of Aries and Taurus, who symbolize the vernal impulses, the beginning of the *opus*.—Thomas Aquinas (pseud.), "De alchimia" (MS., 16th cent.)

dim psyche of the dawn of mankind that a loss of instinct ensues. The result is instinctual atrophy and hence disorientation in everyday human situations. But it also follows from the separation that the "children's land" will remain definitely infantile and become a perpetual source of childish inclinations and impulses. These intrusions are naturally most unwelcome to the conscious mind, and it consistently represses them for that reason. But the very consistency of the repression only serves to bring about a still greater alienation from the fountainhead, thus increasing the lack of instinct until it becomes lack of soul. As a result, the conscious mind is either completely swamped by childishness or else constantly obliged to defend itself in vain against the inundation, by means of a cynical affectation of old age or embittered resignation. We must therefore realize that despite its undeniable successes the rational attitude of present-day consciousness is, in many human respects, childishly un-

18. Christ as shepherd.—Mosaic, mausoleum of Galla Placidia, Ravenna
(c. 424–451)

adapted and hostile to life. Life has grown desiccated and cramped, crying out for the rediscovery of the fountainhead. But the fountainhead can only be found if the conscious mind will suffer itself to be led back to the "children's land," there to receive guidance from the unconscious as before. To remain a child too long is childish, but it is just as childish to move away and then assume that childhood no longer exists because we do not see it. But if we return to the "children's land" we succumb to the fear of becoming childish, because we do not understand that everything of psychic origin has a double face. One face looks forward, the other back. It is ambivalent and therefore symbolic, like all living reality.

75　　We stand on a peak of consciousness, believing in a childish way that the path leads upward to yet higher peaks beyond. That is the chimerical rainbow bridge. In order to reach the next peak we must first go down into the land where the paths begin to divide.

11. Dream:

76　　*A voice says, "But you are still a child."*

77　　This dream forces the dreamer to admit that even a highly differentiated consciousness has not by any means finished with childish things, and that a return to the world of childhood is necessary.

134

19. The soul as guide, showing the way.—Watercolour by William Blake for Dante's *Purgatorio,* Canto IV

12. DREAM:

78   *A dangerous walk with Father and Mother, up and down many ladders.*

79   A childish consciousness is always tied to father and mother, and is never by itself. Return to childhood is always the return to father and mother, to the whole burden of the psychic non-ego as represented by the parents, with its long and momentous history. Regression spells disintegration into our historical and hereditary determinants, and it is only with the greatest effort that we can free ourselves from their embrace. Our psychic pre-history is in truth the spirit of gravity, which needs steps and ladders because, unlike the disembodied airy intellect, it cannot fly at will. Disintegration into the jumble of historical determinants is like losing one's way, where even what is right seems an alarming mistake.

80   As hinted above, the steps and ladders theme (cf. figs. 14, 15) points to the process of psychic transformation, with all its ups and downs. We find a classic example of this in Zosimos' ascent and descent of the fifteen steps of light and darkness.[16]

81   It is of course impossible to free oneself from one's childhood without devoting a great deal of work to it, as Freud's researches have long since shown. Nor can it be achieved through intellectual knowledge only; what is alone effective is a remembering that is also a re-experiencing. The swift passage of the years and the overwhelming inrush of the newly discovered world leave a mass of material behind that is never dealt with. We do not shake this off; we merely remove ourselves from it. So that when, in later years, we return to the memories of childhood we find bits of our personality still alive, which cling round us and suffuse us with the feeling of earlier times. Being still in their childhood state, these fragments are very powerful in their effect. They can lose their infantile aspect and be corrected only when they are reunited with adult consciousness. This "personal unconscious" must always be dealt with first, that is, made conscious, otherwise the gateway to the collective unconscious cannot be opened. The journey with father and mother up and down many ladders represents the making conscious of infantile contents that have not yet been integrated.

16 Berthelot, *Collection des anciens alchimistes grecs,* III, i, 2. Cf. also Jung, "The Visions of Zosimos."

13. DREAM:

82   *The father calls out anxiously, "That is the seventh!"*

83   During the walk over many ladders some event has evidently taken place which is spoken of as "the seventh" (fig. 20). In the language of initiation, "seven" stands for the highest stage of illumination and would therefore be the coveted goal of all desire (cf. fig. 28). But to the conventional mind the *solificatio* is an outlandish, mystical idea bordering on madness. We assume that it was only in the dark ages of misty superstition that people thought in such a nonsensical fashion, but that the lucid and hygienic mentality of our own enlightened days has long since outgrown such nebulous notions, so much so, indeed, that this particular kind of "illumination" is to be found nowadays only in a lunatic asylum. No wonder the father is scared and anxious, like a hen that has hatched out ducklings and is driven to despair by the aquatic proclivities of its young. If this interpretation—that the "seventh" represents the highest stage of illumination—is correct, it would mean in principle that the process of integrating the personal unconscious was actually at an end. Thereafter the collective unconscious would begin to open up, which would suffice to explain the anxiety the father felt as the representative of the traditional spirit.

84   Nevertheless the return to the dim twilight of the unconscious does not mean that we should entirely abandon the precious acquisition of our forefathers, namely the intellectual differentiation of consciousness. It is rather a question of the *man* taking the place of the *intellect*—not the man whom the dreamer imagines himself to be, but someone far more rounded and complete. This would mean assimilating all sorts of things into the sphere of his personality which the dreamer still rejects as disagreeable or even impossible. The father who calls out so anxiously, "That is the seventh!" is a psychic component of the dreamer himself, and the anxiety is therefore his own. So the interpretation must bear in mind the possibility that the "seventh" means not only a sort of culmination but something rather ominous as well. We come across this theme, for instance, in the fairytale of Tom Thumb and the Ogre. Tom Thumb is the youngest of seven brothers. His dwarflike stature and his cunning are harmless enough, yet he is the one who leads his brothers to the ogre's lair, thus proving his own dangerous double nature as a bringer of good and bad luck; in other words,

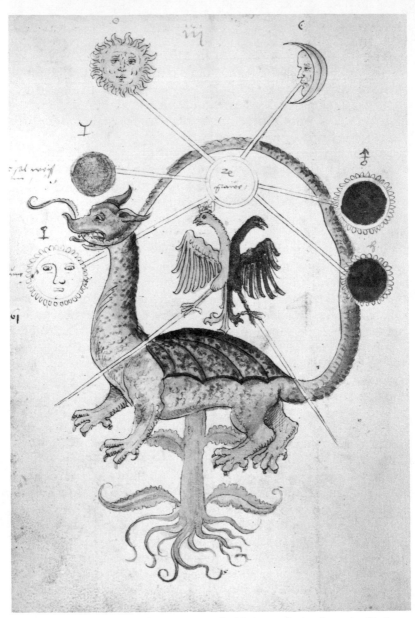

20. The six planets united in the seventh, Mercury, depicted as the Uroboros, and the red-and-white (hermaphroditic) double eagle.—Thomas Aquinas (pseud.), "De alchimia" (MS., 16th cent.)

21. The seven gods of the planets in Hades.—Mylius, *Philosophia reformata* (1622)

he is also the ogre himself. Since olden times "the seven" have represented the seven gods of the planets (fig. 20); they form what the Pyramid inscriptions call a *paut neteru*, a "company of gods" [17] (cf. figs. 21, 23). Although a company is described as "nine," it often proves to be not nine at all but ten, and sometimes even more. Thus Maspero[18] tells us that the first and last members of the series can be added to, or doubled, without injury to the number nine. Something of the sort happened to the classical *paut* of the Greco-Roman or Babylonian gods in the postclassical age, when the gods were degraded to demons and retired partly to the distant stars and partly to the metals inside the earth. It then transpired that Hermes or Mercurius possessed a double nature, being a chthonic god of revelation and also the spirit of quicksilver, for which reason he was represented as a hermaphrodite (fig. 22). As the planet Mercury, he is

[17] Budge, in *Gods of the Egyptians*, I, p. 87, uses this expression.
[18] *Études de mythologie*, II, p. 245.

22. Mercurius in the "philosopher's egg" (the alchemical vessel). As *filius* he stands on the sun and moon, tokens of his dual nature. The birds betoken spiritualization, while the scorching rays of the sun ripen the homunculus in the vessel.—*Mutus liber* (1702)

nearest to the sun, hence he is pre-eminently related to gold. But, as quicksilver, he dissolves the gold and extinguishes its sunlike brilliance. All through the Middle Ages he was the object of much puzzled speculation on the part of the natural philosophers: sometimes he was a ministering and helpful spirit, a πάρεδρος (literally "assistant, comrade") or *familiaris;* and sometimes the *servus* or *cervus fugitivus* (the fugitive slave or stag), an elusive, deceptive, teasing goblin[19] who drove the alchemists to despair and had many of his attributes in common with the devil. For instance he is dragon, lion, eagle, raven, to mention only the most important of them. In the alchemical hierarchy of gods Mercurius comes lowest as *prima materia* and highest

[19] Cf. the entertaining dialogue between the alchemist and Mercurius in Sendivogius, "Dialogus," *Theatr. chem.,* IV.

as *lapis philosophorum*. The *spiritus mercurialis* (fig. 23) is the alchemists' guide (Hermes Psychopompos: cf. fig. 146), and their tempter; he is their good luck and their ruin. His dual nature enables him to be not only the seventh but also the eighth—the eighth on Olympus "whom nobody thought of" (see infra, par. 204f.).

85 It may seem odd to the reader that anything as remote as medieval alchemy should have relevance here. But the "black art" is not nearly so remote as we think; for as an educated man the dreamer must have read *Faust,* and *Faust* is an alchemical drama from beginning to end, although the educated man of today has only the haziest notion of this. Our conscious mind is far from understanding everything, but the unconscious always keeps an eye on the "age-old, sacred things," however strange they may be, and reminds us of them at a suitable opportunity. No doubt *Faust* affected our dreamer much as Goethe was affected when, as a young man in his Leipzig days, he studied Theophrastus Paracelsus with Fräulein von Klettenberg.[20] It was then, as we certainly may assume, that the mysterious equivalence of seven and eight sank deep into his soul, without his conscious mind ever unravelling the mystery. The following dream will show that this reminder of *Faust* is not out of place.

14. DREAM:

86 *The dreamer is in America looking for an employee with a pointed beard. They say that everybody has such an employee.*

87 America is the land of practical, straightforward thinking, uncontaminated by our European sophistication. The intellect would there be kept, very sensibly, as an employee. This naturally sounds like *lèse-majesté* and might therefore be a serious matter. So it is consoling to know that everyone (as is always the case in America) does the same. The "man with a pointed beard" is our time-honoured Mephisto whom Faust "employed" and who was not permitted to triumph over him in the end, despite the fact that Faust had dared to descend into the dark chaos of the historical psyche and steep himself in the ever-changing, seamy side of life that rose up out of that bubbling cauldron.

88 From subsequent questions it was discovered that the

20 Goethe, *Dichtung und Wahrheit.*

23. The mystic vessel where the two natures unite (*sol* and *luna*, *caduceus*) to produce the *filius hermaphroditus*, Hermes Psychopompos, flanked by the six gods of the planets.—"Figurarum Aegyptiorum secretarum" (MS., 18th cent.)

dreamer himself had recognized the figure of Mephistopheles in the "man with the pointed beard." Versatility of mind as well as the inventive gift and scientific leanings are attributes of the astrological Mercurius. Hence the man with the pointed beard represents the intellect, which is introduced by the dream as a real *familiaris,* an obliging if somewhat dangerous spirit. The intellect is thus degraded from the supreme position it once occupied and is put in the second rank, and at the same time branded as daemonic. Not that it had ever been anything but daemonic—only the dreamer had not noticed before how possessed he was by the intellect as the tacitly recognized supreme power. Now he has a chance to view this function, which till then had been the uncontested dominant of his psychic life, at somewhat closer quarters. Well might he exclaim with Faust: "So that's what was inside the poodle!" Mephistopheles is the diabolical aspect of every psychic function that has broken loose from the hierarchy of the total psyche and now enjoys independence and absolute power (fig. 36). But this aspect can be perceived only when the function becomes a separate entity and is objectivated or personified, as in this dream.

89   Amusingly enough, the "man with the pointed beard" also crops up in alchemical literature, in one of the "Parabolae" contained in the "Güldenen Tractat vom philosophischen Stein," [21] written in 1625, which Herbert Silberer[22] has analysed from a psychological point of view. Among the company of old white-bearded philosophers there is a young man with a black pointed beard. Silberer is uncertain whether he should assume this figure to be the devil.

90   Mercurius as quicksilver is an eminently suitable symbol for the "fluid," i.e., mobile, intellect (fig. 24). Therefore in alchemy Mercurius is sometimes a "spirit" and sometimes a "water," the so-called *aqua permanens,* which is none other than *argentum vivum.*

15. DREAM:

91   *The dreamer's mother is pouring water from one basin into another.* (The dreamer only remembered in connection with vision 28 of the next series that this basin belonged to his sister.)

21 Printed in *Geheime Figuren der Rosenkreuzer.*
22 *Problems of Mysticism and Its Symbolism.*

24. The activities presided over by Mercurius.—Tübingen MS. (*c.* 1400)

25. The fountain of life as *fons mercurialis.—Rosarium philosophorum* (1550)

This action is performed with great solemnity: it is of the highest significance for the outside world. Then the dreamer is rejected by his father.

92   Once more we meet with the theme of "exchange" (cf. dream 1): one thing is put in the place of another. The "father" has been dealt with; now begins the action of the "mother." Just as the father represents collective consciousness, the traditional spirit, so the mother stands for the collective unconscious, the source of the water of life[23] (fig. 25). (Cf. the maternal significance of πηγή,[24] the *fons signatus*,[25] as an attribute of the Virgin Mary, etc.—fig. 26.) The unconscious has altered the locus of the life forces, thus indicating a change of attitude. The dreamer's subsequent recollection enables us to see who is now

[23] For water as origin, cf. Egyptian cosmogony, among others.
[24] Wirth, *Aus orientalischen Chroniken,* p. 199.
[25] "A fountain sealed": Song of Songs 4 : 12.

145

26. The Virgin Mary surrounded by her attributes, the quadrangular enclosed garden, the round temple, tower, gate, well and fountain, palms and cypresses (trees of life), all feminine symbols.—17th-century devotional picture

the source of life: it is the "sister." The mother is superior to the son, but the sister is his equal. Thus the deposition of the intellect frees the dreamer from the domination of the unconscious and hence from his infantile attitude. Although the sister is a remnant of the past, we know definitely from later dreams that she was the carrier of the anima-image. We may therefore assume that the transferring of the water of life to the sister really means that the mother has been replaced by the anima.[26]

93   The anima now becomes a life-giving factor, a psychic reality which conflicts strongly with the world of the father. Which of us could assert, without endangering his sanity, that he had accepted the guidance of the unconscious in the conduct of his life, assuming that anyone exists who could imagine what that would mean? Anyone who could imagine it at all would certainly have no difficulty in understanding what a monstrous affront such a *volte face* would offer to the traditional spirit, especially to the spirit that has put on the earthly garment of the Church. It was this subtle change of psychic standpoint that caused the old alchemists to resort to deliberate mystification, and that sponsored all kinds of heresies. Hence it is only logical for the father to reject the dreamer—it amounts to nothing less than excommunication. (Be it noted that the dreamer is a Roman Catholic.) By acknowledging the reality of the psyche and making it a co-determining ethical factor in our lives, we offend against the spirit of convention which for centuries has regulated psychic life from outside by means of institutions as well as by reason. Not that unreasoning instinct rebels of itself against firmly established order; by the strict logic of its own inner laws it is itself of the firmest structure imaginable and, in addition, the creative foundation of all binding order. But just because this foundation is creative, all order which proceeds from it—even in its most "divine" form—is a phase, a stepping-stone. Despite appearances to the contrary, the establishment of order and the dissolution of what has been established are at

---

[26] This is really a normal life-process, but it usually takes place quite unconsciously. The anima is an archetype that is always present. (Cf. Jung, *Psychological Types*, Defs. 48, 49, and "The Relations between the Ego and the Unconscious," pars. 296ff.) The mother is the first carrier of the anima-image, which gives her a fascinating quality in the eyes of the son. It is then transferred, via the sister and similar figures, to the beloved.

bottom beyond human control. The secret is that only that which can destroy itself is truly alive. It is well that these things are difficult to understand and thus enjoy a wholesome concealment, for weak heads are only too easily addled by them and thrown into confusion. From all these dangers dogma—whether ecclesiastical, philosophical, or scientific—offers effective protection, and, looked at from a social point of view, excommunication is a necessary and useful consequence.

94   The water that the mother, the unconscious, pours into the basin belonging to the anima is an excellent symbol for the living power of the psyche (cf. fig. 152). The old alchemists never tired of devising new and expressive synonyms for this water. They called it *aqua nostra, mercurius vivus, argentum vivum, vinum ardens, aqua vitae, succus lunariae,* and so on, by which they meant a living being not devoid of substance, as opposed to the rigid immateriality of mind in the abstract. The expression *succus lunariae* (sap of the moon-plant) refers clearly enough to the nocturnal origin of the water, and *aqua nostra,* like *mercurius vivus,* to its earthliness (fig. 27). *Acetum fontis* is a powerful corrosive water that dissolves all created things and at the same time leads to the most durable of all products, the mysterious *lapis.*

95   These analogies may seem very far-fetched. But let me refer the reader to dreams 13 and 14 in the next section (pars. 154 and 158), where the water symbolism is taken up again. The importance of the action "for the outside world," noted by the dreamer himself, points to the collective significance of the dream, as also does the fact—which had a far-reaching influence on the conscious attitude of the dreamer—that he is "rejected by the father."

96   The saying "extra ecclesiam nulla salus"—outside the Church there is no salvation—rests on the knowledge that an institution is a safe, practicable highway with a visible or definable goal, and that no paths and no goals can be found outside it. We must not underestimate the devastating effect of getting lost in the chaos, even if we know that it is the *sine qua non* of any regeneration of the spirit and the personality.

27. Life-renewing influence of the conjoined sun and moon on the bath.—Milan,
Biblioteca Ambrosiana, Codex I

16. DREAM:

97   An ace of clubs lies before the dreamer. A seven appears beside it.

98   The ace, as "1," is the lowest card but the highest in value. The ace of clubs, being in the form of a cross, points to the Christian symbol.[27] Hence in Swiss-German the club is often called *Chrüüz* (cross). At the same time the three leaves contain an allusion to the threefold nature of the one God. Lowest and highest are beginning and end, alpha and omega.

99   The seven appears after the ace of clubs and not before. Presumably the idea is: first the Christian conception of God, and then the seven (stages). The seven stages symbolize the transformation (fig. 28) which begins with the symbolism of Cross and Trinity, and, judging by the earlier archaic allusions in dreams 7 and 13, culminates in the *solificatio*. But this solution is not hinted at here. Now, we know that the regression to the Helios of antiquity vainly attempted by Julian the Apostate was succeeded in the Middle Ages by another movement that was expressed in the formula "per crucem ad rosam" (through the cross to the rose), which was later condensed into the "Rosie Crosse" of the Rosicrucians. Here the essence of the heavenly Sol descends into the flower—earth's answer to the sun's countenance (fig. 29). The solar quality has survived in the symbol of the "golden flower" of Chinese alchemy.[28] The well-known "blue flower" of the Romantics might well be the last nostalgic perfume of the "rose"; it looks back in true Romantic fashion to the medievalism of ruined cloisters, yet at the same time modestly proclaims something new in earthly loveliness. But even

[27] Cf. dream 23 of second series (par. 212, also par. 220).

[28] Concerning the "golden flower" of medieval alchemy (cf. fig. 30), see Adolphus Senior, *Azoth*. The golden flower comes from the Greek χρυσάνθιον (Berthelot, *Alch. grecs*, III, xlix, 19) and χρυσάνθεμον = 'golden flower', a magical plant like the Homeric μῶλυ, which is often mentioned by the alchemists. The golden flower is the noblest and purest essence of gold. The same name is sometimes given to pyrites. (Cf. Lippmann, *Entstehung und Ausbreitung der Alchemie*, I, p. 70.) The strength of the *aqua permanens* is also called *flos*, 'flower' (*Turba*, ed. Ruska, p. 214, 20). *Flos* is used by later alchemists to express the mystical transforming substance. (Cf. "flos citrinus" in *Aurora consurgens*; "flos aeris aureus" in "Consil. coniug., Ars chemica," p. 167; "flos est aqua nummosa [Mercurius]" in "Allegoriae sapientum," p. 81; "flos operis est lapis" in Mylius, *Philosophia reformata*, p. 30.)

28. Capture of the Leviathan with the sevenfold tackle of the line of David, with the crucifix as bait.—Herrad of Landsberg's *Hortus deliciarum* (12th cent.)

29. Seven-petalled rose as allegory of the seven planets, the seven stages of transformation, etc.—Fludd, *Summum bonum* (1629), frontispiece

the golden brilliance of the sun had to submit to a descent, and it found its analogy in the glitter of earthly gold—although, as *aurum nostrum,* this was far removed from the gross materiality of the metal, at least for subtler minds. One of the most interesting of the alchemical texts is the *Rosarium philosophorum,* subtitled *Secunda pars alchimiae de lapide philosophico vero modo praeparando. . . . Cum figuris rei perfectionem ostendentibus* (1550).[29] The anonymous author was very definitely a "philosopher" and was apparently aware that alchemy was not concerned with ordinary goldmaking but with a philosophical secret. For these alchemists the gold undoubtedly had a symbolic nature[30] and was therefore distinguished by such attributes as *vitreum* or *philosophicum.* It was probably owing to its all too

[29] Reprinted in *Artis auriferae,* II, pp. 204ff. (1593) and *Bibliotheca chemica curiosa,* II, pp. 87ff. (1702). My quotations are usually taken from the 1593 version.

[30] As the *Rosarium* says: "Aurum nostrum non est aurum vulgi" (Our gold is not the common gold). *Art. aurif.,* II, p. 220.

obvious analogy with the sun that gold was denied the highest philosophical honour, which fell instead to the *lapis philoso- phorum.* The transformer is above the transformed, and trans- formation is one of the magical properties of the marvellous stone. The *Rosarium philosophorum* says: "For our stone, namely the living western quicksilver which has placed itself above the gold and vanquished it, is that which kills and quick- ens." [31] As to the "philosophical" significance of the *lapis,* the following quotation from a treatise ascribed to Hermes is par- ticularly enlightening: "Understand, ye sons of the wise, what this exceeding precious stone proclaims . . . 'And my light conquers every light, and my virtues are more excellent than all virtues. . . . I beget the light, but the darkness too is of my na- ture. . . .' " [32]

17. DREAM:

100   *The dreamer goes for a long walk, and finds a blue flower on the way.*

101   To go for a walk is to wander along paths that lead no- where in particular; it is both a search and a succession of changes. The dreamer finds a blue flower blossoming aimlessly by the wayside, a chance child of nature, evoking friendly memories of a more romantic and lyrical age, of the youthful season when it came to bud, when the scientific view of the world had not yet broken away from the world of actual ex- perience—or rather when this break was only just beginning and the eye looked back to what was already the past. The flower is in fact like a friendly sign, a numinous emanation from the unconscious, showing the dreamer, who as a modern man has been robbed of security and of participation in all the things that lead to man's salvation, the historical place where he can meet friends and brothers of like mind, where he can find the seed that wants to sprout in him too. But the dreamer knows nothing as yet of the old solar gold which connects the innocent

---

31 "Quia lapis noster scilicet argentum vivum occidentale, quod praetulit se auro et vicit illud, est illud quod occidit et vivere facit."—Ibid., p. 223.

32 "Intelligite, filii sapientum, quod hic lapis preciosissimus clamat, . . . et lumen meum omne lumen superat ac mea bona omnibus bonis sunt sublimiora. . . . Ego gigno lumen, tenebrae autem naturae meae sunt. . . ." Ibid., p. 239. Con- cerning the Hermes quotations in *Rosarium,* see infra, par. 140, n. 17.

30. The red-and-white rose, the "golden flower" of alchemy, as birthplace of the *filius philosophorum.*—"Ripley Scrowle" (MS., 1588)

flower with the obnoxious black art of alchemy and with the blasphemous pagan idea of the *solificatio.* For the "golden flower of alchemy" (fig. 30) can sometimes be a blue flower: "The sapphire blue flower of the hermaphrodite." [33]

18. DREAM:

102   *A man offers him some golden coins in his outstretched hand. The dreamer indignantly throws them to the ground and immediately afterwards deeply regrets his action. A variety performance then takes place in an enclosed space.*

103   The blue flower has already begun to drag its history after it. The "gold" is offered and is indignantly refused. Such a misinterpretation of the *aurum philosophicum* is easy to understand. But hardly has it happened when there comes a pang of remorse that the precious secret has been rejected and a wrong answer given to the riddle of the Sphinx. The same thing happened to the hero in Meyrink's *Golem,* when the ghost offered him a handful of grain which he spurned. The gross materiality of the yellow metal with its odious fiscal flavour, and the mean look of the grain, make both rejections comprehensible enough —but that is precisely why it is so hard to find the *lapis:* it is *exilis,* uncomely, it is thrown out into the street or on the dung-

[33] "Epistola ad Hermannum," *Theatr. chem.,* V, p. 899.

hill, it is the commonest thing to be picked up anywhere—
"in planitie, in montibus et aquis." It has this "ordinary" aspect
in common with Spitteler's jewel in *Prometheus and Epime-
theus,* which, for the same reason, was also not recognized by the
worldly wise. But "the stone which the builders rejected, the
same is become the head of the corner," and the intuition of this
possibility arouses the liveliest regret in the dreamer.

104   It is all part of the banality of its outward aspect that the
gold is minted, i.e., shaped into coins, stamped, and valued. Applied psychologically, this is just what Nietzsche refuses to do in
his *Zarathustra:* to give names to the virtues. By being shaped
and named, psychic life is broken down into coined and valued
units. But this is possible only because it is intrinsically a great
variety of things, an accumulation of unintegrated hereditary
units. Natural man is not a "self"—he is the mass and a parti-
cle in the mass, collective to such a degree that he is not even
sure of his own ego. That is why since time immemorial he has
needed the transformation mysteries to turn him into something, and to rescue him from the animal collective psyche,
which is nothing but a *variété.*

105   But if we reject this unseemly *variété* of man "as he is," it is
impossible for him to attain integration, to become a self.[34] And
that amounts to spiritual death. Life that just happens in and
for itself is not real life; it is real only when it is *known.* Only
a unified personality can experience life, not that personality
which is split up into partial aspects, that bundle of odds and
ends which also calls itself "man." The dangerous plurality already hinted at in dream 4 (par. 58) is compensated in vision 5
(par. 62), where the snake describes a magic circle and thus
marks off the taboo area, the *temenos* (fig. 31). In much the same
way and in a similar situation the *temenos* reappears here, drawing the "many" together for a united variety performance—a
gathering that has the appearance of an entertainment, though
it will shortly lose its entertaining character: the "play of goats"
will develop into a "tragedy." According to all the analogies, the
satyr play was a mystery performance, from which we may as-

---

[34] This does not mean that the self is created, so to speak, only during the
course of life; it is rather a question of its becoming conscious. The self exists
from the very beginning, but is latent, that is, unconscious. Cf. my later explanations.

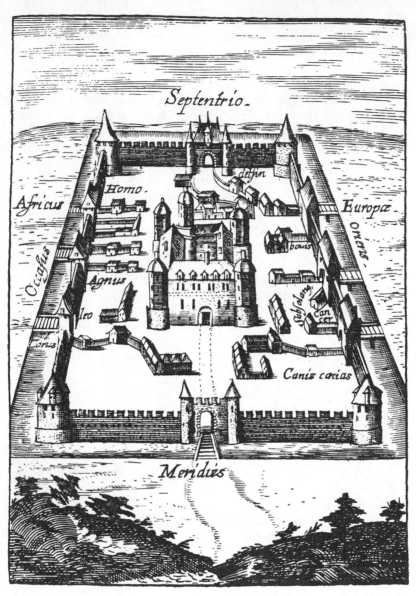

31. The symbolic city as centre of the earth, its four protecting walls laid out in a square: a typical *temenos*.—Maier, *Viatorium* (1651)

sume that its purpose, as everywhere, was to re-establish man's connection with his natural ancestry and thus with the source of life, much as the obscene stories, αἰσχρολογία, told by Athenian ladies at the mysteries of Eleusis, were thought to promote the earth's fertility.[35] (Cf. also Herodotus' account[36] of the exhibitionistic performances connected with the Isis festivities at Bubastis.)

106   The allusion to the compensatory significance of the *temenos,* however, is still wrapped in obscurity for the dreamer. As might be imagined, he is much more concerned with the danger of spiritual death, which is conjured up by his rejection of the historical context.

19. Visual impression:

107   *A death's-head. The dreamer wants to kick it away, but cannot. The skull gradually changes into a red ball, then into a woman's head which emits light.*

108   The skull soliloquies of Faust and of Hamlet are reminders of the appalling senselessness of human life when "sicklied o'er with the pale cast of thought." It was traditional opinions and judgments that caused the dreamer to dash aside the doubtful and uninviting-looking offerings. But when he tries to ward off the sinister vision of the death's-head it is transformed into a red ball, which we may take as an allusion to the rising sun, since it at once changes into the shining head of a woman, reminding us directly of vision 7 (par. 67). Evidently an enantiodromia, a play of opposites,[37] has occurred: after being rejected the unconscious insists on itself all the more strongly. First it produces the classical symbol for the unity and divinity of the self, the sun; then it passes to the motif of the unknown woman who personifies the unconscious. Naturally this motif includes not merely the archetype of the anima but also the dreamer's relationship to a real woman, who is both a human personality and a vessel for psychic projections. ("Basin of the sister" in dream 15, par. 91.)

109   In Neoplatonic philosophy the soul has definite affinities

35 Foucart, *Les Mystères d'Eleusis.*
36 [*Histories,* II, 58; trans. Powell, I, p. 137.]
37 See *Psychological Types,* Def. 18.

with the sphere. The soul substance is laid round the concentric spheres of the four elements above the fiery heaven.[38]

20. VISUAL IMPRESSION:

110   *A globe. The unknown woman is standing on it and worshipping the sun.*

111   This impression, too, is an amplification of vision 7 (par. 67). The rejection in dream 18 evidently amounted to the destruction of the whole development up to that point. Consequently the initial symbols reappear now, but in amplified form. Such enantiodromias are characteristic of dream-sequences in general. Unless the conscious mind intervened, the unconscious would go on sending out wave after wave without result, like the treasure that is said to take nine years, nine months, and nine nights to come to the surface and, if not found on the last night, sinks back to start all over again from the beginning.

112   The globe probably comes from the idea of the red ball. But, whereas this is the sun, the globe is rather an image of the earth, upon which the anima stands worshipping the sun (fig. 32). Anima and sun are thus distinct, which points to the fact that the sun represents a different principle from that of the anima. The latter is a personification of the unconscious, while the sun is a symbol of the source of life and the ultimate wholeness of man (as indicated in the *solificatio*). Now, the sun is an antique symbol that is still very close to us. We know also that the early Christians had some difficulty in distinguishing the ἥλιος ἀνατολῆς (the rising sun) from Christ.[39] The dreamer's anima still seems to be a sun-worshipper, that is to say, she belongs to the ancient world, and for the following reason: the conscious mind with its rationalistic attitude has taken little or no interest in her and therefore made it impossible for the

---

[38] Cf. Fleischer, *Hermes Trismegistus*, p. 6; also the spherical form of Plato's Original Man and the σφαῖρος of Empedocles. As in the *Timaeus*, the alchemical *anima mundi*, like the "soul of the substances," is spherical, and so is the gold (cf. fig. 209). (See Maier, *De circulo physico*, pp. 11f.) For the connection between the *rotundum* and the skull or head, see Jung, "Transformation Symbolism in the Mass," pp. 239ff.

[39] Cf. St. Augustine's argument that God is not this sun but he who made the sun (*In Joannis Evang. Tract.*, XXXIV, 2) and the evidence of Eusebius, who actually witnessed "Christian" sun-worship (*Constantini Oratio ad Sanctorum Coelum*, VI; Migne, *P.G.*, vol. 20, cols. 1245–50).

32. *Coniunctio solis et lunae.*—Trismosin, "Splendor solis" (MS., 1582)

anima to become modernized (or better, Christianized). It almost seems as if the differentiation of the intellect that began in the Christian Middle Ages, as a result of scholastic training, had driven the anima to regress to the ancient world. The Renaissance gives us evidence enough for this, the clearest of all being the *Hypnerotomachia* of Francesco Colonna, where Poliphilo meets his anima, the lady Polia, at the court of Queen Venus, quite untouched by Christianity and graced with all the "virtues" of antiquity. The book was rightly regarded as a mystery text.[40] With this anima, then, we plunge straight into the ancient world. So that I would not think anyone mistaken who interpreted the rejection of the gold in dream 18 *ex effectu* as an attempt to escape this regrettable and unseemly regression to antiquity. Certain vital doctrines of alchemical philosophy go back textually to late Greco-Roman syncretism, as Ruska, for instance, has sufficiently established in the case of the *Turba*. Hence any allusion to alchemy wafts one back to the ancient world and makes one suspect regression to pagan levels.

113   It may not be superfluous to point out here, with due emphasis, that consciously the dreamer had no inkling of all this. But in his unconscious he is immersed in this sea of historical associations, so that he behaves in his dreams as if he were fully cognizant of these curious excursions into the history of the human mind. He is in fact an unconscious exponent of an autonomous psychic development, just like the medieval alchemist or the classical Neoplatonist. Hence one could say—*cum grano salis* —that history could be constructed just as easily from one's own unconscious as from the actual texts.

21. VISUAL IMPRESSION:

114   *The dreamer is surrounded by nymphs. A voice says, "We were always there, only you did not notice us"* (fig. 33).

115   Here the regression goes back even further, to an image that is unmistakably classical. At the same time the situation of dream 4 (par. 58) is taken up again and also the situation of dream 18, where the rejection led to the compensatory enantiodromia in vision 19. But here the image is amplified by the hallucinatory recognition that the drama has always existed al-

40 Béroalde de Verville, in his introduction ["Recueil stéganographique"] to the French translation (1600) of *Hypnerotomachia,* plainly adopts this view.

33. Poliphilo surrounded by nymphs.—Béroalde de Verville, *Le Songe de Poli-phile* (1600)

though unnoticed until now. The realization of this fact joins the unconscious psyche to consciousness as a coexistent entity. The phenomenon of the "voice" in dreams always has for the dreamer the final and indisputable character of the αὐτὸς ἔφα,[41] i.e., the voice expresses some truth or condition that is beyond all doubt. The fact that a sense of the remote past has been established, that contact has been made with the deeper layers of the psyche, is accepted by the unconscious personality of the dreamer and communicates itself to his conscious mind as a feeling of comparative security.

116   Vision 20 represents the anima as a sun-worshipper. She has as it were stepped out of the globe or spherical form (cf. fig. 32). But the first spherical form was the skull. According to tradition the head or brain is the seat of the *anima intellectualis*. For this reason too the alchemical vessel must be round like the head, so that what comes out of the vessel shall be equally

41 "He said [it] himself." The phrase originally alluded to the authority of Pythagoras.

34. The *nigredo* standing on the *rotundum*, i.e., *sol niger.*—Mylius, *Philosophia reformata* (1622)

"round," i.e., simple and perfect like the *anima mundi.*[42] The work is crowned by the production of the *rotundum,* which, as the *materia globosa,* stands at the beginning and also at the end, in the form of gold (fig. 34; cf. also figs. 115, 164, 165). Possibly the nymphs who "were always there" are an allusion to this. The regressive character of the vision is also apparent from the fact that there is a multiplicity of female forms, as in dream 4 (par. 58). But this time they are of a classical nature, which, like the sun-worship in vision 20, points to an historical regression. The splitting of the anima into many figures is equivalent to dissolution into an indefinite state, i.e., into the unconscious, from which we may conjecture that a relative dissolution of the conscious mind is running parallel with the historical regression (a

42 Cf. "Liber Platonis quartorum," *Theatr. chem.,* V, pp. 149ff., 174. This treatise is a Harranite text of great importance for the history of alchemy. It exists in Arabic and Latin, but the latter version is unfortunately very corrupt. The original was probably written in the 10th cent. Cf. Steinschneider, *Die europäischen Übersetzungen aus dem Arabischen.*

process to be observed in its extreme form in schizophrenia). The dissolution of consciousness or, as Janet calls it, *abaissement du niveau mental,* comes very close to the primitive state of mind. A parallel to this scene with the nymphs is to be found in the Paracelsan *regio nymphididica,* mentioned in the treatise *De vita longa* as the initial stage of the individuation process.[43]

22. VISUAL IMPRESSION:

117   *In a primeval forest. An elephant looms up menacingly. Then a large ape-man, bear, or cave-man threatens to attack the dreamer with a club* (fig. 35). *Suddenly the "man with the pointed beard" appears and stares at the aggressor, so that he is spellbound. But the dreamer is terrified. The voice says, "Everything must be ruled by the light."*

118   The multiplicity of nymphs has broken down into still more primitive components; that is to say, the animation of the psychic atmosphere has very considerably increased, and from this we must conclude that the dreamer's isolation from his contemporaries has increased in proportion. This intensified isolation can be traced back to vision 21, where the union with the unconscious was realized and accepted as a fact. From the point of view of the conscious mind this is highly irrational; it constitutes a secret which must be anxiously guarded, since the justification for its existence could not possibly be explained to any so-called reasonable person. Anyone who tried to do so would be branded as a lunatic. The discharge of energy into the environment is therefore considerably impeded, the result being a surplus of energy on the side of the unconscious: hence the abnormal increase in the autonomy of the unconscious figures, culminating in aggression and real terror. The earlier entertaining variety performance is beginning to become uncomfortable. We find it easy enough to accept the classical figures of nymphs thanks to their aesthetic embellishments; but we have no idea that behind these gracious figures there lurks the Dionysian mystery of antiquity, the satyr play with its tragic implications: the bloody dismemberment of the god who has become an animal. It needed a Nietzsche to expose in all its feebleness Europe's schoolboy attitude to the ancient world. But what did Dionysus mean to Nietzsche? What he says about it must be taken seriously; what

43 Cf. "Paracelsus as a Spiritual Phenomenon," par. 214.

35. A medieval version of the "wild man."—Codex Urbanus Latinus 899 (15th cent.)

it did to him still more so. There can be no doubt that he knew, in the preliminary stages of his fatal illness, that the dismal fate of Zagreus was reserved for him. Dionysus is the abyss of impassioned dissolution, where all human distinctions are merged in the animal divinity of the primordial psyche—a blissful and terrible experience. Humanity, huddling behind the walls of its culture, believes it has escaped this experience, until it succeeds in letting loose another orgy of bloodshed. All well-meaning people are amazed when this happens and blame high finance, the armaments industry, the Jews, or the Freemasons.[44]

[44] I wrote this passage in spring, 1935.

119   At the last moment, friend "Pointed Beard" appears on the scene as an obliging *deus ex machina* and exorcizes the annihilation threatened by the formidable ape-man. Who knows how much Faust owed his imperturbable curiosity, as he gazed on the spooks and bogeys of the classical *Walpurgisnacht,* to the helpful presence of Mephisto and his matter-of-fact point of view! Would that more people could remember the scientific or philosophical reflections of the much-abused intellect at the right moment! Those who abuse it lay themselves open to the suspicion of never having experienced anything that might have taught them its value and shown them why mankind has forged this weapon with such unprecedented effort. One has to be singularly out of touch with life not to notice such things. The intellect may be the devil (fig. 36), but the devil is the "strange son of chaos" who can most readily be trusted to deal effectively with his mother. The Dionysian experience will give this devil plenty to do should he be looking for work, since the resultant settlement with the unconscious far outweighs the labours of Hercules. In my opinion it presents a whole world of problems which the intellect could not settle even in a hundred years—the very reason why it so often goes off for a holiday to recuperate on lighter tasks. And this is also the reason why the psyche is forgotten so often and so long, and why the intellect makes such frequent use of magical apotropaic words like "occult" and "mystic," in the hope that even intelligent people will think that these mutterings really mean something.

120   The voice finally declares, "Everything must be ruled by the light," which presumably means the light of the discerning, conscious mind, a genuine *illuminatio* honestly acquired. The dark depths of the unconscious are no longer to be denied by ignorance and sophistry—at best a poor disguise for common fear—nor are they to be explained away with pseudo-scientific rationalizations. On the contrary it must now be admitted that things exist in the psyche about which we know little or nothing at all, but which nevertheless affect our bodies in the most obstinate way, and that they possess at least as much reality as the things of the physical world which ultimately we do not understand either. No line of research which asserted that its subject was unreal or a "nothing but" has ever made any contribution to knowledge.

36. The devil as aerial spirit and ungodly intellect.—Illustration by Eugène Delacroix (1799–1863) for *Faust*, Part I

121   With the active intervention of the intellect a new phase of the unconscious process begins: the conscious mind must now come to terms with the figures of the unknown woman ("anima"), the unknown man ("the shadow"), the wise old man ("mana personality"),[45] and the symbols of the self. The last named are dealt with in the following section.

[45] For these concepts see Jung, "The Relations between the Ego and the Unconscious."

37. The seven-petalled flower.
—Boschius, *Symbolographia* (1702)

38. Mercurius as *virgo* standing on the gold (*sol*) and silver (*luna*) fountain, with the dragon as her son.—Thomas Aquinas (pseud.), "De alchimia" (MS., 16th cent.)

39. Shri-Yantra

3. THE SYMBOLISM OF THE MANDALA

I. CONCERNING THE MANDALA

122   As I have already said, I have put together, out of a continuous series of some four hundred dreams and visions, all those that I regard as mandala dreams. The term "mandala" was chosen because this word denotes the ritual or magic circle used in Lamaism and also in Tantric yoga as a *yantra* or aid to contemplation (fig. 39). The Eastern mandalas used in ceremonial

are figures fixed by tradition; they may be drawn or painted or, in certain special ceremonies, even represented plastically.[1]

123   In 1938, I had the opportunity, in the monastery of Bhutia Busty, near Darjeeling, of talking with a Lamaic *rimpoche*, Lingdam Gomchen by name, about the *khilkor* or mandala. He explained it as a *dmigs-pa* (pronounced "migpa"), a mental image which can be built up only by a fully instructed lama through the power of imagination. He said that no mandala is like any other, they are all individually different. Also, he said, the mandalas to be found in monasteries and temples were of no particular significance because they were external representations only. The true mandala is always an inner image, which is gradually built up through (active) imagination, at such times when psychic equilibrium is disturbed or when a thought cannot be found and must be sought for, because it is not contained in holy doctrine. The aptness of this explanation will become apparent in the course of my exposition. The alleged free and individual formation of the mandala, however, should be taken with a considerable grain of salt, since in all Lamaic mandalas there predominates not only a certain unmistakable style but also a traditional structure. For instance they are all based on a quaternary system, a *quadratura circuli*, and their contents are invariably derived from Lamaic dogma. There are texts, such as the Shri-Chakra-Sambhara Tantra,[2] which contain directions for the construction of these "mental images." The *khilkor* is strictly distinguished from the so-called *sidpe-korlo*, or World Wheel (fig. 40), which represents the course of human existence in its various forms as conceived by the Buddhists. In contrast to the *khilkor*, the World Wheel is based on a ternary system in that the three world-principles are to be found in its centre: the cock, equalling concupiscence; the serpent, hatred or envy; and the pig, ignorance or unconsciousness (*avidya*). Here we come upon the dilemma of three and four, which also crops up in Buddhism. We shall meet this problem again in the further course of our dream-series.

124   It seems to me beyond question that these Eastern symbols originated in dreams and visions, and were not invented by some Mahayana church father. On the contrary, they are among the

1 Cf. Wilhelm and Jung, *Secret of the Golden Flower*, and Zimmer, *Myths and Symbols in Indian Art and Civilization*.   2 Avalon, *The Serpent Power*, VII.

40. Tibetan World Wheel (*sidpe-korlo*)

oldest religious symbols of humanity (figs. 41–44) and may even
have existed in paleolithic times (cf. the Rhodesian rock-paint-
ings). Moreover they are distributed all over the world, a point
I need not insist on here. In this section I merely wish to show
from the material at hand how mandalas come into existence.

125   The mandalas used in ceremonial are of great significance
because their centres usually contain one of the highest religious
figures: either Shiva himself—often in the embrace of Shakti——

171

41. The Aztec "Great Calendar Stone"

or the Buddha, Amitabha, Avalokiteshvara, or one of the great
Mahayana teachers, or simply the *dorje*, symbol of all the divine
forces together, whether creative or destructive (fig. 43). The
text of the *Golden Flower*, a product of Taoist syncretism, speci-
fies in addition certain "alchemical" properties of this centre
after the manner of the *lapis* and the *elixir vitae*, so that it is in
effect a φάρμακον ἀθανασίας.[3]

126 It is not without importance for us to appreciate the high
value set upon the mandala, for it accords very well with the
paramount significance of individual mandala symbols which
are characterized by the same qualities of a—so to speak—"metaphysical" nature.[4] Unless everything deceives us, they signify

[3] Cf. Reitzenstein, *Die hellenistischen Mysterienreligionen.*
[4] The quotation marks indicate that I am not positing anything by the term
"metaphysical": I am only using it figuratively, in the psychological sense, to
characterize the peculiar statements made by dreams.

172

42. Mandala containing the Infant Christ carrying the Cross.—Mural painting by Albertus Pictor in the church of Harkeberga, Sweden (*c.* 1480)

nothing less than a psychic centre of the personality not to be identified with the ego. I have observed these processes and their products for close on thirty years on the basis of very extensive material drawn from my own experience. For fourteen years I neither wrote nor lectured about them so as not to prejudice my observations. But when, in 1929, Richard Wilhelm laid the text of the *Golden Flower* before me, I decided to publish at least a foretaste of the results. One cannot be too cautious in these matters, for what with the imitative urge and a positively morbid avidity to possess themselves of outlandish feathers and deck themselves out in this exotic plumage, far too many people are misled into snatching at such "magical" ideas and applying them externally, like an ointment. People will do anything, no matter how absurd, in order to avoid facing their

43. Lamaic Vajramandala.—Cf. Jung, "Concerning Mandala Symbolism," fig. 1

44. Mexican calendar.—Herrliberger, *Heilige Ceremonien* (1748)

own souls. They will practise Indian yoga and all its exercises, observe a strict regimen of diet, learn theosophy by heart, or mechanically repeat mystic texts from the literature of the whole world—all because they cannot get on with themselves and have not the slightest faith that anything useful could ever come out of their own souls. Thus the soul has gradually been turned into a Nazareth from which nothing good can come. Therefore let us fetch it from the four corners of the earth—the more far-fetched and bizarre it is the better! I have no wish to disturb such people at their pet pursuits, but when anybody who expects to be taken seriously is deluded enough to think that I use yoga methods and yoga doctrines or that I get my patients, whenever possible, to draw mandalas for the purpose of bringing them to the "right

175

point"—then I really must protest and tax these people with having read my writings with the most horrible inattention. The doctrine that all evil thoughts come from the heart and that the human soul is a sink of iniquity must lie deep in the marrow of their bones. Were that so, then God had made a sorry job of creation, and it were high time for us to go over to Marcion the Gnostic and depose the incompetent demiurge. Ethically, of course, it is infinitely more convenient to leave God the sole responsibility for such a Home for Idiot Children, where no one is capable of putting a spoon into his own mouth. But it is worth man's while to take pains with himself, and he has something in his soul that can grow.[5] It is rewarding to watch patiently the silent happenings in the soul, and the most and the best happens when it is not regulated from outside and from above. I readily admit that I have such a great respect for what happens in the human soul that I would be afraid of disturbing and distorting the silent operation of nature by clumsy interference. That was why I even refrained from observing this particular case myself and entrusted the task to a beginner who was not handicapped by my knowledge—anything rather than disturb the process. The results which I now lay before you are the unadulterated, conscientious, and exact self-observations of a man of unerring intellect, who had nothing suggested to him from outside and who would in any case not have been open to suggestion. Anyone at all familiar with psychic material will have no difficulty in recognizing the authentic character of the results.

[5] As Meister Eckhart says, "It is not outside, it is inside: wholly within."—Trans. Evans, p. 8.

45. Hermes as psychopomp.
—Gem in a Roman ring

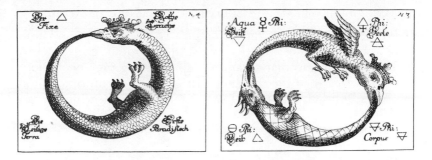

46, 47. Crowned dragon as tail-eater; two dragons forming a circle and, in the four corners, signs of the four elements.—Eleazar, *Uraltes chymisches Werk* (1760)

II. THE MANDALAS IN THE DREAMS

127   For the sake of completeness I will recapitulate the mandala symbols which occur in the initial dreams and visions already discussed:

1. The snake that described a circle round the dreamer (5).

2. The blue flower (17).

3. The man with the gold coins in his hand, and the enclosed space for a variety performance (18).

4. The red ball (19).

5. The globe (20).

128   The next mandala symbol occurs in the first dream of the new series:[6]

6. DREAM:

An unknown woman is pursuing the dreamer. He keeps running round in a circle.

129   The snake in the first mandala dream was anticipatory, as is often the case when a figure personifying a certain aspect of the unconscious does or experiences something that the subject himself will experience later. The snake anticipates a circular movement in which the subject is going to be involved; i.e., something is taking place in the unconscious which is perceived

6 [Inasmuch as the five mandala dreams and visions listed in par. 127 necessarily figure in this new series (though actually part of the first dream-series), the author initiated the number sequence of the new—i.e., the mandala—series with them. —EDITORS.]

177

as a circular movement, and this occurrence now presses into consciousness so forcefully that the subject himself is gripped by it. The unknown woman or anima representing the unconscious continues to harass the dreamer until he starts running round in circles. This clearly indicates a potential centre which is not identical with the ego and round which the ego revolves.

7. DREAM:

¹³⁰ *The anima accuses the dreamer of paying too little attention to her. There is a clock that says five minutes to the hour.*

¹³¹ The situation is much the same: the unconscious pesters him like an exacting woman. The situation also explains the clock, for a clock's hands go round in a circle. Five minutes to the hour implies a state of tension for anybody who lives by the clock: when the five minutes are up he must do something or other. He might even be pressed for time. (The symbol of circular movement—cf. fig. 13—is always connected with a feeling of tension, as we shall see later.)

8. DREAM:

¹³² *On board ship. The dreamer is occupied with a new method of taking his bearings. Sometimes he is too far away and sometimes too near: the right spot is in the middle. There is a chart on which is drawn a circle with its centre.*

¹³³ Obviously the task set here is to find the centre, the right spot, and this is the centre of a circle. While the dreamer was writing down this dream he remembered that he had dreamed shortly before of shooting at a target (fig. 48): sometimes he shot too high, sometimes too low. The right aim lay in the middle. Both dreams struck him as highly significant. The target is a circle with a centre. Bearings at sea are taken by the apparent rotation of the stars round the earth. Accordingly the dream describes an activity whose aim is to construct or locate an objective centre—a centre outside the subject.

9. DREAM:

¹³⁴ *A pendulum clock that goes forever without the weights running down.*

¹³⁵ This is a species of clock whose hands move unceasingly, and, since there is obviously no loss due to friction, it is a *per-*

48. The *putrefactio* without which the "goal" of the *opus* cannot be reached (hence the target-shooting).—Stolcius de Stolcenberg, *Viridarium chymicum* (1624)

petuum mobile, an everlasting movement in a circle. Here we meet with a "metaphysical" attribute. As I have already said, I use this word in a psychological sense, hence figuratively. I mean by this that eternity is a quality predicated by the unconscious, and not a hypostasis. The statement made by the dream will obviously offend the dreamer's scientific judgment, but this is just what gives the mandala its peculiar significance. Highly significant things are often rejected because they seem to contradict reason and thus set it too arduous a test. The movement without friction shows that the clock is cosmic, even transcendental; at any rate it raises the question of a quality which leaves us in some doubt whether the psychic phenomenon expressing itself in the mandala is under the laws of space and time. And this points to something so entirely different from the empirical ego that the gap between them is difficult to bridge; i.e., the other centre of personality lies on a different plane from the ego since, unlike this, it has the quality of "eternity" or relative timelessness.

10. DREAM:

136   *The dreamer is in the Peterhofstatt in Zurich with the doctor, the man with the pointed beard, and the "doll woman."
The last is an unknown woman who neither speaks nor is
spoken to. Question: To which of the three does the woman belong?*

137   The tower of St. Peter's in Zurich has a clock with a strikingly large face. The Peterhofstatt is an enclosed space, a *temenos* in the truest sense of the word, a precinct of the church.
The four of them find themselves in this enclosure. The circular
dial of the clock is divided into four quarters, like the horizon.
In the dream the dreamer represents his own ego, the man with
the pointed beard the "employed" intellect (Mephisto), and the
"doll woman" the anima. Since the doll is a childish object it is
an excellent image for the non-ego nature of the anima, who is
further characterized as an object by "not being spoken to." This
negative element (also present in dreams 6 and 7 above) indicates an inadequate relationship between the conscious mind
and the unconscious, as also does the question of whom the unknown woman belongs to. The "doctor," too, belongs to the
non-ego; he probably contains a faint allusion to myself, although at that time I had no connections with the dreamer.[7]
The man with the pointed beard, on the other hand, belongs
to the ego. This whole situation is reminiscent of the relations
depicted in the diagram of functions (fig. 49). If we think of the
psychological functions[8] as arranged in a circle, then the most
differentiated function is usually the carrier of the ego and,
equally regularly, has an auxiliary function attached to it. The
"inferior" function, on the other hand, is unconscious and for
that reason is projected into a non-ego. It too has an auxiliary
function. Hence it would not be impossible for the four persons
in the dream to represent the four functions as components of
the total personality (i.e., if we include the unconscious). But
this totality is ego plus non-ego. Therefore the centre of the
circle which expresses such a totality would correspond not to
the ego but to the self as the summation of the total personality.
(The centre with a circle is a very well-known allegory of the na-

7 As the dream at most alludes to me and does not name me, the unconscious
evidently has no intention of emphasizing my personal role.
8 Cf. Jung, *Psychological Types,* ch. X.

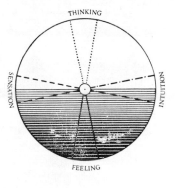

49. Diagram showing the four functions of consciousness. Thinking, the superior function in this case, occupies the centre of the light half of the circle, whereas feeling, the inferior function, occupies the dark half. The two auxiliary functions are partly in the light and partly in the dark

ture of God.) In the philosophy of the Upanishads the Self is in one aspect the *personal* atman, but at the same time it has a cosmic and metaphysical quality as the *suprapersonal* Atman.[9]

138 We meet with similar ideas in Gnosticism: I would mention the idea of the Anthropos, the Pleroma, the Monad, and the spark of light (Spinther) in a treatise of the Codex Brucianus:

> This same is he [Monogenes] who dwelleth in the Monad, which is in the Setheus, and which came from the place of which none can say where it is. . . . From Him it is the Monad came, in the manner of a ship, laden with all good things, and in the manner of a field, filled or planted with every kind of tree, and in the manner of a city, filled with all races of mankind. . . . This is the fashion of the Monad, all these being in it: there are twelve Monads as a crown upon its head. . . . And to its veil which surroundeth it in the manner of a defence [πύργος = tower] there are twelve gates. . . . This same is the Mother-City [μητρόπολις] of the Only-begotten [μονογενής].[10]

139 By way of explanation I should add that "Setheus" is a name for God, meaning "creator." The Monogenes is the Son of God. The comparison of the Monad with a field and a city corresponds to the idea of the *temenos* (fig. 50). Also, the Monad is crowned (cf. the hat which appears in dream 1 of the first series [par. 52] and dream 35 of this series [par. 254]). As "metropolis" (cf. fig. 51) the Monad is feminine, like the *padma* or lotus, the basic form of the Lamaic mandala (the Golden Flower in China and the Rose or Golden Flower in the West). The Son of

9 Deussen, *Allgemeine Geschichte der Philosophie,* I.
10 Baynes, *A Coptic Gnostic Treatise,* p. 89.

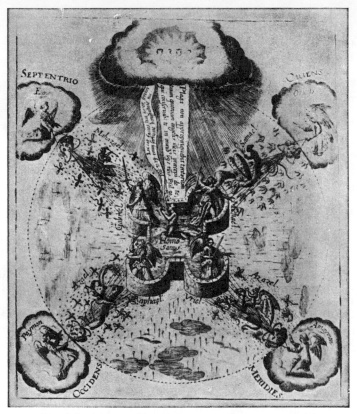

50. Baneful spirits attacking the Impregnable Castle.—Fludd,
Summum bonum (1629)

God, God made manifest, dwells in the flower.[11] In the Book of
Revelation, we find the Lamb in the centre of the Heavenly Je-
rusalem. And in our Coptic text we are told that Setheus dwells
in the innermost and holiest recesses of the Pleroma, a city with
four gates (equivalent to the Hindu City of Brahma on the
world-mountain Meru). In each gate there is a Monad.[12] The

[11] The Buddha, Shiva, etc., in the lotus (fig. 52); Christ in the rose, in the womb
of Mary (ample material on this theme in Salzer, *Die Sinnbilder und Beiworte
Mariens*); the seeding-place of the diamond body in the golden flower. Cf. the
circumambulation of the square in dream 16, par. 164.

[12] Baynes, *A Coptic Gnostic Treatise*, p. 58. Cf. the Vajramandala (fig. 43), where
the great *dorje* is found in the centre surrounded by the twelve smaller *dorjes*,

51. The Lapis Sanctuary, also a labyrinth, surrounded by the planetary orbits.—
Van Vreeswyck, *De Groene Leeuw* (1672)

limbs of the Anthropos born of the Autogenes (= Monogenes)
correspond to the four gates of the city. The Monad is a spark
of light (Spinther) and an image of the Father, identical with the
Monogenes. An invocation runs: "Thou art the House and the
Dweller in the House." [13] The Monogenes stands on a *tetra-
peza*,[14] a table or platform with four pillars corresponding to the
quaternion of the four evangelists.[15]

140   The idea of the *lapis* has several points of contact with all
this. In the *Rosarium* the *lapis* says, quoting Hermes:[16] "I beget
the light, but the darkness too is of my nature . . . therefore

---

like the one Monad with the "twelve Monads as a crown upon its head." Moreover there is a *dorje* in each of the four gates.

[13] Baynes, p. 94.

[14] Ibid., p. 70. Similar to the tetramorph, the steed of the Church (fig. 53).

[15] Cf. Irenaeus, *Adversus haereses*, III, xi, and Clement of Alexandria, *Stromata*,
V, vi.

[16] *Art. aurif.*, II, pp. 239f. The Hermes quotations come from the fourth chapter of "Tractatus aureus" (*Ars chemica*, pp. 23f., or *Bibl. chem.*, I, pp. 427f.).

nothing better or more worthy of veneration can come to pass in the world than the conjunction of myself and my son." [17] Similarly, the Monogenes is called the "dark light," [18] a reminder of the *sol niger*, the black sun of alchemy[19] (fig. 34).

141   The following passage from chapter 4 of the "Tractatus aureus" provides an interesting parallel to the Monogenes who dwells in the bosom of the Mother-City and is identical with the crowned and veiled Monad:

But the king reigns, as is witnessed by his brothers, [and] says: "I am crowned, and I am adorned with the diadem; I am clothed with the royal garment, and I bring joy to the heart; for, being chained to the arms and breast of my mother, and to her substance, I cause my substance to hold together and rest; and I compose the invisible from the visible, making the occult to appear; and everything that the philosophers have concealed will be generated from us. Hear then these words, and understand them; keep them, and meditate upon them, and seek for nothing more. Man is generated from the principle of Nature whose inward parts are fleshy, and from no other substance."

52. Harpokrates on the lotus.
—Gnostic gem

[17] "Ego gigno lumen, tenebrae autem naturae meae sunt . . . me igitur et filio meo conjuncto, nihil melius ac venerabilius in mundo fieri potest." The Hermes sayings as quoted by the anonymous author of the *Rosarium* contain deliberate alterations that have far more significance than mere faulty readings. They are authentic recastings, to which he lends higher authority by attributing them to Hermes. I have compared the three printed editions of the "Tractatus aureus," 1566, 1610, and 1702, and found that they all agree. The *Rosarium* quotation runs as follows in the "Tractatus aureus": "Iam Venus ait: Ego genero lumen, nec tenebrae meae naturae sunt . . . me igitur et fratri meo iunctis nihil melius ac venerabilius" (Venus says: I beget the light, and the darkness is not of my nature . . . therefore nothing is better or more worthy of veneration than the conjunction of myself and my brother).
[18] Baynes, p. 87.   [19] Cf. Mylius, *Philosophia reformata*, p. 19.

53. The tetramorph, the steed of the Church.—Crucifixion in Herrad of Landsberg's *Hortus deliciarum* (12th cent.) detail

142   The "king" refers to the *lapis*. That the *lapis* is the "master" is evident from the following Hermes quotation in the *Rosarium:* [20] "Et sic Philosophus non est Magister lapidis, sed potius minister" (And thus the philosopher is not the master of the stone but rather its minister). Similarly the final production of the *lapis* in the form of the crowned hermaphrodite is called the *aenigma regis.*[21] A German verse refers to the *aenigma* as follows (fig. 54):

> Here now is born the emperor of all honour
> Than whom there cannot be born any higher,
> Neither by art nor by the work of nature
> Out of the womb of any living creature.
> Philosophers speak of him as their son
> And everything they do by him is done.[22]

143   The last two lines might easily be a direct reference to the above quotation from Hermes.

144   It looks as if the idea had dawned on the alchemists that the Son who, according to classical (and Christian) tradition, dwells eternally in the Father and reveals himself as God's gift to mankind, was something that man could produce out of his own nature—with God's help, of course (*Deo concedente*). The heresy of this idea is obvious.

145   The feminine nature of the inferior function derives from its contamination with the unconscious. Because of its feminine characteristics the unconscious is personified by the anima (that is to say, in men; in women it is masculine).[23]

146   If we assume that this dream and its predecessors really do mean something that justly arouses a feeling of significance in the dreamer, and if we further assume that this significance is more or less in keeping with the views put forward in the commentary, then we would have reached here a high point of introspective intuition whose boldness leaves nothing to be desired. But even the everlasting pendulum clock is an indigestible morsel for a consciousness unprepared for it, and likely to hamper any too lofty flight of thought.

---

[20] *Art. aurif.*, II, p. 356.   [21] Ibid., p. 359.   [22] Ibid.
[23] Cf. Jung, "The Relations between the Ego and the Unconscious," pars. 296ff.

Ænigma Regis.

**Sie ist geboren der Keyser aller ehren/
Kein höher mag vber jn geboren werden.**

54. Hermaphrodite with three serpents and one serpent.
Below, the three-headed Mercurial dragon.—*Rosarium
philosophorum*, in *Artis auriferae* (1593)

11. DREAM:

147   *The dreamer, the doctor, a pilot, and the unknown woman
are travelling by airplane. A croquet ball suddenly smashes the
mirror, an indispensable instrument of navigation, and the airplane crashes to the ground. Here again there is the same doubt:
to whom does the unknown woman belong?*

148   Doctor, pilot, and unknown woman are characterized as
belonging to the non-ego by the fact that all three of them are
strangers. Therefore the dreamer has retained possession only
of the differentiated function, which carries the ego; that is,
the unconscious has gained ground considerably. The croquet
ball is part of a game where the ball is driven under a hoop.
Vision 8 of the first series (par. 69) said that people should not
go over the rainbow (fly?), but must go *under* it. Those who go
over it fall to the ground. It looks as though the flight had been

too lofty after all. Croquet is played on the ground and not in the air. We should not rise above the earth with the aid of "spiritual" intuitions and run away from hard reality, as so often happens with people who have brilliant intuitions. We can never reach the level of our intuitions and should therefore not identify ourselves with them. Only the gods can pass over the rainbow bridge; mortal men must stick to the earth and are subject to its laws (cf. fig. 16). In the light of the possibilities revealed by intuition, man's earthliness is certainly a lamentable imperfection; but this very imperfection is part of his innate being, of his reality. He is compounded not only of his best intuitions, his highest ideals and aspirations, but also of the odious conditions of his existence, such as heredity and the indelible sequence of memories that shout after him: "You did it, and that's what you are!" Man may have lost his ancient saurian's tail, but in its stead he has a chain hanging on to his psyche which binds him to the earth—an anything-but-Homeric chain[24] of given conditions which weigh so heavy that it is better to remain bound to them, even at the risk of becoming neither a hero nor a saint. (History gives us some justification for not attaching any absolute value to these collective norms.) That we are bound to the earth does not mean that we cannot grow; on the contrary it is the *sine qua non* of growth. No noble, well-grown tree ever disowned its dark roots, for it grows not only upward but downward as well. The question of where we are going is of course extremely important; but equally important, it seems to me, is the question of *who* is going where. The "who" always implies a "whence." It takes a certain greatness to gain lasting possession of the heights, but anybody can overreach himself. The difficulty lies in striking the dead centre (cf. dream 8, par. 132). For this an awareness of the two sides of man's personality is essential, of their respective aims and origins. These two aspects must never be separated through arrogance or cowardice.

149   The "mirror" as an "indispensable instrument of navigation" doubtless refers to the intellect, which is able to think

24 The Homeric chain in alchemy is the series of great wise men, beginning with Hermes Trismegistus, which links earth with heaven. At the same time it is the chain of substances and different chemical states that appear in the course of the alchemical process. Cf. *Aurea catena Homeri.*

and is constantly persuading us to identify ourselves with its insights ("reflections"). The mirror is one of Schopenhauer's favourite similes for the intellect. The term "instrument of navigation" is an apt expression for this, since it is indeed man's indispensable guide on pathless seas. But when the ground slips from under his feet and he begins to speculate in the void, seduced by the soaring flights of intuition, the situation becomes dangerous (fig. 55).

150 Here again the dreamer and the three dream figures form a quaternity. The unknown woman or anima always represents the "inferior," i.e., the undifferentiated function, which in the case of our dreamer is feeling. The croquet ball is connected with the "round" motif and is therefore a symbol of wholeness, that is, of the self, here shown to be hostile to the intellect (the mirror). Evidently the dreamer "navigates" too much by the intellect and thus upsets the process of individuation. In *De vita longa,* Paracelsus describes the "four" as *Scaiolae,* but the self as Adech (from Adam = the first man). Both, as Paracelsus emphasizes, cause so many difficulties in the "work" that one can almost speak of Adech as hostile.[25]

12. DREAM:

151 *The dreamer finds himself with his father, mother, and sister in a very dangerous situation on the platform of a tram-car.*

152 Once more the dreamer forms a quaternity with the other dream figures. He has fallen right back into childhood, a time when we are still a long way from wholeness. Wholeness is represented by the family, and its components are still projected upon the members of the family and personified by them. But this state is dangerous for the adult because regressive: it denotes a splitting of personality which primitive man experiences as the perilous "loss of soul." In the break-up the personal components that have been integrated with such pains are once more sucked into the outside world. The individual loses his guilt and exchanges it for infantile innocence; once more he can blame the wicked father for this and the unloving mother for that, and all the time he is caught in this inescapable causal nexus like a fly in a spider's web, without noticing that he has

---

25 Jung, "Paracelsus as a Spiritual Phenomenon," pars. 209ff.

55. Faust before the magic mirror.—Rembrandt, etching (c. 1652).

lost his moral freedom.[26] But no matter how much parents and grandparents may have sinned against the child, the man who is really adult will accept these sins as his own condition which has to be reckoned with. Only a fool is interested in other people's guilt, since he cannot alter it. The wise man learns only from his own guilt. He will ask himself: Who am I that all this should happen to me? To find the answer to this fateful question he will look into his own heart.

153   As in the previous dream the vehicle was an airplane, so in this it is a tram. The type of vehicle in a dream illustrates the kind of movement or the manner in which the dreamer moves forward in time—in other words, how he lives his psychic life, whether individually or collectively, whether on his own or on borrowed means, whether spontaneously or mechanically. In the airplane he is flown by an unknown pilot; i.e., he is borne along on intuitions emanating from the unconscious. (The mistake is that the "mirror" is used too much to steer by.) But in this dream he is in a collective vehicle, a tram, which anybody can ride in; i.e., he moves or behaves just like everybody else. All the same he is again one of four, which means that he is in both vehicles on account of his unconscious striving for wholeness.

13. DREAM:

154   *In the sea there lies a treasure. To reach it, he has to dive through a narrow opening. This is dangerous, but down below he will find a companion. The dreamer takes the plunge into the dark and discovers a beautiful garden in the depths, symmetrically laid out, with a fountain in the centre (fig. 56).*

155   The "treasure hard to attain" lies hidden in the ocean of the unconscious, and only the brave can reach it. I conjecture that the treasure is also the "companion," the one who goes through life at our side—in all probability a close analogy to the lonely ego who finds a mate in the self, for at first the self is the strange non-ego. This is the theme of the magical travelling companion,

---

26 Meister Eckhart says: " 'I came not upon earth to bring peace but a sword; to cut away all things, to part thee from brother, child, mother and friend, which are really thy foes.' For verily thy comforts are thy foes. Doth thine eye see all things and thine ear hear all things and thy heart remember them all, then in these things thy soul is destroyed."—Trans. Evans, I, pp. 12–13.

of whom I will give three famous examples: the disciples on the road to Emmaus, Krishna and Arjuna in the Bhagavad Gita, Moses and El-Khidr in Sura 18 of the Koran.[27] I conjecture further that the treasure in the sea, the companion, and the garden with the fountain are all one and the same thing: the self. For the garden is another *temenos,* and the fountain is the source of "living water" mentioned in John 7 : 38, which the Moses of the Koran also sought and found, and beside it El-Khidr,[28] "one of Our servants whom We had endowed with Our grace and wisdom" (Sura 18). And the legend has it that the ground round about El-Khidr blossomed with spring flowers, although it was desert. In Islam, the plan of the *temenos* with the fountain developed under the influence of early Christian architecture into the court of the mosque with the ritual wash-house in the centre (e.g., Ahmed ibn-Tulun in Cairo). We see much the same thing in our Western cloisters with the fountain in the garden. This is also the "rose garden of the philosophers," which we know from the treatises on alchemy and from many beautiful engravings. "The Dweller in the House" (cf. commentary to dream 10, par. 139) is the "companion." The centre and the circle, here represented by fountain and garden, are analogues of the *lapis,* which is among other things a living being (cf. figs. 25, 26). In the *Rosarium* the *lapis* says: "Protege me, protegam te. Largire mihi ius meum, ut te adiuvem" (Protect me and I will protect you. Give me my due that I may help you).[29] Here the *lapis* is nothing less than a good friend and helper who helps those that help him, and this points to a compensatory relationship. (I would call to mind what was said in the commentary to dream 10, pars. 138ff., more particularly the Monogenes-*lapis*-self parallel.)

156   The crash to earth thus leads into the depths of the sea, into the unconscious, and the dreamer reaches the shelter of the *temenos* as a protection against the splintering of personality caused by his regression to childhood. The situation is rather like that of dream 4 and vision 5 in the first series (pars. 58 and 62) where the magic circle warded off the lure of the unconscious and its plurality of female forms. (The dangers of temptation

---

[27] Cf. Jung, "Concerning Rebirth," pp. 135ff.   [28] Vollers, "Chidher," p. 235.
[29] *Art. aurif.,* II, p. 239. This is a Hermes quotation from the "Tractatus aureus," but in the edition of 1566 (*Ars chemica*) it runs: "Largiri vis mihi meum ut adiuvem te" (You want to give me freely what is mine, that I may help you).

56. Fountain of youth.—Codex de Sphaera (Modena, 15th cent.)

approach Poliphilo in much the same way at the beginning of his *nekyia*.)

157   The source of life is, like El-Khidr, a good companion, though it is not without its dangers, as Moses of old found to his cost, according to the Koran. It is the symbol of the life force that eternally renews itself (fig. 57; cf. also figs. 25–27, 84) and of the clock that never runs down. An uncanonical saying of our Lord runs: "He who is near unto me is near unto the fire." [30] Just as this esoteric Christ is a source of fire (fig. 58)—probably not without reference to the πῦρ ἀεὶ ζῶον of Heraclitus—so the alchemical philosophers conceive their *aqua nostra* to be *ignis* (fire).[31] The source means not only the flow of life but its warmth, indeed its heat, the secret of passion, whose synonyms are always fiery.[32] The all-dissolving *aqua nostra* is an essential ingredient in the production of the *lapis*. But the source is underground and therefore the way leads underneath: only down below can we find the fiery source of life. These depths constitute the natural history of man, his causal link with the world of instinct (cf. fig. 16). Unless this link be rediscovered no *lapis* and no self can come into being.

14. DREAM:

158   *The dreamer goes into a chemist's shop with his father. Valuable things can be got there quite cheap, above all a special water. His father tells him about the country the water comes from. Afterwards he crosses the Rubicon by train.*

159   The traditional apothecary's shop, with its carboys and gallipots, its waters, its *lapis divinus* and *infernalis* and its magisteries, is the last visible remnant of the kitchen paraphernalia

---

[30] A quotation from Aristotle in the *Rosarium, Art. aurif.*, II, p. 317, says: "Elige tibi pro lapide, per quem reges venerantur in Diadematibus suis . . . quia ille est propinquus igni" (Choose for your stone that through which kings are venerated in their crowns . . . because that [stone] is near to the fire).

[31] Cf. the treatise of Komarios, in which Cleopatra explains the meaning of the water (Berthelot, *Collection des anciens alchimistes grecs*, IV, xx).

[32] *Rosarium, Art. aurif.*, II, p. 378: "Lapis noster hic est ignis ex igne creatus et in ignem vertitur, et anima eius in igne moratur" (This our stone is fire, created of fire, and turns into fire; its soul dwells in fire). This may have been based on the following: "Item lapis noster, hoc est ignis ampulla, ex igne creatus est, et in eum vertitur" (Likewise this our stone, i.e., the flask of fire, is created out of fire and turns back into it).—"Allegoriae sapientum," *Bibl. chem. curiosa*, I, p. 468a.

57. Imperial bath with the miraculous spring of water, beneath the influence of
sun and moon.—"De balneis Puteolanis" (MS., 14th cent.)

58. Christ as the source of fire, with the "flaming" stigmata.—14th-cent. stained-glass window, church at Königsfelden, Aargau, Switzerland

of those alchemists who saw in the *donum spiritus sancti*—the precious gift—nothing beyond the chimera of goldmaking. The "special water" is literally the *aqua nostra non vulgi*.[33] It is easy

[33] *Aqua nostra* is also called *aqua permanens*, corresponding to the ὕδωρ θεῖον of the Greeks: "aqua permanens, ex qua quidem aqua lapis noster pretiosissimus generatur," we read in the "Turba philosophorum," *Art. aurif.*, I, p. 14. "Lapis enim est haec ipsa permanens aqua et dum aqua est, lapis non est" (For the stone is this selfsame permanent water; and while it is water it is not the stone). —Ibid., p. 16. The commonness of the "water" is very often emphasized, as for instance in ibid., p. 30. "Quod quaerimus publice minimo pretio venditur, et si nosceretur, ne tantillum venderent mercatores" (What we are seeking is sold publicly for a very small price, and if it were recognized, the merchants would not sell it for so little).

to understand why it is his father who leads the dreamer to the source of life, since he is the natural source of the latter's life. We could say that the father represents the country or soil from which that life sprang. But figuratively speaking, he is the "informing spirit" who initiates the dreamer into the meaning of life and explains its secrets according to the teachings of old. He is a transmitter of the traditional wisdom. But nowadays the fatherly pedagogue fulfils this function only in the dreams of his son, where he appears as the archetypal father figure, the "wise old man."

160 The water of life is easily had: everybody possesses it, though without knowing its value. "Spernitur a stultis"—it is despised by the stupid, because they assume that every good thing is always outside and somewhere else, and that the source in their own souls is a "nothing but." Like the *lapis,* it is "pretio quoque vilis," of little price, and therefore, like the jewel in Spitteler's *Prometheus,* it is rejected by everyone from the high priest and the academicians down to the very peasants, and "in viam eiectus," flung out into the street, where Ahasuerus picks it up and puts it into his pocket. The treasure has sunk down again into the unconscious.

161 But the dreamer has noticed something and with vigorous determination crosses the Rubicon. He has realized that the flux and fire of life are not to be underrated and are absolutely necessary for the achievement of wholeness. But there is no recrossing the Rubicon.

15. DREAM:

162 *Four people are going down a river: the dreamer, his father, a certain friend, and the unknown woman.*

163 In so far as the "friend" is a definite person well known to the dreamer, he belongs, like the father, to the conscious world of the ego. Hence something very important has happened: in dream 11 the unconscious was three against one, but now the situation is reversed and it is the dreamer who is three against one (the latter being the unknown woman). The unconscious has been depotentiated. The reason for this is that by "taking the plunge" the dreamer has connected the upper and the lower regions—that is to say, he has decided not to live only as a bodiless abstract being but to accept the body and the world of instinct,

the reality of the problems posed by love and life, and to act accordingly.[34] This was the Rubicon that was crossed. Individuation, becoming a self, is not only a spiritual problem, it is the problem of all life.

16. DREAM:

164   *Many people are present. They are all walking to the left around a square. The dreamer is not in the centre but to one side. They say that a gibbon is to be reconstructed.*

165   Here the square appears for the first time. Presumably it arises from the circle with the help of the four people. (This will be confirmed later.) Like the *lapis,* the *tinctura rubea,* and the *aurum philosophicum,* the squaring of the circle was a problem that greatly exercised medieval minds. It is a symbol of the *opus alchymicum* (fig. 59), since it breaks down the original chaotic unity into the four elements and then combines them again in a higher unity. Unity is represented by a circle and the four elements by a square. The production of one from four is the result of a process of distillation and sublimation which takes the so-called "circular" form: the distillate is subjected to sundry distillations[35] so that the "soul" or "spirit" shall be extracted in its purest state. The product is generally called the "quintessence," though this is by no means the only name for the ever-hoped-for and never-to-be-discovered "One." It has, as the alchemists say, a "thousand names," like the *prima materia.* Heinrich Khunrath has this to say about the circular distillation: "Through Circumrotation or a Circular Philosophical revolving of the Quaternarius, it is brought back to the highest and purest Simplicity of the plusquamperfect Catholic Monad. . . . Out of the gross and impure One there cometh an exceeding pure and subtile One," and so forth.[36] Soul and spirit must be separated from the body, and this is equivalent to death: "Therefore Paul of Tarsus saith, Cupio dissolvi, et esse cum

---

[34] The alchemists give only obscure hints on this subject, e.g., the quotation from Aristotle in *Rosarium* (*Art. aurif.,* II, p. 318): "Fili, accipere debes de pinguiori carne" (Son, you must take of the fatter flesh). And in the "Tractatus aureus," ch. IV, we read: "Homo a principio naturae generatur, cuius viscera carnea sunt" (Man is generated from the principle of Nature whose inward parts are fleshy).
[35] Cf. "Paracelsus as a Spiritual Phenomenon," pars. 185ff.
[36] *Von hylealischen Chaos,* p. 204.

59. "All things do live in the three / But in the four they merry be." (Squaring the circle.)—Jamsthaler, *Viatorium spagyricum* (1625)

Christo.[37] Therefore, my dear Philosopher, must thou catch the Spirit and Soul of the Magnesia." [38] The spirit (or spirit and soul) is the *ternarius* or number three which must first be separated from its body and, after the purification of the latter, infused back into it.[39] Evidently the body is the fourth. Hence Khunrath refers to a passage from Pseudo-Aristotle,[40] where the circle re-emerges from a triangle set in a square.[41] This circular

[37] ". . . having a desire to be dissolved and to be with Christ" (Phil. (D.V.) 1 : 23).
[38] The "magnesia" of the alchemists has nothing to do with magnesia (MgO). In Khunrath (ibid., p. 161) it is the "materia coelestis et divina," i.e., the "materia lapidis Philosophorum," the arcane or transforming substance.
[39] Ibid., p. 203.   [40] Ibid., p. 207.
[41] There is a figurative representation of this idea in Maier, *Scrutinium chymicum*: Emblema XXI. But Maier interprets the *ternarius* differently (cf. fig. 60). He says (p. 63): "Similiter volunt Philosophi quadrangulum in triangulum ducendum esse, hoc est, in corpus, spiritum et animam, quae tria in trinis coloribus ante rubedinem praeviis apparent, utpote corpus seu terra in Saturni nigredine, spiritus in lunari albedine, tanquam aqua, anima sive aer in solari citrinitate.

199

60. Squaring of the circle to make the two sexes one whole.—Maier, *Scrutinium
chymicum* (1687)

figure, together with the Uroboros—the dragon devouring itself
tail first—is the basic mandala of alchemy.

166   The Eastern and more particularly the Lamaic mandala
usually contains a square ground-plan of the stupa (fig. 43).
We can see from the mandalas constructed in solid form that
it is really the plan of a *building*. The square also conveys the
idea of a house or temple, or of an inner walled-in space[42] (cf.

Tum triangulus perfectus erit, sed hic vicissim in circulum mutari debet, hoc
est in rubedinem invariabilem." (Similarly the philosophers maintain that the
quadrangle is to be reduced to a triangle, that is, to body, spirit, and soul. These
three appear in three colours which precede the redness: the body, or earth, in
Saturnine blackness; the spirit in lunar whiteness, like water; and the soul, or
air, in solar yellow. Then the triangle will be perfect, but in its turn it must
change into a circle, that is into unchangeable redness.) Here the fourth is fire,
and an *everlasting* fire.

42 Cf. "city" and "castle" in commentary to dream 10, pars. 137ff. (See figs. 31,

below). According to the ritual, stupas must always be circumambulated to the right, because a leftward movement is evil. The left, the "sinister" side, is the unconscious side. Therefore a leftward movement is equivalent to a movement in the direction of the unconscious, whereas a movement to the right is "correct" and aims at consciousness. In the East these unconscious contents have gradually, through long practice, come to assume definite forms which have to be accepted as such and retained by the conscious mind. Yoga, so far as we know it as an established practice, proceeds in much the same way: it impresses fixed forms on consciousness. Its most important Western parallel is the *Exercitia spiritualia* of Ignatius Loyola, which likewise impress fixed concepts about salvation on the psyche. This procedure is "right" so long as the symbol is still a valid expression of the unconscious situation. The psychological rightness of both Eastern and Western yoga ceases only when the unconscious process—which anticipates future modifications of consciousness—has developed so far that it produces shades of meaning which are no longer adequately expressed by, or are at variance with, the traditional symbol. Then and only then can one say that the symbol has lost its "rightness." Such a process signifies a gradual shift in man's unconscious view of the world over the centuries and has nothing whatever to do with intellectual criticisms of this view. Religious symbols are phenomena of life, plain facts and not intellectual opinions. If the Church clung for so long to the idea that the sun rotates round the earth, and then abandoned this contention in the nineteenth century, she can always appeal to the psychological truth that for millions of people the sun did revolve round the earth and that it was only in the nineteenth century that any major portion of mankind became sufficiently sure of the intellectual function to grasp the proofs of the earth's planetary nature. Unfortunately there is no "truth" unless there are people to understand it.

167　　Presumably the leftward circumambulation of the square indicates that the squaring of the circle is a stage on the way to the unconscious, a point of transition leading to a goal lying as yet unformulated beyond it. It is one of those paths to the centre

---

50, 51.) The alchemists similarly understand the *rotundum* arising out of the square as the *oppidum* (city). See Aegidius de Vadis, "Dialogus inter naturam et filium Philosophiae," *Theatr. chem.*, II, p. 115.

of the non-ego which were also trodden by the medieval investigators when producing the *lapis*. The *Rosarium* says:[43] "Out of
man and woman make a round circle and extract the quadrangle
from this and from the quadrangle the triangle. Make a round
circle and you will have the philosophers' stone"[44] (figs. 59, 60).

168   The modern intellect naturally regards all this as poppy-
cock. But this estimate fails to get rid of the fact that such con-
catenations of ideas do exist and that they even played an
important part for many centuries. It is up to psychology to *understand* these things, leaving the layman to rant about poppy-
cock and obscurantism. Many of my critics who call themselves
"scientific" behave exactly like the bishop who excommunicated
the cockchafers for their unseemly proliferation.

169   Just as the stupas preserve relics of the Buddha in their
innermost sanctuary, so in the interior of the Lamaic quadrangle, and again in the Chinese earth-square, there is a Holy
of Holies with its magical agent, the cosmic source of energy, be

43 A quotation attributed to Pseudo-Aristotle ("Tractatus Aristotelis," *Theatr.
chem.*, V, pp. 88off.), but not traceable.

44 In the *Tractatus aureus . . . cum Scholiis Dominici Gnosii* (1610), p. 43, there
is a drawing of the "secret square of the sages." In the centre of the square is a
circle surrounded by rays of light. The scholium gives the following explanation:
"Divide lapidem tuum in quatuor elementa . . . et coniunge in unum et totum
habebis magisterium" (Reduce your stone to the four elements . . . and unite
them into one and you will have the whole magistery)—a quotation from Pseudo-
Aristotle. The circle in the centre is called "mediator, pacem faciens inter inim-
icos sive elementa imo hic solus efficit quadraturam circuli" (the mediator, making peace between enemies, or [the four] elements; nay rather he alone effects
the squaring of the circle).—Ibid., p. 44. The circumambulation has its parallel
in the "circulatio spirituum sive distillatio circularis, hoc est exterius intro, interius foras: item inferius et superius, simul in uno circulo conveniant, neque
amplius cognoscas, quid vel exterius, vel interius, inferius vel superius fuerit:
sed omnia sint unum in uno circulo sive vase. Hoc enim vas est Pelecanus verus
Philosophicus, nec alius est in toto mundo quaerendus." (. . . circulation of
spirits or circular distillation, that is, the outside to the inside, the inside to the
outside, likewise the lower and the upper; and when they meet
together in one circle, you could no longer recognize what was
outside or inside, or lower or upper; but all would be one
thing in one circle or vessel. For this vessel is the true philosophical Pelican, and there is no other to be sought for in all
the world.) This process is elucidated by the accompanying
drawing. The little circle is the "inside," and the circle divided into four is the "outside": four rivers flowing in and
out of the inner "ocean."—Ibid., pp. 262f.

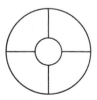

61. The pearl as symbol of Ch'ien, surrounded by the four cosmic effluences (dragons).—Chinese bronze mirror of the T'ang Period (7th to 9th cent.)

it the god Shiva, the Buddha, a bodhisattva, or a great teacher. In China it is Ch'ien—heaven—with the four cosmic effluences radiating from it (fig. 61). And equally in the Western mandalas of medieval Christendom the deity is enthroned at the centre, often in the form of the triumphant Redeemer together with the four symbolical figures of the evangelists (fig. 62). The symbol in our dream presents the most violent contrast to these highly metaphysical ideas, for it is a gibbon, unquestionably an ape, that is to be reconstructed in the centre. Here we meet again the ape who first turned up in vision 22 of the first series (par. 117). In that dream he caused a panic, but he also brought about the helpful intervention of the intellect. Now he is to be "reconstructed," and this can only mean that the anthropoid—man as

203

62. Rectangular mandala with cross, the Lamb in the centre, surrounded by the four evangelists and the four rivers of Paradise. In the medallions, the four cardinal virtues.—Zwiefalten Abbey breviary (12th cent.)

an archaic fact—is to be put together again. Clearly the left-hand path does not lead upwards to the kingdom of the gods and eternal ideas, but down into natural history, into the bestial instinctive foundations of human existence. We are therefore dealing, to put it in classical language, with a Dionysian mystery.

170   The square corresponds to the *temenos* (fig. 31), where a drama is taking place—in this case a play of apes instead of satyrs. The inside of the "golden flower" is a "seeding-place" where the "diamond body" is produced. The synonymous term "the ancestral land" [45] may actually be a hint that this product is the result of integrating the ancestral stages.

171   The ancestral spirits play an important part in primitive rites of renewal. The aborigines of central Australia even identify themselves with their mythical ancestors of the *alcheringa* period, a sort of Homeric age. Similarly the Pueblo Indians of Taos, in preparation for their ritual dances, identify with the sun, whose sons they are. This atavistic identification with human and animal ancestors can be interpreted psychologically as an integration of the unconscious, a veritable bath of renewal in the life-source where one is once again a fish, unconscious as in sleep, intoxication, and death. Hence the sleep of incubation, the Dionysian orgy, and the ritual death in initiation. Naturally the proceedings always take place in some hallowed spot. We can easily translate these ideas into the concretism of Freudian theory: the *temenos* would then be the womb of the mother and the rite a regression to incest. But these are the neurotic misunderstandings of people who have remained partly infantile and who do not realize that such things have been practised since time immemorial by adults whose activities cannot possibly be explained as a mere regression to infantilism. Otherwise the highest and most important achievements of mankind would ultimately be nothing but the perverted wishes of children, and the word "childish" would have lost its *raison d'être*.

172   Since the philosophical side of alchemy was concerned with problems that are very closely related to those which interest the most modern psychology, it might perhaps be worth while to probe a little deeper into the dream motif of the ape that is to be reconstructed in the square. In the overwhelming majority of cases alchemy identifies its transforming substance with the

[45] Wilhelm and Jung, *Secret of the Golden Flower* (1962 edn.), p. 22.

63. Hermes.—Greek vase painting (Hamilton Collection)

argentum vivum or Mercurius. Chemically this term denotes quicksilver, but philosophically it means the *spiritus vitae,* or even the world-soul (cf. fig. 91), so that Mercurius also takes on the significance of Hermes, god of revelation. (This question has been discussed in detail elsewhere.[46]) Hermes is associated with the idea of roundness and also of squareness, as can be seen particularly in Papyrus V (line 401) of the *Papyri Graecae Magicae,*[47] where he is named στρογγύλος καὶ τετράγωνος, "round and square." He is also called τετραγλώχιν, "quadrangular." He is in general connected with the number four; hence there is a Ἑρμῆς τετρακέφαλος, a "four-headed Hermes." [48] These attributes were known also in the Middle Ages, as the work of Cartari,[49] for instance, shows. He says:

Again, the square figures of Mercury [Hermes] [fig. 63], made up of nothing but a head and a virile member, signify that the Sun is the head of the world, and scatters the seed of all things; while the four sides of the square figure have the same significance as the four-stringed sistrum which was likewise attributed to Mercury, namely, the four quarters of the world or the four seasons of the year; or

46 Cf. Jung, "The Spirit Mercurius."
47 Ed. Preisendanz, *Papyri Graecae Magicae,* I, p. 195.
48 Cf. Bruchmann, *Epitheta deorum,* s.v.   49 *Les Images des dieux,* p. 403.

64. Christ as Anthropos, standing on the globe, flanked by the four elements.
—Glanville, *Le Propriétaire des choses* (1482)

again, that the two equinoxes and the two solstices make up between them the four parts of the whole zodiac.

173   It is easy to see why such qualities made Mercurius an eminently suitable symbol for the mysterious transforming substance of alchemy; for this is round and square, i.e., a totality consisting of four parts (four elements). Consequently the Gnostic quadripartite original man[50] (fig. 64) as well as Christ Pantokrator is an *imago lapidis* (fig. 65). Western alchemy is mainly of Egyptian origin, so let us first of all turn our attention to the Hellenistic figure of Hermes Trismegistus, who, while standing sponsor to the medieval Mercurius, derives ultimately from the ancient Egyptian Thoth (fig. 66). The attribute of Thoth was the baboon, or again he was represented outright as an ape.[51] This idea was visibly preserved all through the numberless editions of the Book of the Dead right down to the most

50 "Paracelsus as a Spiritual Phenomenon," pars. 168, 206ff.
51 Budge, *The Gods of the Egyptians,* I, pp. 21 and 404.

65. Tetramorph (Anthropos symbol) standing on two wheels, symbols of the Old and New Testaments.—Mosaic, Vatopedi Monastery, Mt. Athos (1213)

recent times. It is true that in the existing alchemical texts—which with few exceptions belong to the Christian era—the ancient connection between Thoth-Hermes and the ape has disappeared, but it still existed at the time of the Roman Empire. Mercurius, however, had several things in common with the devil—which we will not enter upon here—and so the ape once more crops up in the vicinity of Mercurius as the *simia Dei* (fig. 67). It is of the essence of the transforming substance to be on the one hand extremely common, even contemptible (this is expressed in the series of attributes it shares with the devil, such as serpent, dragon, raven, lion, basilisk, and eagle), but on the other hand to mean something of great value, not to say divine. For the transformation leads from the depths to the heights, from the bestially archaic and infantile to the mystical *homo maximus*.

174   The symbolism of the rites of renewal, if taken seriously, points far beyond the merely archaic and infantile to man's innate psychic disposition, which is the result and deposit of all ancestral life right down to the animal level—hence the ancestor

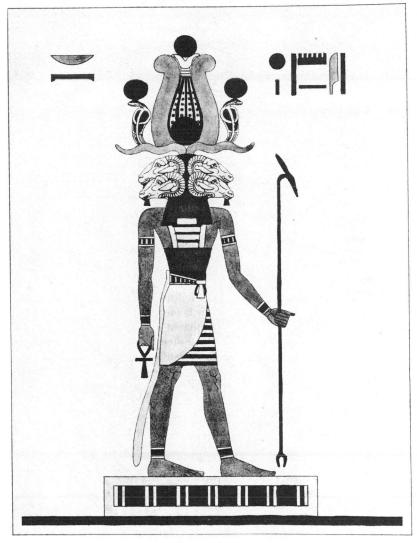

66. Ammon-Ra, the Egyptian spirit of the four elements.—Temple of Esneh, Ptolemaic, from Champollion, *Panthéon égyptien*

67. Demon in the shape of a monkey.—"Speculum humanae salvationis"
(Cod. Lat. 511, Paris, 14th cent.)

and animal symbolism. The rites are attempts to abolish the separation between the conscious mind and the unconscious, the real source of life, and to bring about a reunion of the individual with the native soil of his inherited, instinctive make-up. Had these rites of renewal not yielded definite results they would not only have died out in prehistoric times but would never have arisen in the first place. The case before us proves that even if the conscious mind is miles away from the ancient conceptions of the rites of renewal, the unconscious still strives to bring them closer in dreams. It is true that without the qualities of autonomy and autarky there would be no consciousness at all, yet these qualities also spell the danger of isolation and stagnation since, by splitting off the unconscious, they bring about an unbearable alienation of instinct. Loss of instinct is the source of endless error and confusion.

175   Finally the fact that the dreamer is "not in the centre but to one side" is a striking indication of what will happen to his ego: it will no longer be able to claim the central place but must presumably be satisfied with the position of a satellite, or at least of a planet revolving round the sun. Clearly the important place in the centre is reserved for the gibbon about to be reconstructed. The gibbon belongs to the anthropoids and, on account of its kinship with man, is an appropriate symbol for that part of the psyche which goes down into the subhuman. Further, we have seen from the cynocephalus or dog-headed baboon associated with Thoth-Hermes (fig. 68), the highest among the apes known to the Egyptians, that its godlike affinities make it an equally appropriate symbol for that part of the unconscious which transcends the conscious level. The assumption that the human psyche possesses layers that lie *below* consciousness is not likely to arouse serious opposition. But that there could just as well be layers lying *above* consciousness seems to be a surmise which borders on a *crimen laesae majestatis humanae*. In my experience the conscious mind can claim only a relatively central position and must accept the fact that the unconscious psyche transcends and as it were surrounds it on all sides. Unconscious contents connect it *backwards* with physiological states on the one hand and archetypal data on the other. But it is extended *forwards* by intuitions which are determined partly by archetypes and partly by subliminal perceptions depending on the

relativity of time and space in the unconscious. I must leave it to the reader, after thorough consideration of this dream-series and the problems it opens up, to form his own judgment as to the possibility of such an hypothesis.

176   The following dream is given unabridged, in its original text:

17. DREAM:

All the houses have something theatrical about them, with stage scenery and decorations. The name of Bernard Shaw is mentioned. The play is supposed to take place in the distant future. There is a notice in English and German on one of the sets:

This is the universal Catholic Church.
It is the Church of the Lord.
All those who feel that they are the instruments of the Lord
may enter.

Under this is printed in smaller letters: "The Church was founded by Jesus and Paul"—like a firm advertising its long standing.

I say to my friend, "Come on, let's have a look at this." He replies, "I do not see why a lot of people have to get together when they're feeling religious." I answer, "As a Protestant you will never understand." A woman nods emphatic approval. Then I see a sort of proclamation on the wall of the church. It runs:

Soldiers!

When you feel you are under the power of the Lord, do not address him directly. The Lord cannot be reached by words. We also strongly advise you not to indulge in any discussions among yourselves concerning the attributes of the Lord. It is futile, for everything valuable and important is ineffable.

(Signed) Pope . . . (Name illegible)

Now we go in. The interior resembles a mosque, more particularly the Hagia Sophia: no seats—wonderful effect of space; no images, only framed texts decorating the walls (like the Koran texts in the Hagia Sophia). One of the texts reads "Do not flatter your benefactor." The woman who had agreed with me before bursts into tears and cries, "Then there's nothing

68. Thoth as cynocephalus.—From
tomb of Amen-her-khopshef, near
Der el-Medina, Luxor (XXth dy-
nasty, 12th cent. B.C.)

left!" I reply, "I find it quite right!" but she vanishes. At first I stand with a pillar in front of me and can see nothing. Then I change my position and see a crowd of people. I do not belong to them and stand alone. But they are quite distinct, so that I can see their faces. They all say in unison, "We confess that we are under the power of the Lord. The Kingdom of Heaven is within us." They repeat this three times with great solemnity. Then the organ starts to play and they sing a Bach fugue with chorale. But the original text is omitted; sometimes there is only a sort of coloratura singing, then the words are repeated: "Everything else is paper" (meaning that it does not make a living impression on me). When the chorale has faded away the gemütlich *part of the ceremony begins; it is almost like a students' party. The people are all cheerful and equable. We move about, converse, and greet one another, and wine (from an episcopal seminary) is served with other refreshments. The health of the Church is drunk and, as if to express everybody's pleasure at the increase in membership, a loudspeaker blares out a ragtime melody with the refrain, "Charles is also with us now." A priest explains to me: "These somewhat trivial amusements are officially approved and permitted. We must adapt a little to American methods. With a large crowd such as we have here this is inevitable. But we differ in principle from the American churches by our decidedly anti-ascetic tendency." Thereupon I awake with a feeling of great relief.*

177   Unfortunately I must refrain from commenting on this dream as a whole[52] and confine myself to our theme. The *temenos* has become a sacred building (in accordance with the hint given earlier). The proceedings are thus characterized as "religious." The grotesque-humorous side of the Dionysian mystery comes out in the so-called *gemütlich* part of the ceremony, where wine is served and a toast drunk to the health of the Church. An inscription on the floor of an Orphic-Dionysian shrine puts it very aptly: μόνον μὴ ὕδωρ (Only no water!).[53] The

---

[52] It was considered at length in my "Psychology and Religion," pp. 24ff.
[53] Orphic mosaic from Tramithia (Eisler, *Orpheus—the Fisher*, pp. 271f.). We can take this inscription as a joke without offending against the spirit of the ancient mysteries. (Cf. the frescoes in the Villa dei Misteri in Pompeii—Maiuri, *La Villa dei Misteri*—where drunkenness and ecstasy are not only closely related but actually one and the same thing.) But, since initiations have been connected

Dionysian relics in the Church, such as the fish and wine symbolism, the Damascus chalice, the seal-cylinder with the crucifix and the inscription ΟΡΦΕΟϹ ΒΑΚΚΙΚΟϹ,[54] and much else besides, can be mentioned only in passing.

178   The "anti-ascetic" tendency clearly marks the point of difference from the Christian Church, here defined as "American" (cf. commentary to dream 14 of the first series). America is the ideal home of the reasonable ideas of the practical intellect, which would like to put the world to rights by means of a "brain trust." [55] This view is in keeping with the modern formula "intellect = spirit," but it completely forgets the fact that "spirit" was never a human "activity," much less a "function." The movement to the left is thus confirmed as a withdrawal from the modern world of ideas and a regression to pre-Christian Dionysos worship, where "asceticism" in the Christian sense is unknown. At the same time the movement does not lead right out of the sacred spot but remains within it; in other words it does not lose its sacramental character. It does not simply fall into chaos and anarchy, it relates the Church directly to the Dionysian sanctuary just as the historical process did, though from the opposite direction. We could say that this regressive development faithfully retreads the path of history in order to reach the pre-Christian level. Hence it is not a relapse but a kind of systematic descent *ad inferos* (fig. 69), a psychological *nekyia*.[56]

179   I encountered something very similar in the dream of a clergyman who had a rather problematical attitude to his faith: *Coming into his church at night, he found that the whole wall of the choir had collapsed. The altar and ruins were overgrown with vines hanging full of grapes, and the moon was shining in through the gap.*

180   Again, a man who was much occupied with religious problems had the following dream: *An immense Gothic cathedral, almost completely dark. High Mass is being celebrated. Suddenly the whole wall of the aisle collapses. Blinding sunlight bursts into the interior together with a large herd of bulls and*

---

with healing since their earliest days, the advice may possibly be a warning against water drinking, for it is well known that the drinking water in southern regions is the mother of dysentery and typhoid fever.

54 Eisler, *Orpheus—the Fisher.*   55 This is roughly the opinion of the dreamer.
56 Cf. figs. 170, 171, 172, 174, 176, 177 in *Psychology and Alchemy.*

69. Dante and Virgil on their journey to the underworld.—Illumination for the *Inferno*, Canto XVII, Codex Urbanus Latinus 365 (15th cent.)

cows. This setting is evidently more Mithraic, but Mithras is associated with the early Church in much the same way Dionysos is.

181   Interestingly enough, the church in our dream is a syncretistic building, for the Hagia Sophia is a very ancient Christian church which, however, served as a mosque until quite recently. It therefore fits in very well with the purpose of the dream: to attempt a combination of Christian and Dionysian religious ideas. Evidently this is to come about without the one excluding the other, without any values being destroyed. This is extremely important, since the reconstruction of the "gibbon" is to take place in the sacred precincts. Such a sacrilege might easily lead to the dangerous supposition that the leftward movement is a *diabolica fraus* and the gibbon the devil—for the devil is in fact regarded as the "ape of God." The leftward movement would then be a perversion of divine truth for the purpose of setting up "His Black Majesty" in place of God. But the uncon-

scious has no such blasphemous intentions; it is only trying to restore the lost Dionysos who is somehow lacking in modern man (*pace* Nietzsche!) to the world of religion. At the end of vision 22 (par. 117), where the ape first appears, it was said that "everything must be ruled by the light," and everything, we might add, includes the Lord of Darkness with his horns and cloven hoof—actually a Dionysian corybant who has rather unexpectedly risen to the rank of Prince.

182   The Dionysian element has to do with emotions and affects which have found no suitable religious outlets in the predominantly Apollonian cult and ethos of Christianity. The medieval carnivals and *jeux de paume* in the Church were abolished relatively early; consequently the carnival became secularized and with it divine intoxication vanished from the sacred precincts. Mourning, earnestness, severity, and well-tempered spiritual joy remained. But intoxication, that most direct and dangerous form of possession, turned away from the gods and enveloped the human world with its exuberance and pathos. The pagan religions met this danger by giving drunken ecstasy a place within their cult. Heraclitus doubtless saw what was at the back of it when he said, "But Hades is that same Dionysos in whose honour they go mad and keep the feast of the wine-vat." For this very reason orgies were granted religious license, so as to exorcise the danger that threatened from Hades. Our solution, however, has served to throw the gates of hell wide open.

18. DREAM:

183   *A square space with complicated ceremonies going on in it, the purpose of which is to transform animals into men. Two snakes, moving in opposite directions, have to be got rid of at once. Some animals are there, e.g., foxes and dogs. The people walk round the square and must let themselves be bitten in the calf by these animals at each of the four corners (cf. fig. 118). If they run away all is lost. Now the higher animals come on the scene—bulls and ibexes. Four snakes glide into the four corners. Then the congregation files out. Two sacrificial priests carry in a huge reptile and with this they touch the forehead of a shapeless animal lump or life-mass. Out of it there instantly rises a human head, transfigured. A voice proclaims: "These are attempts at being."*

217

70. Pagan rites of transformation in the Middle Ages, with serpents.—
Gnostic design

184   One might almost say that the dream goes on with the "explanation" of what is happening in the square space. Animals are to be changed into men; a "shapeless life-mass" is to be turned into a transfigured (illuminated) human head by magic contact with a reptile. The animal lump or life-mass stands for the mass of the inherited unconscious which is to be united with consciousness. This is brought about by the ceremonial use of a reptile, presumably a snake. The idea of transformation and renewal by means of a serpent is a well-substantiated archetype (fig. 70). It is the healing serpent, representing the god (cf. figs. 203, 204). It is reported of the mysteries of Sabazius: "Aureus coluber in sinum demittitur consecratis et eximitur rursus ab inferioribus partibus atque imis" (A golden snake is let down into the lap of the initiated and taken away again from the lower parts).[57] Among the Ophites, Christ was the serpent. Probably the most significant development of serpent symbolism as regards renewal of personality is to be found in Kundalini yoga.[58] The shepherd's experience with the snake in Nietzsche's *Zarathustra* would accordingly be a fatal omen (and not the only one of its kind—cf. the prophecy at the death of the rope-dancer).

185   The "shapeless life-mass" immediately recalls the ideas of the alchemical "chaos," [59] the *massa* or *materia informis* or *confusa*

57 Arnobius, *Adversus gentes*, V, 21 (Migne, *P.L.*, vol. 5, col. 1125). For similar practices during the Middle Ages, cf. Hammer-Purgstall, *Mémoire sur deux coffrets gnostiques du moyen âge*. See fig. 70.

58 Avalon, *The Serpent Power;* Woodroffe, *Shakti and Shakta.*

59 The alchemists refer to Lactantius, *Opera*, I, p. 14, 20: "a chao, quod est rudis inordinataeque materiae confusa congeries" (from the chaos, which is a confused assortment of crude disordered matter).

71. Creation of Adam from the clay of the *prima materia.*—Schedel, *Das Buch
der Chroniken* (1493)

which has contained the divine seeds of life ever since the Creation. According to a midrashic view, Adam was created in
much the same way: in the first hour God collected the dust, in
the second made a shapeless mass out of it, in the third fashioned
the limbs, and so on[60] (fig. 71).

186   But if the life-mass is to be transformed a *circumambulatio*
is necessary, i.e., exclusive concentration on the centre, the place
of creative change. During this process one is "bitten" by animals; in other words, we have to expose ourselves to the animal
impulses of the unconscious without identifying with them and
without "running away"; for flight from the unconscious would
defeat the purpose of the whole proceeding. We must hold our
ground, which means here that the process initiated by the

[60] Dreyfuss, *Adam und Eva,* quoted by Reitzenstein, *Poimandres,* p. 258.

dreamer's self-observation must be experienced in all its rami-
fications and then articulated with consciousness to the best of
his understanding. This often entails an almost unbearable tension because of the utter incommensurability between conscious
life and the unconscious process, which can be experienced only
in the innermost soul and cannot touch the visible surface of life
at any point. The principle of conscious life is: "Nihil est in in-
tellectu, quod non prius fuerit in sensu." But the principle of
the unconscious is the autonomy of the psyche itself, reflecting
in the play of its images not the world but *itself,* even though it
utilizes the illustrative possibilities offered by the sensible world
in order to make its images clear. The sensory datum, however,
is not the *causa efficiens* of this; rather, it is autonomously selected and exploited by the psyche, with the result that the ra-
tionality of the cosmos is constantly being violated in the most
distressing manner. But the sensible world has an equally devastating effect on the deeper psychic processes when it breaks into
them as a *causa efficiens.* If reason is not to be outraged on the
one hand and the creative play of images not violently suppressed on the other, a circumspect and farsighted synthetic procedure is required in order to accomplish the paradoxical union
of irreconcilables (fig. 72). Hence the alchemical parallels in our
dreams.

187   The focusing of attention on the centre demanded in this
dream and the warning about "running away" have clear parallels in the *opus alchymicum:* the need to concentrate on the
work and to meditate upon it is stressed again and again. The
tendency to run away, however, is attributed not to the operator
but to the transforming substance. Mercurius is evasive and is
labelled *servus* (servant) or *cervus fugitivus* (fugitive stag). The
vessel must be well sealed so that what is within may not escape.
Eirenaeus Philalethes[61] says of this *servus:* "You must be very
wary how you lead him, for if he can find an opportunity he will
give you the slip, and leave you to a world of misfortune." [62] It
did not occur to these philosophers that they were chasing a projection, and that the more they attributed to the substance the
further away they were getting from the psychological source of

[61] Pseudonymous author ("peaceable lover of truth") who lived in England at
the beginning of the 17th century.
[62] Philalethes, *Ripley Reviv'd,* p. 100.

72. The "union of irreconcilables": marriage of water and fire. The two figures each have four hands to symbolize their many different capabilities.—After an Indian painting

their expectations. From the difference between the material in this dream and its medieval predecessors we can measure the psychological advance: the running away is now clearly apparent as a characteristic of the dreamer, i.e., it is no longer projected into the unknown substance. Running away thus becomes a moral question. This aspect was recognized by the alchemists in so far as they emphasized the need for a special religious devotion at their work, though one cannot altogether clear them of the suspicion of having used their prayers and pious exercises for the purpose of forcing a miracle—there are even some who aspired to have the Holy Ghost as their familiar! [63] But, to do

63 [Cf. *Mysterium Coniunctionis*, p. 288, n. 116.—Editors.]

them justice, one should not overlook the fact that there is more than a little evidence in the literature that they realized it was a matter of their own transformation. For instance, Gerhard Dorn exclaims, "Transmutemini in vivos lapides philosophicos!" (Transform yourselves into living philosophical stones!)

188   Hardly have conscious and unconscious touched when they fly asunder on account of their mutual antagonism. Hence, right at the beginning of the dream, the snakes that are making off in opposite directions have to be removed; i.e., the conflict between conscious and unconscious is at once resolutely stopped and the conscious mind is forced to stand the tension by means of the *circumambulatio*. The magic circle thus traced will also prevent the unconscious from breaking out again, for such an eruption would be equivalent to psychosis. "Nonnulli perierunt in opere nostro": "Not a few have perished in our work," we can say with the author of the *Rosarium*. The dream shows that the difficult operation of thinking in paradoxes—a feat possible only to the superior intellect—has succeeded. The snakes no longer run away but settle themselves in the four corners, and the process of transformation or integration sets to work. The "transfiguration" and illumination, the conscious recognition of the centre, has been attained, or at least anticipated, in the dream. This potential achievement—if it can be maintained, i.e., if the conscious mind does not lose touch with the centre again[64]—means a renewal of personality. Since it is a subjective state whose reality cannot be validated by any external criterion, any further attempt to describe and explain it is doomed to failure, for only those who have had this experience are in a position to understand and attest its reality. "Happiness," for example, is such a noteworthy reality that there is nobody who does not long for it, and yet there is not a single objective criterion which would prove beyond all doubt that this condition necessarily exists. As so often with the most important things, we have to make do with a subjective judgment.

189   The arrangement of the snakes in the four corners is indicative of an order in the unconscious. It is as if we were confronted with a pre-existent ground plan, a kind of Pythagorean

---

[64] Cf. the commentary to dream 10, second series, par. 141: "And, being chained to the arms and breast of my mother, and to her substance, I cause my substance to hold together and rest." ("Tractatus aureus," ch. IV.)

73. The deliverance of man from the power of the dragon.—Codex Palatinus
Latinus 412 (15th cent.)

tetraktys. I have very frequently observed the number four in this connection. It probably explains the universal incidence and magical significance of the cross or of the circle divided into four. In the present case the point seems to be to capture and regulate the animal instincts so as to exorcise the danger of falling into unconsciousness. This may well be the empirical basis of the cross as that which vanquishes the powers of darkness (fig. 73).

190   In this dream the unconscious has managed to stage a powerful advance by thrusting its contents dangerously near to the conscious sphere. The dreamer appears to be deeply entangled in the mysterious synthetic ceremony and will unfailingly carry a lasting memory of the dream into his conscious life. Experience shows that this results in a serious conflict for the conscious mind, because it is not always either willing or able to put forth the extraordinary intellectual and moral effort needed to take a paradox seriously. Nothing is so jealous as a truth.

191   As a glance at the history of the medieval mind will show, our whole modern mentality has been moulded by Christianity. (This has nothing to do with whether we believe the truths of Christianity or not.) Consequently the reconstruction of the ape in the sacred precincts as proposed by the dream comes as such a shock that the majority of people will seek refuge in blank incomprehension. Others will heedlessly ignore the abysmal depths of the Dionysian mystery and will welcome the rational Darwinian core of the dream as a safeguard against mystic exaltation. Only a very few will feel the collision of the two worlds and realize what it is all about. Yet the dream says plainly enough that in the place where, according to tradition, the deity dwells, the ape is to appear. This substitution is almost as bad as a Black Mass.

192   In Eastern symbolism the square—signifying the earth in China, the *padma* or lotus in India—has the character of the *yoni:* femininity. A man's unconscious is likewise feminine and is personified by the anima.[65] The anima also stands for the "in-

---

[65] The idea of the anima as I define it is by no means a novelty but an archetype which we meet in the most diverse places. It was also known in alchemy, as the following scholium proves ("Tractatus aureus," in *Bibl. chem. curiosa,* I, p. 417): "Quemadmodum in sole ambulantis corpus continuo sequitur umbra . . . sic hermaphroditus noster Adamicus, quamvis in forma masculi appareat semper

74. Heaven fertilizing Earth and begetting mankind.—Thenaud, "Traité de la cabale" (MS., 16th cent.)

ferior" function[66] and for that reason frequently has a shady character; in fact she sometimes stands for evil itself. She is as a rule the *fourth* person (cf. dreams 10, 11, 15; pars. 136, 147, 162). She is the dark and dreaded maternal womb (fig. 74), which is of an essentially ambivalent nature. The Christian deity is one in three persons. The fourth person in the heavenly drama is undoubtedly the devil. In the more harmless psychological version he is merely the inferior function. On a moral

tamen in corpore occultatam Evam sive foeminam suam secum circumfert" (As the shadow continually follows the body of one who walks in the sun, so our hermaphroditic Adam, though he appears in the form of a male, nevertheless always carries about with him Eve, or his wife, hidden in his body).
66 Cf. Jung, *Psychological Types*, Def. 30.

valuation he is a man's sin, a function belonging to him and presumably masculine. The feminine element in the deity is kept very dark, the interpretation of the Holy Ghost as Sophia being considered heretical. Hence the Christian metaphysical drama, the "Prologue in Heaven," has only masculine actors, a point it shares with many of the ancient mysteries. But the feminine element must obviously be somewhere—so it is presumably to be found in the dark. At any rate that is where the ancient Chinese philosophers located it: in the *yin*.[67] Although man and woman unite they nevertheless represent irreconcilable opposites which, when activated, degenerate into deadly hostility. This primordial pair of opposites symbolizes every conceivable pair of opposites that may occur: hot and cold, light and dark, north and south, dry and damp, good and bad, conscious and unconscious. In the psychology of the functions there are two conscious and therefore masculine functions, the differentiated function and its auxiliary, which are represented in dreams by, say, father and son, whereas the unconscious functions appear as mother and daughter. Since the conflict between the two auxiliary functions is not nearly as great as that between the differentiated and the inferior function, it is possible for the third function—that is, the unconscious auxiliary one—to be raised to consciousness and thus made masculine. It will, however, bring with it traces of its contamination with the inferior function, thus acting as a kind of link with the darkness of the unconscious. It was in keeping with this psychological fact that the Holy Ghost should be heretically interpreted as Sophia, for he was the mediator of birth in the flesh, who enabled the deity to shine forth in the darkness of the world. No doubt it was this association that caused the Holy Ghost to be suspected of femininity, for Mary was the dark earth of the field—"illa terra virgo nondum pluviis irrigata" (that virgin earth not yet watered by the rains), as Tertullian called her.[68]

¹⁹³ The fourth function is contaminated with the unconscious and, on being made conscious, drags the whole of the uncon-

---

[67] "Tractatus aureus," *Ars chemica*, p. 12: "Verum masculus est coelum foeminae et foemina terra masculi" (The male is the heaven of the female, and the female is the earth of the male).

[68] *Adversus Judaeos*, 13 (Migne, *P.L.*, vol. 2, col. 655).

scious with it. We must then come to terms with the unconscious and try to bring about a synthesis of opposites.[69] At first
a violent conflict breaks out, such as any reasonable man would
experience when it became evident that he had to swallow a lot
of absurd superstitions. Everything in him would rise up in re-
volt and he would defend himself desperately against what
looked to him like murderous nonsense. This situation explains
the following dreams.

19. DREAM:

194   *Ferocious war between two peoples.*

195   This dream depicts the conflict. The conscious mind is de-
fending its position and trying to suppress the unconscious. The
first result of this is the expulsion of the fourth function, but,
since it is contaminated with the third, there is a danger of the
latter disappearing as well. Things would then return to the
state that preceded the present one, when only two functions
were conscious and the other two unconscious.

20. DREAM:

196   *There are two boys in a cave. A third falls in as if through
a pipe.*

197   The cave represents the darkness and seclusion of the unconscious; the two boys correspond to the two unconscious functions. Theoretically the third must be the auxiliary function,
which would indicate that the conscious mind had become completely absorbed in the differentiated function. The odds now
stand 1 : 3, greatly in favour of the unconscious. We may therefore expect a new advance on its part and a return to its former
position. The "boys" are an allusion to the dwarf motif (fig. 77),
of which more later.

[69] Alchemy regarded this synthesis as one of its chief tasks. The *Turba philosophorum* (ed. Ruska, p. 26) says: "Coniungite ergo masculinum servi rubei filium
suae odoriferae uxori et iuncti artem gignunt" (Join therefore the male son of
the red slave to his sweet-scented wife, and joined together they will generate
the Art). This synthesis of opposites was often represented as a brother-and-
sister incest, which version undoubtedly goes back to the "Visio Arislei," *Art.
aurif.,* I (see fig. 167), where the cohabitation of Thabritius and Beya, the children of the *Rex marinus,* is described (see infra, pars. 434ff.).

21. DREAM:

198   *A large transparent sphere containing many little spheres.*
A green plant is growing out of the top.

199   The sphere is a whole that embraces all its contents; life
which has been brought to a standstill by useless struggle becomes possible again. In Kundalini yoga the "green womb" is
a name for Ishvara (Shiva) emerging from his latent condition.

75. Trimurti picture. The triangle symbolizes the tendency of the universe to
converge towards the point of unity. The
tortoise represents Vishnu; the lotus growing out of the skull between two flames,
Shiva. The shining sun of Brahma forms
the background. The whole picture corresponds to the alchemical *opus,* the tortoise symbolizing the *massa confusa,* the
skull the *vas* of transformation, and the
flower the "self" or wholeness.—After an
Indian painting

22. DREAM:

200   *The dreamer is in an American hotel. He goes up in the lift*
to about the third or fourth floor. He has to wait there with a lot
of other people. A friend (an actual person) is also there and
says that the dreamer should not have kept the dark unknown
woman waiting so long below, since he had put her in his (the
dreamer's) charge. The friend now gives him an unsealed note
for the dark woman, on which is written: "Salvation does not
come from refusing to take part or from running away. Nor does
it come from just drifting. Salvation comes from complete sur-
render, with one's eyes always turned to the centre." On the mar-
gin of the note there is a drawing: a wheel or wreath with eight
spokes. Then a lift-boy appears and says that the dreamer's room
is on the eighth floor. He goes on up in the lift, this time to the
seventh or eighth floor. An unknown red-haired man, standing
there, greets him in a friendly way. Then the scene changes.
There is said to be a revolution in Switzerland: the military
party is making propaganda for "completely throttling the left."
The objection that the left is weak enough anyway is met by the

answer that this is just why it ought to be throttled completely. Soldiers in old-fashioned uniforms now appear, who all resemble the red-haired man. They load their guns with ramrods, stand in a circle, and prepare to shoot at the centre. But in the end they do not shoot and seem to march away. The dreamer wakes up in terror.

201   The tendency to re-establish a state of wholeness—already indicated in the foregoing dream—once more comes up against a consciousness with a totally different orientation. It is therefore appropriate that the dream should have an American background. The lift is going up, as is right and proper when something is coming "up" from the "sub-"conscious. What is coming up is the unconscious content, namely the mandala characterized by the number four (cf. figs. 61, 62). Therefore the lift should rise to the fourth floor; but, as the fourth function is taboo, it only rises to "about the third or fourth." This happens not to the dreamer alone but to many others as well, who must all wait like him until the fourth function can be accepted. A good friend then calls his attention to the fact that he should not have kept the dark woman, i.e., the anima who stands for the tabooed function, waiting "below," i.e., in the unconscious, which was just the reason why the dreamer himself had to wait upstairs with the others. It is in fact not merely an individual but a collective problem, for the animation of the unconscious which has become so noticeable in recent times has, as Schiller foresaw, raised questions which the nineteenth century never even dreamed of. Nietzsche in his *Zarathustra* decided to reject the "snake" and the "ugliest man," thus exposing himself to an heroic cramp of consciousness which led, logically enough, to the collapse foretold in the same book.

202   The advice given in the note is as profound as it is to the point, so that there is really nothing to add. After it has been more or less accepted by the dreamer the ascent can be resumed. We must take it that the problem of the fourth function was accepted, at least broadly, for the dreamer now reaches the seventh or eighth floor, which means that the fourth function is no longer represented by a quarter but by an eighth, and is apparently reduced by a half.

203   Curiously enough, this hesitation before the last step to wholeness seems also to play a part in *Faust II,* where, in the

Cabiri scene, "resplendent mermaids" come from over the water:[70]

NEREIDS AND TRITONS:	Bear we, on the waters riding, That which brings you all glad tiding. In Chelone's giant shield Gleams a form severe revealed: These are gods that we are bringing; Hail them, you high anthems singing.
SIRENS:	Little in length, Mighty in strength! Time-honoured gods Of shipwreck and floods.
NEREIDS AND TRITONS:	Great Cabiri do we bear, That our feast be friendly fair: Where their sacred powers preside Neptune's rage is pacified.

76. The tortoise: an alchemical instrument.
—Porta, *De distillationibus* (1609)

A "form severe" is brought by "mermaids," feminine figures (cf. figs. 10, 11, 12, 157) who represent as it were the sea and the waves of the unconscious. The word "severe" reminds us of "severe" architectural or geometrical forms which illustrate a definite idea without any romantic (feeling-toned) trimmings.

---

[70] [Based on the translation by Philip Wayne (*Faust, Part Two*, pp. 145f.). Slight modifications have been necessary to accommodate his version to Jung's commentary.—TRANS.]

It "gleams" from the shell of a tortoise[71] (fig. 76), which, primitive and cold-blooded like the snake, symbolizes the instinctual side of the unconscious. The "image" is somehow identical with the unseen, creative dwarf-gods (fig. 77), hooded and cloaked

77. Telesphorus, one of the Cabiri, the *familiaris* of Aesculapius: (*a*) Bronze figure from Roman Gaul; (*b*) Marble statuette from Austria.

manikins who are kept hidden in the dark *cista,* but who also appear on the seashore as little figures about a foot high, where, as kinsmen of the unconscious, they protect navigation, i.e., the venture into darkness and uncertainty. In the form of the Dactyls they are also the gods of invention, small and apparently insignificant like the impulses of the unconscious but endowed with the same mighty power. (*El gabir* is "the great, the mighty one.")

NEREIDS AND TRITONS:	Three have followed where we led,
	But the fourth refused to call;
	He the rightful seer, he said,
	His to think for one and all.

[71] The *testudo* (tortoise) is an alchemical instrument, a shallow bowl with which the cooking-vessel was covered on the fire. See Rhenanus, *Solis e puteo emergentis,* p. 40.

SIRENS: A god may count it sport
To set a god at naught.
Honour the grace they bring,
And fear their threatening.

204   It is characteristic of Goethe's feeling-toned nature that the fourth should be the thinker. If the supreme principle is "feeling is all," then thinking has to play an unfavourable role and be submerged. *Faust I* portrays this development. Since Goethe acted as his own model, thinking became the fourth (taboo) function. Because of its contamination with the unconscious it takes on the grotesque form of the Cabiri, for the Cabiri, as dwarfs, are chthonic gods and misshapen accordingly. ("I call them pot-bellied freaks of common clay.") They thus stand in grotesque contrast to the heavenly gods and poke fun at them (cf. the "ape of God"). The Nereids and Tritons sing:

                Seven there should really be.

SIRENS: Where, then, stay the other three?

NEREIDS AND   That we know not. You had best
TRITONS: On Olympus make your quest.
                There an eighth may yet be sought
                Though none other gave him thought.
                Well inclined to us in grace,
                Not all perfect yet their race.
                Beings there beyond compare,
                Yearning, unexplainable,
                Press with hunger's pang to share
                In the unattainable.

205   We learn that there are "really" seven of them; but again there is some difficulty with the eighth as there was before with the fourth. Similarly, in contradiction to the previous emphasis placed on their lowly origin in the dark, it now appears that the Cabiri are actually to be found on Olympus; for they are eternally striving from the depths to the heights and are therefore always to be found both below *and* above. The "severe image" is obviously an unconscious content that struggles towards the light. It seeks, and itself is, what I have elsewhere called "the treasure hard to attain." [72] This hypothesis is immediately confirmed:

[72] Jung, *Symbols of Transformation*, index, s.v.

SIRENS: Fame is dimmed of ancient time,
Honour droops in men of old;
Though they have the Fleece of Gold,
Ye have the Cabiri.

206   The Golden Fleece is the coveted goal of the argosy, the perilous quest that is one of the numerous synonyms for attaining the unattainable. Thales makes this wise remark about it:

> That is indeed what men most seek on earth:
> 'Tis rust alone that gives the coin its worth!

207   The unconscious is always the fly in the ointment, the skeleton in the cupboard of perfection, the painful lie given to all idealistic pronouncements, the earthliness that clings to our human nature and sadly clouds the crystal clarity we long for. In the alchemical view rust, like verdigris, is the metal's sickness. But at the same time this leprosy is the *vera prima materia*, the basis for the preparation of the philosophical gold. The *Rosarium* says:

> Our gold is not the common gold. But thou hast inquired concerning the greenness [*viriditas,* presumably verdigris], deeming the bronze to be a leprous body on account of the greenness it hath upon it. Therefore I say unto thee that whatever is perfect in the bronze is that greenness only, because that greenness is straightway changed by our magistery into our most true gold.[73]

208   The paradoxical remark of Thales that the rust alone gives the coin its true value is a kind of alchemical quip, which at bottom only says that there is no light without shadow and no psychic wholeness without imperfection. To round itself out, life calls not for perfection but for completeness; and for this the "thorn in the flesh" is needed, the suffering of defects without which there is no progress and no ascent.

209   The problem of three and four, seven and eight, which Goethe has tackled here was a great puzzle to alchemy and goes back historically to the texts ascribed to Christianos.[74] In the

---

[73] *Art. aurif.*, II, p. 220: a quotation from Senior. *Viriditas* is occasionally called *azoth*, which is one of the numerous synonyms for the stone.
[74] According to Berthelot (*Origines de l'alchimie,* p. 100), the anonymous author called Christianos was a contemporary of Stephanos of Alexandria, and must therefore have lived about the beginning of the 7th century.

78. Maria Prophetissa. In the background, the union (*coniunctio*) of upper and lower.—Maier, *Symbola aureae mensae* (1617)

treatise on the production of the "mythical water" it is said: "Therefore the Hebrew prophetess cried without restraint, 'One becomes two, two becomes three, and out of the third comes the One as the fourth.' " [75] In alchemical literature this prophetess is taken to be Maria Prophetissa[76] (fig. 78), also called the Jewess, sister of Moses, or the Copt, and it is not unlikely that she is connected with the Maria of Gnostic tradition. Epiphanius testifies to the existence of writings by this Maria, namely the "Interrogationes magnae" and "Interrogationes parvae," said to describe a vision of how Christ, on a mountain, caused a woman to come forth from his side and how he mingled himself with her.[77] It is probably no accident that the trea-

---

[75] Berthelot, *Alchimistes grecs*, VI, v, 6. The almost bestial κραυγάζειν (shriek) points to an ecstatic condition.

[76] A treatise (of Arabic origin?) is ascribed to her under the title "Practica Mariae Prophetissae in artem alchemicam," *Art. aurif.*, I, pp. 319ff.

[77] *Panarium*, XXVI. Concerning further possible connections with Mariamne and with the Mary Magdalene of the *Pistis Sophia*, cf. Leisegang, *Die Gnosis*, pp. 113f., and Schmidt, "Gnostische Schriften," pp. 596ff. [On *Panarium*, cf. *Aion*, pars. 314ff.]

tise of Maria (see n. 76) deals with the theme of the *matrimonium alchymicum* in a dialogue with the philosopher Aros,[78] from which comes the saying, often repeated later: "Marry gum with gum in true marriage." [79] Originally it was "gum arabic," and it is used here as a secret name for the transforming substance, on account of its adhesive quality. Thus Khunrath[80] declares that the "red" gum is the "resin of the wise"—a synonym for the transforming substance. This substance, as the life force (*vis animans*), is likened by another commentator to the "glue of the world" (*glutinum mundi*), which is the medium between mind and body and the union of both.[81] The old treatise "Consilium coniugii" explains that the "philosophical man" consists of the "four natures of the stone." Of these three are earthy or in the earth, but "the fourth nature is the water of the stone, namely the viscous gold which is called red gum and with which the three earthy natures are tinted." [82] We learn here that gum is the critical fourth nature: it is duplex, i.e., masculine and feminine, and at the same time the one and only *aqua mercurialis*. So the union of the two is a kind of self-fertilization, a characteristic always ascribed to the mercurial dragon.[83] From these hints it can easily be seen who the philosophical man is: he is the androgynous original man or Anthropos of Gnosticism[84] (cf. figs. 64, 82, 117, 195), whose parallel in India is *purusha*. Of him the Brihadaranyaka Upanishad says: "He was as large as a man and woman embracing. He divided his self

---

[78] Aros = Horos. Ἴσις προφῆτις τῷ υἱῷ αὐτῆς (Berthelot, *Alchimistes grecs*, I, xiii) may be an earlier version of the Maria dialogue. Isis and Maria were easy to confuse.
[79] "Matrimonifica gummi cum gummi vero matrimonio."—*Art. aurif.*, I, p. 320.
[80] *Von hylealischen Chaos*, pp. 239f.
[81] "Aphorismi Basiliani," *Theatr. chem.*, IV, p. 368.
[82] *Ars chemica*, pp. 247, 255.
[83] Arnaldus de Villanova ("Carmen," *Theatr. chem.*, IV, p. 614) has summed up the quintessence of Maria's treatise very aptly in the following verses:

> "Maria mira sonat breviter, quod talia tonat.
> Gummis cum binis fugitivum figit in imis. . . .
> Filia Plutonis consortia iungit amoris,
> Gaudet in assata sata per tria sociata."

(Maria utters brief wonders because such are the things that she thunders.
She fixes what runs to the bottom with double-strong gums. . . .
This daughter of Pluto unites love's affinities,
Delighting in everything sown, roasted, assembled by threes.)
[84] Cf. my remarks on Paracelsus' "Adech" in "Paracelsus as a Spiritual Phenomenon," pars. 168, 203ff.

[Atman] in two, and thence arose husband and wife. He united himself with her and men were born," etc.[85] The common origin of these ideas lies in the primitive notion of the bisexual original man.

210   The fourth nature—to return to the text of the "Consilium coniugii"—leads straight to the Anthropos idea that stands for man's wholeness, that is, the conception of a unitary being who existed before man and at the same time represents man's goal. The one joins the three as the fourth and thus produces the synthesis of the four in a unity[86] (fig. 196). We seem to be dealing with much the same thing in the case of seven and eight, though this motif occurs much less frequently in the literature. It is, however, to be found in Paracelsus' *Ein ander Erklärung der gantzen Astronomie,*[87] to which Goethe had access. "One is powerful, Six are subjects, the Eighth is also powerful"—and somewhat more so than the first. One is the king, the six are his servants and his son; so here we have King Sol and the six planets or metallic homunculi as depicted in the *Pretiosa margarita novella* of Petrus Bonus (Lacinius edition, 1546)[88] (fig. 79). As a matter of fact the eighth does not appear in this text; Paracelsus seems to have invented it himself. But since the eighth is even more "powerful" than the first, the crown is presumably bestowed on him. In *Faust II,* the eighth who dwells on Olympus is a direct reference to the Paracelsan text in so far as this describes the "astrology of Olympus" (that is, the structure of the *corpus astrale*).[89]

211   Returning now to our dream, we find at the critical point— the seventh or eighth floor—the red-haired man, a synonym for

---

[85] 1. 4. 3. (Cf. Max Müller, *The Upanishads,* II, pp. 85–86.)

[86] There is a rather different formulation in Distinction XIV of the "Allegoriae sapientum" (*Theatr. chem.,* V, p. 86): "Unum et est duo, et duo et sunt tria, et tria et sunt quatuor, et quatuor et sunt tria, et tria et sunt duo, et duo et sunt unum" (One, and it is two; and two, and it is three; and three, and it is four; and four, and it is three; and three, and it is two; and two, and it is one). This evidently represents the quartering (tetrameria) of the one and the synthesis of the four in one.

[87] In Sudhoff/Matthiessen, XII.

[88] Folio VIII^v. The *aqua mercurialis* is characterized here as the "bright and clear fluid of Bacchus." The king and the son are united in the operation, so that at the end only the renewed king and his five servants are left. The *senarius* (sixth) plays a modest role only in later alchemy.

[89] Paracelsus, *Opera,* ed. Huser, I, p. 503.

79. King Sol with his six planet-sons.—Bonus, *Pretiosa margarita novella* (1546)

the "man with the pointed beard" and hence for the shrewd Mephisto, who magically changes the scene because he is concerned with something that Faust himself never saw: the "severe image," symbolizing the supreme treasure, the immortal self.[90] He changes himself into the soldiers, representatives of uniformity, of collective opinion, which is naturally dead against tolerating anything "unsuitable." For collective opinion the numbers three and seven are, on the highest authority, sacred; but four and eight are the very devil, something inferior—"common clay"—that in the stern judgment of bonzes of every hue has no right to exist. The "left" is to be "completely throttled," meaning the unconscious and all the "sinister" things that come from it. An antiquated view, no doubt, and one that uses antiquated methods; but even muzzle-loaders can hit the mark. For reasons unknown, i.e., not stated in the dream, the destructive attack on the "centre"—to which, according to the advice in the note, "one's eyes must always be turned"—peters out. In the drawing on the margin of the note this centre is portrayed as a wheel with eight spokes (cf. fig. 80).

[90] The angels bear Faust's "immortal part" to heaven, after cheating the devil of it. This, in the original version, is "Faust's entelechy."

80. Mercurius turning the eight-spoked wheel which symbolizes the process. In one hand he holds the *telum passionis.*—"Speculum veritatis" (MS., 17th cent.)

23. DREAM:

212   *In the square space. The dreamer is sitting opposite the unknown woman whose portrait he is supposed to be drawing. What he draws, however, is not a face but three-leaved clovers or distorted crosses in four different colours: red, yellow, green, and blue.*

213   In connection with this dream the dreamer spontaneously drew a circle with quarters tinted in the above colours. It was a wheel with eight spokes. In the middle there was a four-petalled blue flower. A great many drawings now followed at short intervals, all dealing with the curious structure of the "centre," and arising from the dreamer's need to discover a configuration that adequately expresses the nature of this centre. The drawings were based partly on visual impressions, partly on intuitive perceptions, and partly on dreams.

214   It is to be noted that the wheel is a favourite symbol in alchemy for the circulating process, the *circulatio.* By this is meant firstly the *ascensus* and *descensus,* for instance the ascending and descending birds symbolizing the precipitation of vapours,[91] and secondly the rotation of the universe as a model for the work,

91 Cf. the movements of the transforming substance in the "Tabula smaragdina" (*De alchemia,* p. 363).

and hence the cycling of the year in which the work takes place. The alchemist was not unaware of the connection between the *rotatio* and his drawings of circles. The contemporary moral allegories of the wheel emphasize that the *ascensus* and *descensus* are, among other things, God's descent to man and man's ascent to God. (On the authority of one of St. Bernard's sermons: "By his descent he established for us a joyful and wholesome ascent." [92]) Further, the wheel expresses virtues that are important for the work: *constantia, obedientia, moderatio, aequalitas,* and *humilitas.*[93] The mystical associations of the wheel play no small part in Jakob Böhme. Like the alchemists he too operates with the wheels of Ezekiel, saying: "Thus we see that the spiritual life stands turned in upon itself, and that the natural life stands turned out of and facing itself. We can then liken it to a round spherical wheel that goes on all its sides, as the wheel in Ezekiel shows." [94] He goes on to explain: "The wheel of nature turns in upon itself from without; for God dwells within himself and has such a figure, not that it can be painted, it being only a natural likeness, the same as when God paints himself in the figure of this world; for God is everywhere entire, and so dwells in himself. Mark: the outer wheel is the zodiac with the stars, and after it come the seven planets," etc.[95] "Albeit this figure is not fashioned sufficiently, it is nevertheless a meditation: and we could make a fine drawing of it on a great circle for the meditation of those of less understanding. Mark therefore, desire goes in upon itself to the heart, which is God," etc. But Böhme's wheel is also the "impression" (in alchemical terms, the *informatio*) of the eternal will. It is Mother Nature, or the "mind [*Gemüth*] of the mother, from whence she continually creates and works; and these are the stars with the planetary orb [after the model] of the eternal *astrum,* which is only a spirit, and the eternal mind in the wisdom of God, viz., the Eternal Nature, from whence the eternal spirits proceeded and entered into a creaturely being." [96] The "property" of the wheel is *life* in the form of "four bailiffs"

---

[92] "Suo nobis descensu suavem ac salubrem dedicavit ascensum." *Sermo IV de Ascensione Domini* (Migne, *P.L.*, vol. 183, col. 312).
[93] Picinelli, *Mundus symbolicus*, s.v. "rota."
[94] "Vom irdischen und himmlischen Mysterium," ch. V, 1f.
[95] *Von dem dreyfachen Leben*, ch. IX, 58f.
[96] *De signatura rerum*, ch. XIV, 15 (trans. Bax, p. 179).

who "manage the dominion in the life-giving mother." These bailiffs are the four elements "to which the wheel of the mind, viz., the *astrum*, affords will and desire; so that this whole essence is but one thing only, like the mind of a man. Even as he is in soul and body, so also is this whole essence"; for he is created in the likeness of this "whole essence." But nature in her four elements is also a whole essence with a soul.[97] This "sulphurean wheel" is the origin of good and evil, or rather it leads into them and out of them.[98]

215   Böhme's mysticism is influenced by alchemy in the highest degree. Thus he says: "The form of the birth is as a turning wheel, which Mercurius causes in the sulphur." [99] The "birth" is the "golden child" (*filius philosophorum* = archetype of the divine child [100]) whose "master-workman" is Mercurius.[101] Mercurius himself is the "fiery wheel of the essence" in the form of a serpent. Similarly the (unenlightened) soul is just "such a fiery Mercurius." Vulcan kindles the fiery wheel of the essence in the soul when it "breaks off" from God; whence come desire and sin, which are the "wrath of God." The soul is then a "worm" like the "fiery serpent," a "larva" and a "monster." [102]

216   The interpretation of the wheel in Böhme reveals something of the mystical secret of alchemy and is thus of considerable importance in this respect as well as from the psychological point of view: the wheel appears here as a concept for wholeness which represents the essence of mandala symbolism and therefore includes the *mysterium iniquitatis*.

217   The idea of the "centre," which the unconscious has been repeatedly thrusting upon the conscious mind of the dreamer, is beginning to gain foothold there and to exercise a peculiar fascination. The next drawing is again of the blue flower (cf. fig. 85), but this time subdivided into eight; then follow pictures of four mountains round a lake in a crater, also of a red ring lying on the ground with a withered tree standing in it, round which a green snake (cf. fig. 13) creeps up with a leftward movement.

218   The layman may be rather puzzled by the serious attention devoted to this problem. But a little knowledge of yoga and of

97 Ibid., 16 (p. 179).   98 Ibid.   99 Ibid., IV, 28 (Bax, p. 37).
100 Cf. Jung, "The Psychology of the Child Archetype."
101 Böhme, *De signatura rerum*, ch. IV, 27 (Bax, p. 37).
102 Böhme, *Gespräch einer erleuchteten und unerleuchteten Seele*, 11–24.

the medieval philosophy of the *lapis* would help him to understand. As we have already said, the squaring of the circle was one of the methods for producing the *lapis;* another was the use of *imaginatio,* as the following text unmistakably proves:

> And take care that thy door be well and firmly closed, so that he who is within cannot escape, and—God willing—thou wilt reach the goal. Nature performeth her operations gradually; and indeed I would have thee do the same: let thy imagination be guided wholly by nature. And observe according to nature, through whom the substances regenerate themselves in the bowels of the earth. And imagine this with true and not with fantastic imagination.[103]

219   The *vas bene clausum* (well-sealed vessel) is a precautionary measure very frequently mentioned in alchemy, and is the equivalent of the magic circle. In both cases the idea is to protect what is within from the intrusion and admixture of what is without, as well as to prevent it from escaping.[104] The *imaginatio* is to be understood here as the real and literal power to create images (*Einbildungskraft* = imagination)—the classical use of the word in contrast to *phantasia,* which means a mere "conceit" in the sense of insubstantial thought. In the *Satyricon* this connotation is more pointed still: *phantasia* means something ridiculous.[105] *Imaginatio* is the active evocation of (inner) images *secundum naturam,* an authentic feat of thought or ideation, which does not spin aimless and groundless fantasies "into the blue"—does not, that is to say, just play with its objects, but tries to grasp the inner facts and portray them in images true to their nature. This activity is an *opus,* a work. And we cannot call the manner in which the dreamer handles the objects of his inner experience anything but true work, considering how conscientiously, accurately, and carefully he records and elaborates the content now pushing its way into consciousness. The resemblance to the *opus* is obvious enough to anyone familiar with alchemy. Moreover

---

103 *Rosarium, Art. aurif.,* II, p. 214.

104 Ibid., p. 213: "Nec intrat in eum [lapidem], quod non sit ortum ex eo, quoniam si aliquid extranei sibi apponatur, statim corrumpitur" (Nothing enters into it [the stone] that did not come from it; since, if anything extraneous were to be added to it, it would at once be spoilt).

105 Petronius, *Satyricon,* par. 38: "Phantasia non homo" (He's a fantasy, not a man).

81. "Sol et eius umbra." The earth is midway between light and darkness.
—Maier, *Scrutinium chymicum* (1687)

the analogy is borne out by the dreams themselves, as dream 24 will show.

220   The present dream, from which the above-mentioned drawings originated, shows no signs of the "left" having been in any way "throttled." On the contrary, the dreamer finds himself once more in the *temenos* facing the unknown woman who personifies the fourth or "inferior" function.[106] His drawing of the

[106] Prescription for preparation of the *lapis* (Hermes quotation in *Rosarium, Art. aurif.*, II, p. 317): "Fili, extrahe a radio suam umbram: accipe ergo quartam partem sui, hoc est, unam partem de fermento et tres partes de corpore imperfecto," etc. (Son, extract from the ray its shadow: then take a fourth part of it, i.e., one part of the ferment and three parts of the imperfect body, etc.). For *umbra*, see ibid., p. 233: "Fundamentum artis est sol et eius umbra" (The basis of the art is the sun and its shadow) (fig. 81). The above quotation gives only the sense of the "Tractatus aureus" and is not literal.

wheel with a four-petalled blue flower in the middle was anticipated by the dream: what the dream represents in personified form the dreamer reproduces as an abstract ideogram. This might well be a hint that the *meaning* of the personification could also be represented in quite another form. This "other form" (three-leaved clover, distorted cross) refers back to the ace of clubs in dream 16 of the first series (par. 97), where we pointed out its analogy with the irregular cross. The analogy is confirmed here. In this dream, however, the symbol of the Christian Trinity has been overshadowed or "coloured" by the alchemical quaternity. The colours appear as a concretization of the *tetraktys*. The *Rosarium* quotes a similar statement from the "Tractatus aureus": "Vultur[107] . . . clamat voce magna, inquiens: Ego sum albus niger et rubeus citrinus" [108] (The vulture . . . exclaims in a loud voice: I am the white black and the red yellow). On the other hand it is stressed that the *lapis* unites *omnes colores* in itself. We can thus take it that the quaternity represented by the colours is a kind of preliminary stage of the *lapis*. This is confirmed by the *Rosarium:* "Our stone is from the four elements." [109] (Cf. figs. 64, 82, 117.) The same applies to the *aurum philosophicum:* "In the gold the four elements are contained in equal proportions." [110] The fact is that the four colours in the dream represent the transition from trinity to quaternity and thus to the squared circle (figs. 59, 60), which, according to the alchemists, comes nearest to the *lapis* on account of its roundness or perfect simplicity. For this reason a recipe for the preparation of the *lapis,* attributed to Raymundus, says:

Take of the body that is most simple and round, and do not take of the triangle or quadrangle but of the round, for the round is nearer to simplicity than the triangle. Hence it is to be noted that

---

107 Cf. dream 58, par. 304. The alchemical vulture, eagle, and crow are all essentially synonymous.

108 This quotation from Hermes is likewise an arbitrary reading. The passage runs literally: "Ego sum albus nigri et rubeus albi et citrinus rubei et certe veridicus sum" (I am the white of the black, and the red of the white, and the yellow of the red, and I speak very truth). In this way three meanings are expressed by four colours, in contrast to the formula of Hortulanus which attributes four natures and three colours to the *lapis.—De alchemia,* p. 372.

109 *Art. aurif.,* II, p. 207: "Lapis noster est ex quatuor elementis."

110 Ibid., p. 208: "In auro sunt quatuor elementa in aequali proportione aptata."

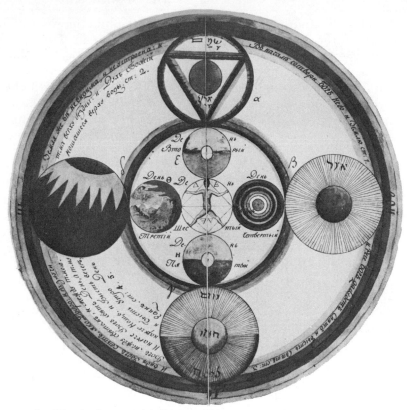

82. The Anthropos with the four elements.—Russian MS. (18th cent.)

a simple body has no corners, for it is the first and last among the planets, like the sun among the stars.[111]

24. DREAM:

221   *Two people are talking about crystals, particularly about a diamond.*

222   Here one can hardly avoid thinking of the *lapis*. In fact this dream discloses the historical background and indicates that we really are dealing with the coveted *lapis*, the "treasure hard

111 Ibid., p. 317: "Recipe de simplicissimo et de rotundo corpore, et noli recipere de triangulo vel quadrangulo sed de rotundo: quia rotundum est propinquius simplicitati quam triangulus. Notandum est ergo, quod corpus simplex nullum habens angulum, quia ipsum est primum et posterius in planetis, sicut Sol in stellis."

to attain." The dreamer's *opus* amounts to an unconscious recapitulation of the efforts of Hermetic philosophy. (More about the diamond in dreams 37, 39, 50 below.)

25. DREAM:

²²³ *It is a question of constructing a central point and making the figure symmetrical by reflection at this point.*

²²⁴ The word "constructing" points to the synthetic character of the *opus* and also to the laborious building process that taxes the dreamer's energy. The "symmetry" is an answer to the conflict in dream 22 ("completely throttling the left"). Each side must perfectly balance the other as its mirror-image, and this image is to fall at the "central point," which evidently possesses the property of reflection—it is a *vitrum*,[112] a crystal or sheet of water (cf. fig. 209). This power of reflection seems to be another allusion to the underlying idea of the *lapis*, the *aurum philosophicum*, the elixir, the *aqua nostra*, etc. (cf. fig. 265).

²²⁵ Just as the "right" denotes the world of consciousness and its principles, so by "reflection" the picture of the world is to be turned round to the left, thus producing a corresponding world in reverse. We could equally well say: through reflection the right appears as the reverse of the left. Therefore the left seems to have as much validity as the right; in other words, the unconscious and its—for the most part unintelligible—order becomes the symmetrical counterpart of the conscious mind and its contents, although it is still not clear which of them is reflected and which reflecting (cf. fig. 55). To carry our reasoning a step further, we could regard the centre as the point of intersection of two worlds that correspond but are inverted by reflection.[113]

²²⁶ The idea of creating a symmetry would thus indicate some kind of climax in the task of accepting the unconscious and incorporating it in a general picture of the world. The unconscious here displays a "cosmic" character.

---

112 A quotation from Ademarus (ibid., p. 353): "[Lapis] nihilominus non funditur, nec ingreditur, nec permiscetur, sed vitrificatur" (But [the stone] can neither be melted nor penetrated nor mixed but is made as hard as glass).
113 There are very interesting parapsychological parallels to this, but I cannot enter upon them here.

26. DREAM:

227   *It is night, with stars in the sky. A voice says, "Now it will begin." The dreamer asks, "What will begin?" Whereupon the voice answers, "The circulation can begin." Then a shooting star falls in a curious leftward curve. The scene changes, and the dreamer is in a rather squalid night club. The proprietor, who appears to be an unscrupulous crook, is there with some bedraggled-looking girls. A quarrel starts about left and right. The dreamer then leaves and drives round the perimeter of a square in a taxi. Then he is in the bar again. The proprietor says, "What they said about left and right did not satisfy my feelings. Is there really such a thing as a left and a right side of human society?" The dreamer answers, "The existence of the left does not contradict that of the right. They both exist in everyone. The left is the mirror-image of the right. Whenever I feel it like that, as a mirror-image, I am at one with myself. There is no right and no left side to human society, but there are symmetrical and lopsided people. The lopsided are those who can fulfil only one side of themselves, either left or right. They are still in the childhood state." The proprietor says meditatively, "Now that's much better," and goes about his business.*

228   I have given this dream in full because it is an excellent illustration of how the ideas hinted at in the last dream have been taken up by the dreamer. The idea of symmetrical proportion has been stripped of its cosmic character and translated into psychological terms, expressed in social symbols. "Right" and "left" are used almost like political slogans.

229   The beginning of the dream, however, is still under the cosmic aspect. The dreamer noted that the curious curve of the shooting star corresponded exactly to the line he drew when sketching the picture of the eightfold flower (cf. par. 217). The curve formed the edge of the petals. Thus the shooting star traces the outline, so to speak, of a flower that spreads over the whole starry heaven. What is now beginning is the circulation of the light.[114] This cosmic flower corresponds roughly to the rose in Dante's *Paradiso* (fig. 83).

230   The "cosmic" nature of an experience—as an aspect of some

[114] See pars. 245f., 258f.; and my commentary on *The Secret of the Golden Flower,* ch. I, sec. 2.

246

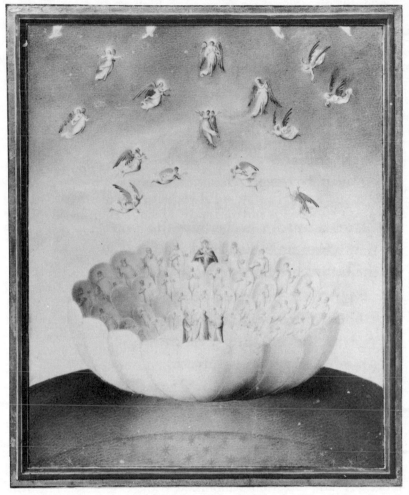

83. Dante being led before God in the heavenly rose.—Illumination for the
Paradiso, Canto XXXI, Codex Urbanus Latinus 365 (15th cent.)

inner occurrence that can only be understood psychologically
—is offensive and at once provokes a reaction "from below."
Evidently the cosmic aspect was too high and is compensated
"downward," so that the symmetry is no longer that of two
world pictures but merely of human society, in fact of the
dreamer himself. When the proprietor remarks that the latter's
psychological understanding is "much better," he is making an
estimate whose conclusion should run: "but still not good
enough."

231   The quarrel about right and left that starts in the bar is the
conflict which breaks out in the dreamer himself when he is
called upon to recognize the symmetry. He cannot do this because the other side looks so suspicious that he would rather not
investigate it too closely. That is the reason for the magical *circumambulatio* (driving round the square): he has to stay inside
and learn to face his mirror-image without running away. He
does this as best he can, though not quite as the other side would
wish. Hence the somewhat chill recognition of his merits.

27. VISUAL IMPRESSION:

232   *A circle with a green tree in the middle. In the circle a
fierce battle is raging between savages. They do not see the tree.*

233   Evidently the conflict between right and left has not yet
ended. It continues because the savages are still in the "childhood state" and therefore, being "lopsided," only know either
the left or the right but not a third that stands above the conflict.

28. VISUAL IMPRESSION:

234   *A circle: within it, steps lead up to a basin with a fountain
inside.*

235   When a condition is unsatisfactory because some essential
aspect of the unconscious content is lacking, the unconscious
process reverts to earlier symbols, as is the case here. The symbolism goes back to dream 13 (par. 154), where we met the mandala garden of the philosophers with its fountain of *aqua nostra*
(fig. 84; cf. also figs. 25, 26, 56). Circle and basin emphasize the
mandala, the rose of medieval symbolism.[115] The "rose garden
of the philosophers" is one of alchemy's favourite symbols.[116]

[115] Valli, "Die Geheimsprache Dantes."
[116] Cf. "Rosarius minor," *De alchemia*, p. 309.

84. The fountain in the walled garden, symbolizing *constantia in adversis* —a situation particularly characteristic of alchemy.—Boschius, *Symbolographia* (1702)

29. Visual impression:

236   *A bunch of roses, then the sign*$\equiv\!\!\!\!\!\!/$*, but it should be*$\ast$

237   A rose bouquet is like a fountain fanning out. The meaning of the first sign—possibly a tree—is not clear, whereas the correction represents the eightfold flower (fig. 85). Evidently a mistake is being corrected which somehow impaired the wholeness of the rose. The aim of the reconstruction is to bring the problem of the mandala—the correct valuation and interpretation of the "centre"—once more into the field of consciousness.

30. Dream:

238   *The dreamer is sitting at a round table with the dark unknown woman.*

239   Whenever a process has reached a culmination as regards either its clarity or the wealth of inferences that can be drawn from it, a regression is likely to ensue. From the dreams that come in between the ones we have quoted here it is evident that the dreamer is finding the insistent demands of wholeness somewhat disagreeable; for their realization will have far-reaching practical consequences, whose personal nature, however, lies outside the scope of our study.

240   The round table again points to the circle of wholeness, and the anima comes in as representative of the fourth function, especially in her "dark" aspect, which always makes itself felt when something is becoming concrete, i.e., when it has to be translated, or threatens to translate itself, into reality. "Dark"

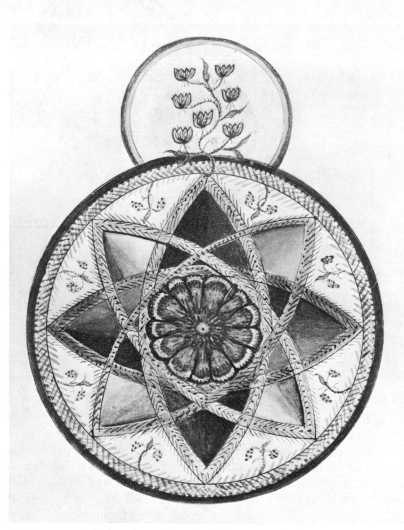

85. The eight-petalled flower as the eighth or the first of seven.—"Recueil de figures astrologiques" (MS., 18th cent.)

means chthonic, i.e., concrete and earthy. This is also the source of the fear that causes the regression.[117]

31. DREAM:

241 *The dreamer is sitting with a certain man of unpleasant aspect at a round table. On it stands a glass filled with a gelatinous mass.*

242 This dream is an advance on the last in that the dreamer has accepted the "dark" as his own darkness, to the extent of producing a real "shadow" belonging to him personally.[118] The anima is thus relieved of the moral inferiority projected upon her and can take up the living and creative function[119] which is properly her own. This is represented by the glass with its peculiar contents which we, like the dreamer, may compare with the undifferentiated "life-mass" in dream 18 (par. 183). It was then a question of the gradual transformation of primitive animality into something human. So we may expect something of the sort here, for it seems as if the spiral of inner development had come round to the same point again, though higher up.

117 "Symbola Pythagore philosophi" in Ficino, *Auctores platonici*, Fol. X, III, says: "Ab eo, quod nigram caudam habet abstine, terrestrium enim deorum est" (Keep your hands from that which has a black tail, for it belongs to the gods of the earth).

118 Although the theme of this study does not permit a full discussion of the psychology of dreams, I must make a few explanatory remarks at this point. Sitting together at one table means relationship, being connected or "put together." The round table indicates that the figures have been brought together for the purpose of wholeness. If the anima figure (the personified unconscious) is separated from ego-consciousness and therefore unconscious, it means that there is an isolating layer of personal unconscious embedded between the ego and the anima. The existence of a personal unconscious proves that contents of a personal nature which could really be made conscious are being kept unconscious for no good reason. There is thus an inadequate or even non-existent consciousness of the shadow. The shadow corresponds to a negative ego-personality and includes all those qualities we find painful or regrettable. Shadow and anima, being unconscious, are then contaminated with each other, a state that is represented in dreams by "marriage" or the like. But if the existence of the anima (or the shadow) is accepted and understood, a separation of these figures ensues, as has happened in the case of our dreamer. The shadow is thus recognized as belonging, and the anima as not belonging, to the ego.

119 Cf. what I have said about the anima in "The Archetypes of the Collective Unconscious," pars. 53ff. In Hermes' treatise, *An die menschliche Seele*, she is called "the highest interpreter and nearest custodian (of the eternal)," which aptly characterizes her function as mediator between conscious and unconscious.

86. The alchemical apparatus for distillation, the *unum vas*, with the serpents of the (double) Mercurius.—Kelley, *Tractatus de Lapide philosophorum* (1676)

243   The glass corresponds to the *unum vas* of alchemy (fig. 86) and its contents to the living, semi-organic mixture from which the body of the *lapis*, endowed with spirit and life, will emerge —or possibly that strange Faustian figure who bursts into flame three times: the Boy Charioteer, the Homunculus who is dashed against the throne of Galatea, and Euphorion (all symbolizing a dissolution of the "centre" into its unconscious elements). We know that the *lapis* is not just a "stone" since it is expressly stated to be composed "de re animali, vegetabili et minerali," and to consist of body, soul, and spirit;[120] moreover, it grows from flesh and blood.[121] For which reason the philosopher (Hermes in the "Tabula smaragdina") says: "The wind hath carried it in his belly" (fig. 210). Therefore "wind is air, air is life, and life is soul." "The stone is that thing midway between perfect and imperfect bodies, and that which nature herself begins is brought to perfection through the art." [122] The stone "is named the stone of invisibility" (*lapis invisibilitatis*).[123]

244   The dream takes up the question of giving the centre life and reality—giving birth to it, so to speak. That this birth can issue from an amorphous mass has its parallel in the alchemical idea of the *prima materia* as a chaotic *massa informis* impregnated by the seeds of life (figs. 162, 163). As we have seen, the qualities of gum arabic and glue are attributed to it, or again it is called *viscosa* and *unctuosa*. (In Paracelsus the "Nostoc" is the arcane substance.) Although modern conceptions of nutrient soil, jelly-like growths, etc., underlie the dreamer's "gelatinous mass," the atavistic associations with far older alchemical ideas

[120] *Rosarium, Art. aurif.*, II, p. 237.   [121] Ibid., p. 238.
[122] P. 236.   [123] P. 231.

87. The Virgin as the *vas* of the divine child.—From a Venetian *Rosario dela gloriosa vergine Maria* (1524)

still persist, and these, although not consciously present, nevertheless exert a powerful unconscious influence on the choice of symbols.

32. DREAM:

245   *The dreamer receives a letter from an unknown woman. She writes that she has pains in the uterus. A drawing is attached to the letter, looking roughly like this:* [124]

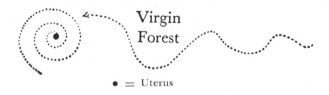

Virgin
Forest

● = Uterus

[124] The uterus is the centre, the life-giving vessel (fig. 87). The stone, like the grail, is itself the creative vessel, the *elixir vitae*. It is surrounded by the spiral, the symbol of indirect approach by means of the *circumambulatio*.

253

In the primeval forest there are swarms of monkeys. Then a panorama of white glaciers opens out.

246   The anima reports that there are painful processes going on in the life-creating centre, which in this case is no longer the "glass" containing the life-mass but a point designated as a "uterus," to be reached—so the spiral suggests—by means of a *circumambulatio*. At all events the spiral emphasizes the centre and hence the uterus, which is a synonym frequently employed for the alchemical vessel, just as it is one of the basic meanings of the Eastern mandala.[125] The serpentine line leading to the vessel is analogous to the healing serpent of Aesculapius (figs. 203, 204) and also to the Tantric symbol of *Shiva bindu*. the creative, latent god without extension in space who, in the form of a point or *lingam,* is encircled three and a half times by the Kundalini serpent.[126] With the primeval forest we meet the animal or ape motif again, which appeared before in vision 22 of the first series (par. 117) and in dreams 16 and 18 of this (pars. 164, 183). In vision 22 it led to the announcement that "everything must be ruled by the light" and, in dream 18, to the "transfigured" head. Similarly the present dream ends with a panorama of white "glaciers," reminding the dreamer of an earlier dream (not included here) in which he beheld the Milky Way and was having a conversation about immortality. Thus the glacier symbol is a bridge leading back again to the cosmic aspect that caused the regression. But, as is nearly always the case, the earlier content does not return in its first simple guise—it brings a new complication with it, which, though it might have been expected logically, is no less repugnant to the intellectual consciousness than the cosmic aspect was. The complication is the memory of the conversation about immortality. This theme was

---

[125] The centre of the mandala corresponds to the calyx of the Indian lotus, seat and birthplace of the gods. This is called the *padma,* and has a feminine significance. In alchemy the *vas* is often understood as the uterus where the "child" is gestated. In the Litany of Loreto, Mary is spoken of three times as the "vas" ("vas spirituale," "honorabile," and "insigne devotionis") and in medieval poetry she is called the "flower of the sea" which shelters the Christ (cf. dream 36). The grail (fig. 88) is closely related to the Hermetic vessel: Wolfram von Eschenbach calls the stone of the grail "lapsit exillis." Arnold of Villanova (d. ?1312) calls the *lapis* "lapis exilis," the uncomely stone (*Rosarium, Art. aurif.,* II, p. 210), which may be of importance for the interpretation of Wolfram's term.
[126] See Avalon, *The Serpent Power.*

88. Vision of the Holy Grail.—"Roman de Lancelot du lac" (MS., Paris, 15th cent.)

already hinted at in dream 9 (par. 134), with its pendulum clock, a *perpetuum mobile*. Immortality is a clock that never runs down, a mandala that revolves eternally like the heavens. Thus the cosmic aspect returns with interest and compound interest. This might easily prove too much for the dreamer, for the "scientific" stomach has very limited powers of digestion.

247   The unconscious does indeed put forth a bewildering profusion of semblances for that obscure thing we call the mandala or "self." It almost seems as if we were ready to go on dreaming in the unconscious the age-old dream of alchemy, and to continue to pile new synonyms on top of the old, only to know as much or as little about it in the end as the ancients themselves. I will not enlarge upon what the *lapis* meant to our forefathers, and what the mandala still means to the Lamaist and Tantrist, Aztec

255

and Pueblo Indian, the "golden pill" [127] to the Taoist, and the "golden seed" to the Hindu. We know the texts that give us a vivid idea of all this. But what does it mean when the unconscious stubbornly persists in presenting such abstruse symbolisms to a cultured European? The only point of view I can apply here is a psychological one. (There may be others with which I am not familiar.) From this point of view, as it seems to me, everything that can be grouped together under the general concept "mandala" expresses the essence of a certain kind of *attitude*. The known attitudes of the conscious mind have definable aims and purposes. But a man's attitude towards the self is the only one that has no definable aim and no visible purpose. It is easy enough to say "self," but exactly what have we said? That remains shrouded in "metaphysical" darkness. I may define "self" as the totality of the conscious and unconscious psyche, but this totality transcends our vision; it is a veritable *lapis invisibilitatis*. In so far as the unconscious exists it is not definable; its existence is a mere postulate and nothing whatever can be predicated as to its possible contents. The totality can only be experienced in its parts and then only in so far as these are contents of consciousness; but *qua* totality it necessarily transcends consciousness. Consequently the "self" is a pure borderline concept similar to Kant's *Ding an sich*. True, it is a concept that grows steadily clearer with experience—as our dreams show—without, however, losing anything of its transcendence. Since we cannot possibly know the boundaries of something unknown to us, it follows that we are not in a position to set any bounds to the self. It would be wildly arbitrary and therefore unscientific to restrict the self to the limits of the individual psyche, quite apart from the fundamental fact that we have not the least knowledge of these limits, seeing that they also lie in the unconscious. We may be able to indicate the limits of consciousness, but the unconscious is simply the unknown psyche and for that very reason illimitable because indeterminable. Such being the case, we should not be in the least surprised if the empirical manifestations of unconscious contents bear all the marks of something illimitable, something not determined by space and time. This quality is numinous and therefore alarming, above all to a cautious mind that knows the value of

[127] Synonymous with the "golden flower."

precisely delimited concepts. One is glad not to be a philosopher or theologian and so under no obligation to meet such numina professionally. It is all the worse when it becomes increasingly clear that numina are psychic *entia* that force themselves upon consciousness, since night after night our dreams practise philosophy on their own account. What is more, when we attempt to give these numina the slip and angrily reject the alchemical gold which the unconscious offers, things do in fact go badly with us, we may even develop symptoms in defiance of all reason, but the moment we face up to the stumbling-block and make it—if only hypothetically—the cornerstone, the symptoms vanish and we feel "unaccountably" well. In this dilemma we can at least comfort ourselves with the reflection that the unconscious is a necessary evil which must be reckoned with, and that it would therefore be wiser to accompany it on some of its strange symbolic wanderings, even though their meaning be exceedingly questionable. It might perhaps be conducive to good health to relearn Nietzsche's "lesson of earlier humanity."

248   The only objection I could make to such rationalistic explanations is that very often they do not stand the test of events. We can observe in these and similar cases how, over the years, the entelechy of the self becomes so insistent that consciousness has to rise to still greater feats if it is to keep pace with the unconscious.

249   All that can be ascertained at present about the symbolism of the mandala is that it portrays an autonomous psychic fact, characterized by a phenomenology which is always repeating itself and is everywhere the same. It seems to be a sort of atomic nucleus about whose innermost structure and ultimate meaning we know nothing. We can also regard it as the actual—i.e., effective—reflection of a conscious attitude that can state neither its aim nor its purpose and, because of this failure, projects its activity entirely upon the virtual centre of the mandala.[128] The compelling force necessary for this projection always lies in some situation where the individual no longer knows how to help himself in any other way. That the mandala is merely a psychological reflex is, however, contradicted firstly by the autonomous nature of this symbol, which sometimes manifests itself

---

[128] Projection is considered here a spontaneous phenomenon, and not the deliberate extrapolation of anything. It is not a phenomenon of the will.

89. The pelican nourishing its young with its own blood, an allegory of Christ.
—Boschius, *Symbolographia* (1702)

with overwhelming spontaneity in dreams and visions, and secondly by the autonomous nature of the unconscious as such, which is not only the original form of everything psychic but also the condition we pass through in early childhood and to which we return every night. There is no evidence for the assertion that the activity of the psyche is merely reactive or reflex. This is at best a biological working hypothesis of limited validity. When raised to a universal truth it is nothing but a materialistic myth, for it overlooks the creative capacity of the psyche, which—whether we like it or not—exists, and in face of which all so-called "causes" become mere occasions.

33. DREAM:

250   *A battle among savages, in which bestial cruelties are perpetrated.*

251   As was to be foreseen, the new complication ("immortality") has started a furious conflict, which makes use of the same symbols as the analogous situation in dream 27 (par. 232).

34. DREAM:

252   *A conversation with a friend. The dreamer says, "I must carry on with the figure of the bleeding Christ before me and persevere in the work of self-redemption."*

253   This, like the previous dream, points to an extraordinary, subtle kind of suffering (fig. 89) caused by the breaking through of an alien spiritual world which we find very hard to accept—hence the analogy with the tragedy of Christ: "My kingdom is not of this world." But it also shows that the dreamer is now continuing his task in deadly earnest. The reference to Christ may well have a deeper meaning than that of a mere moral re-

258

minder: we are concerned here with the process of individuation, a process which has constantly been held up to Western man in the dogmatic and religious model of the life of Christ. The accent has always fallen on the "historicity" of the Saviour's life, and because of this its symbolical nature has remained in the dark, although the Incarnation formed a very essential part of the *symbolon* (creed). The efficacy of dogma, however, by no means rests on Christ's unique historical reality but on its own symbolic nature, by virtue of which it expresses a more or less ubiquitous psychological assumption quite independent of the existence of any dogma. There is thus a "pre-Christian" as well as a "non-Christian" Christ, in so far as he is an autonomous psychological fact. At any rate the doctrine of prefiguration is founded on this idea. In the case of the modern man, who has no religious assumptions at all, it is therefore only logical that the Anthropos or Poimen figure should emerge, since it is present in his own psyche (figs. 117, 195).

35. DREAM:

254   *An actor smashes his hat against the wall, where it looks like this:*

255   As certain material not included here shows, the "actor" refers to a definite fact in the dreamer's personal life. Up to now he had maintained a certain fiction about himself which prevented him from taking himself seriously. This fiction has become incompatible with the serious attitude he has now attained. He must give up the actor, for it was the actor in him who rejected the self. The hat refers to the first dream of all, where he put on a *stranger's* hat. The actor throws the hat against the wall, and the hat proves to be a mandala. So the "strange" hat was the self, which at that time—while he was still playing a fictitious role—seemed like a stranger to him.

36. DREAM:

256   *The dreamer drives in a taxi to the Rathausplatz, but it is called the "Marienhof."*

257   I mention this dream only in passing because it shows the feminine nature of the *temenos,* just as *hortus conclusus* (enclosed garden) is often used as an image for the Virgin Mary in medieval hymns, and *rosa mystica* is one of her attributes in the Litany of Loreto (cf. fig. 26).

37. DREAM:

258   *There are curves outlined in light around a dark centre. Then the dreamer is wandering about in a dark cave, where a battle is going on between good and evil. But there is also a prince who knows everything. He gives the dreamer a ring set with a diamond and places it on the fourth finger of his left hand.*

259   The circulation of light that started in dream 26 reappears more clearly. Light always refers to consciousness, which at present runs only along the periphery. The centre is still dark. It is the dark cave, and to enter it is obviously to set the conflict going again. At the same time it is like the prince who stands aloof, who knows everything and is the possessor of the precious stone. The gift means nothing less than the dreamer's vow to the self— for as a rule the wedding ring is worn on the fourth finger of the left hand. True, the left is the unconscious, from which it is to be inferred that the situation is still largely shrouded in unconsciousness. The prince seems to be the representative of the *aenigma regis* (fig. 54; cf. commentary to dream 10, par. 142). The dark cave corresponds to the vessel containing the warring opposites. The self is made manifest in the opposites and in the conflict between them; it is a *coincidentia oppositorum.* Hence the way to the self begins with conflict.

38. DREAM:

260   *A circular table with four chairs round it. Table and chairs are empty.*

261   This dream confirms the above conjecture. The mandala is not yet "in use."

90. The bear representing the dangerous aspect of the *prima materia.*—Thomas
Aquinas (pseud.), "De alchimia" (MS., 16th cent.)

39. VISUAL IMPRESSION:

262   *The dreamer is falling into the abyss. At the bottom there
is a bear whose eyes gleam alternately in four colours: red, yellow, green, and blue. Actually it has four eyes that change into
four lights. The bear disappears and the dreamer goes through
a long dark tunnel. Light is shimmering at the far end. A treasure is there, and on top of it the ring with the diamond. It is
said that this ring will lead him on a long journey to the east.*

263   This waking dream shows that the dreamer is still preoccupied with the dark centre. The bear stands for the chthonic element that might seize him. But then it becomes clear that the
animal is only leading up to the four colours (cf. dream 23,
par. 212), which in their turn lead to the *lapis,* i.e., the diamond
whose prism contains all the hues of the rainbow. The way to
the east probably points to the unconscious as an antipode. Ac-

261

cording to the legend the Grail-stone comes from the east and must return there again. In alchemy the bear corresponds to the *nigredo* of the *prima materia* (fig. 90), whence comes the colourful *cauda pavonis*.

40. DREAM:

264   *Under the guidance of the unknown woman the dreamer has to discover the Pole at the risk of his life.*

265   The Pole is the point round which everything turns—hence another symbol of the self. Alchemy also took up this analogy: "In the Pole is the heart of Mercurius, who is the true fire, wherein his master rests. When navigating over this great sea . . . he sets his course by the aspect of the North star." [129] Mercurius is the world-soul, and the Pole is its heart (fig. 140). The idea of the *anima mundi* (fig. 91; cf. fig. 8) coincides with that of the collective unconscious whose centre is the self. The symbol of the sea is another synonym for the unconscious.

41. VISUAL IMPRESSION:

266   *Yellow balls rolling round to the left in a circle.*

267   Rotation about a centre, recalling dream 21 (par. 198).

42. DREAM:

268   *An old master points to a spot on the ground illuminated in red.*

269   The *philosophus* shows him the "centre." The redness may mean the dawn, like the *rubedo* in alchemy, which as a rule immediately preceded the completion of the work.

43. DREAM:

270   *A yellow light like the sun looms through the fog, but it is murky. Eight rays go out from the centre. This is the point of penetration: the light ought to pierce through, but has not quite succeeded.*

271   The dreamer himself observed that the point of penetration was identical with the Pole in dream 40. So it is, as we surmised, a question of the sun's appearing, which now turns yellow. But

---

[129] "In polo est cor Mercurii, qui verus est ignis, in quo requies est Domini sui, navigans per mare hoc magnum . . . cursum dirigat per aspectum astri septentrionalis"—Philalethes, "Introitus apertus," *Musaeum hermeticum*, p. 655.

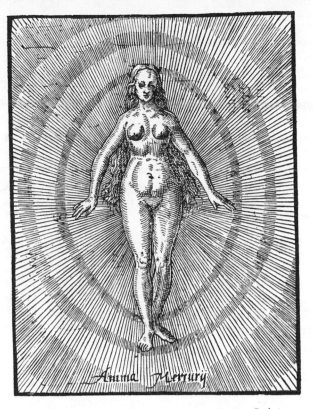

91. *Anima Mundi.*—Thurneisser zum Thurn, *Quinta essentia* (1574)

the light is still murky, which probably means insufficient understanding. The "penetration" alludes to the need for effort in coming to a decision. In alchemy yellow (*citrinitas*) often coincides with the *rubedo*. The "gold" is yellow or reddish yellow.

44. DREAM:

272   *The dreamer is in a square enclosure where he must keep still. It is a prison for Lilliputians (or children?). A wicked woman is in charge of them. The children start moving and begin to circulate round the periphery. The dreamer would like to run away but may not do so. One of the children turns into an animal and bites him in the calf* (fig. 118).

273   The lack of clarity demands further efforts of concentration; hence the dreamer finds himself still in the childhood state

(figs. 95, 96), hence "lopsided" (cf. dream 26, par. 227), and imprisoned in the *temenos* in the charge of a wicked mother-anima. The animal appears as in dream 18 (par. 183) and he is bitten, i.e., he must expose himself and pay the price. The *circumambulatio* means, as always, concentration on the centre. He finds this state of tension almost unendurable. But he wakes up with an intense and pleasant feeling of having solved something, "as if he held the diamond in his hand." The children point to the dwarf motif, which may express Cabiric elements, i.e., it may represent unconscious formative powers (see dreams 56ff., below), or it may at the same time allude to his still childish condition.

45. DREAM:

274   *A parade ground with troops. They are not equipping themselves for war but form an eight-rayed star rotating to the left.*

275   The essential point here is that the conflict seems to be overcome. The star is not in the sky and not a diamond, but a configuration on the earth formed by human beings.

46. DREAM:

276   *The dreamer is imprisoned in the square enclosure. Lions and a wicked sorceress appear.*

277   He cannot get out of the chthonic prison because he is not yet ready to do something that he should. (This is an important personal matter, a duty even, and the cause of much misgiving.) Lions, like all wild animals, indicate latent affects. The lion plays an important part in alchemy and has much the same meaning. It is a "fiery" animal, an emblem of the devil, and stands for the danger of being swallowed by the unconscious.

47. DREAM:

278   *The wise old man shows the dreamer a place on the ground marked in a peculiar way.*

279   This is probably the place on earth where the dreamer belongs if he is to realize the self (similar to dream 42).

48. DREAM:

280   *An acquaintance wins a prize for digging up a potter's wheel.*

281   The potter's wheel rotates on the ground (cf. dream 45) and

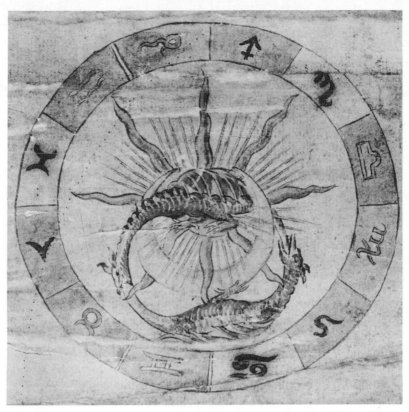

92. The alchemical process in the zodiac.—"Ripley Scrowle" (MS., 1588)

produces earthenware ("earthly") vessels which may figuratively be called "human bodies." Being round, the wheel refers to the self and the creative activity in which it is manifest. The potter's wheel also symbolizes the recurrent theme of circulation.

49. DREAM:

282   *A starry figure rotating. At the cardinal points of the circle there are pictures representing the seasons.*

283   Just as the place was defined before, so now the time. Place and time are the most general and necessary elements in any definition. The determination of time and place was stressed right at the beginning (cf. dreams 7, 8, 9; pars. 130–34). A definite location in place and time is part of a man's reality. The seasons refer to the quartering of the circle which corresponds to

the cycle of the year (fig. 92). The year is a symbol of the original man[130] (figs. 99, 100, 104). The rotation motif indicates that the symbol of the circle is to be thought of not as static but as dynamic.

50. DREAM:

284   *An unknown man gives the dreamer a precious stone. But he is attacked by a gang of apaches. He runs away (nightmare) and is able to escape. The unknown woman tells him afterwards that it will not always be so: sometime he will have to stand his ground and not run away.*

285   When a definite time is added to a definite place one is rapidly approaching reality. That is the reason for the gift of the jewel, but also for the fear of decision, which robs the dreamer of the power to make up his mind.

51. DREAM:

286   *There is a feeling of great tension. Many people are circulating round a large central oblong with four smaller oblongs on its sides. The circulation in the large oblong goes to the left and in the smaller oblongs to the right. In the middle there is the eight-rayed star. A bowl is placed in the centre of each of the smaller oblongs, containing red, yellow, green, and colourless water. The water rotates to the left. The disquieting question arises: Is there enough water?*

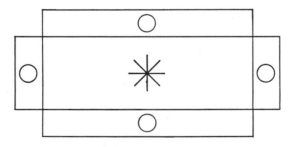

287   The colours point once more to the preliminary stage. The "disquieting" question is whether there is enough water of life —*aqua nostra*, energy, libido—to reach the central star (i.e., the

130 See "Paracelsus as a Spiritual Phenomenon," pars. 229, 237.

"core" or "kernel"; cf. next dream). The circulation in the central oblong is still going to the left, i.e., consciousness is moving towards the unconscious. The centre is therefore not yet sufficiently illuminated. The rightward circulation in the smaller oblongs, which represent the quaternity, seems to suggest that the four functions are becoming conscious. The four are generally characterized by the four colours of the rainbow. The striking fact here is that the blue is missing, and also that the square ground-plan has suddenly been abandoned. The horizontal has extended itself at the cost of the vertical. So we are dealing with a "disturbed" mandala.[131] We might add by way of criticism that the antithetical arrangement of the functions has not yet become sufficiently conscious for their characteristic polarity to be recognized.[132] The predominance of the horizontal over the vertical indicates that the ego-consciousness is uppermost, thus entailing a loss of height and depth.

52. DREAM:

288   *A rectangular dance hall. Everybody is going round the periphery to the left. Suddenly the order is heard: "To the kernels!" But the dreamer has first to go into the adjoining room to crack some nuts. Then the people climb down rope ladders to the water.*

289   The time has come to press on to the "kernel" or core of the matter, but the dreamer still has a few more "hard nuts" to crack in the little rectangle (the "adjoining room"), i.e., in one of the four functions. Meanwhile the process goes on and descends to the "water." The vertical is thus lengthened, and from the incorrect oblong we again get the square which expresses the complete symmetry of conscious and unconscious with all its psychological implications.

---

131 "Disturbed" mandalas occur from time to time. They consist of all forms that deviate from the circle, square, or regular cross, and also of those based not on the number four but on three or five. The numbers six and twelve are something of an exception. Twelve can be based on either four or three. The twelve months and the twelve signs of the zodiac are definite symbolic circles in daily use. And six is likewise a well-known symbol for the circle. Three suggests the predominance of ideation and will (trinity), and five that of the physical man (materialism).

132 Cf. the psychological functions in *Psychological Types,* ch. X.

53. DREAM:

290   *The dreamer finds himself in an empty square room which is rotating. A voice cries, "Don't let him out. He won't pay the tax!"*

291   This refers to the dreamer's inadequate self-realization in the personal matter already alluded to, which in this case was one of the essential conditions of individuation and therefore could not be circumvented. As was to be expected, after the preparatory emphasis on the vertical in the preceding dream, the square is now re-established. The cause of the disturbance was an underestimation of the demands of the unconscious (the vertical), which led to a flattening of the personality (recumbent oblong).

292   After this dream the dreamer worked out six mandalas in which he tried to determine the right length of the vertical, the form of "circulation," and the distribution of colour. At the end of this work came the following dream (given unabridged):

54. DREAM:

293   *I come to a strange, solemn house—the "House of the Gathering." Many candles are burning in the background, arranged in a peculiar pattern with four points running upward. Outside, at the door of the house, an old man is posted. People are going in. They say nothing and stand motionless in order to collect themselves inwardly. The man at the door says of the visitors to the house, "When they come out again they are cleansed." I go into the house myself and find I can concentrate perfectly. Then a voice says: "What you are doing is dangerous. Religion is not a tax to be paid so that you can rid yourself of the woman's image, for this image cannot be got rid of. Woe unto them who use religion as a substitute for another side of the soul's life; they are in error and will be accursed. Religion is no substitute; it is to be added to the other activities of the soul as the ultimate completion. Out of the fulness of life shall you bring forth your religion; only then shall you be blessed!" While the last sentence is being spoken in ringing tones I hear distant music, simple chords on an organ. Something about it reminds me of Wagner's Fire Music. As I leave the house I see a burning mountain and I feel: "The fire that is not put out is a holy fire" (Shaw, St. Joan).*

Labels within the image:

IGNIS.
AERIS.
AQVÆ.
TERRÆ.

V.W.I.W.V.

TINCTVR .
COAGVLATION .
DISTILLATION .
PVTREFACTION .
SOLVTION .
SVBLIMATION .
CALTINATION .

93. The Mountain of the Adepts. The temple of the wise ("House of the Gathering" or of "Self-Collection"), lit by the sun and moon, stands on the seven stages, surmounted by the phoenix. The temple is hidden in the mountain—a hint that the philosophers' stone lies buried in the earth and must be extracted and cleansed. The zodiac in the background symbolizes the duration of the *opus*, while the four elements indicate wholeness. In foreground, blindfolded man and the investigator who follows his natural instinct.—Michelspacher, *Cabala* (1654)

294 The dreamer notes that this dream was a "powerful experience." Indeed it has a numinous quality and we shall therefore not be far wrong if we assume that it represents a new climax of insight and understanding. The "voice" has as a rule an absolutely authoritative character and generally comes at decisive moments.

295 The house probably corresponds to the square, which is a "gathering place" (fig. 93). The four shining points in the background again indicate the quaternity. The remark about cleansing refers to the transformative function of the taboo area. The production of wholeness, which is prevented by the "tax evasion," naturally requires the "image of the woman," since as anima she represents the fourth, "inferior" function, feminine because contaminated with the unconscious. In what sense the "tax" is to be paid depends on the nature of the inferior function and its auxiliary, and also on the attitude type.[133] The payment can be either concrete or symbolic, but the conscious mind is not qualified to decide which form is valid.

296 The dream's view that religion may not be a substitute for "another side of the soul's life" will certainly strike many people as a radical innovation. According to it, religion is equated with wholeness; it even appears as the expression of the integration of the self in the "fulness of life."

297 The faint echo of the Fire Music—the Loki motif—is not out of key, for what does "fulness of life" mean? What does "wholeness" mean? I feel that there is every reason here for some anxiety, since man as a whole being casts a shadow. The fourth was not separated from the three and banished to the kingdom of everlasting fire for nothing. Does not an uncanonical saying of our Lord declare: "Whoso is near unto me is near unto the fire"? [134] (Cf. fig. 58.) Such dire ambiguities are not meant for grown-up children—which is why Heraclitus of old was named "the dark," because he spoke too plainly and called life itself an "ever-living fire." And that is why there are uncanonical sayings for those that have ears to hear.

---

133 *Psychological Types*, pars. 556ff.
134 "Ait autem ipse salvator: Qui iuxta me est, iuxta ignem est. qui longe est a me, longe est a regno" (The Saviour himself says: He that is near me is near the fire. He that is far from me is far from the kingdom).—Origen, *Homiliae in Jeremiam*, XX, 3; cited in James, *Apocryphal New Testament*, p. 35.

94. Etna: "gelat et ardet."—Boschius, *Symbolographia* (1702)

298   The theme of the Fire Mountain (fig. 94) is to be met with in the Book of Enoch.[135] Enoch sees the seven stars chained "like great mountains and burning with fire" at the angels' place of punishment. Originally the seven stars were the seven great Babylonian gods, but at the time of Enoch's revelation they had become the seven Archons, rulers of "this world," fallen angels condemned to punishment. In contrast to this menacing theme there is an allusion to the miracles of Jehovah on Mount Sinai, while according to other sources the number seven is by no means sinister, since it is on the seventh mountain of the western land that the tree with the life-giving fruit is to be found, i.e., the *arbor sapientiae* (cf. fig. 188).[136]

55. DREAM:

299   *A silver bowl with four cracked nuts at the cardinal points.*

300   This dream shows that some of the problems in dream 52 have been settled, though the settlement is not complete. The dreamer pictured the goal that has now been attained as a circle divided into four, with the quadrants painted in the four colours. The circulation is to the left. Though this satisfies the demands of symmetry, the polarity of the functions is still unrecognized —despite the last, very illuminating dream—because, in the painting, red and blue, green and yellow, are side by side instead of opposite one another. From this we must conclude that the "realization" is meeting with strong inner resistances, partly of a philosophical and partly of an ethical nature, the justification

[135] Book of Enoch 18 : 13 and ch. 21 (Charles, *Apocrypha and Pseudepigrapha,* II, pp. 200, 201).
[136] A more detailed commentary on this dream is to be found in Jung, "Psychology and Religion," pars. 59ff.

95. *Ludus puerorum.*—Trismosin, "Splendor solis" (MS., 1582)

96. Pygmies (helpful child-gods).—Fragments of an Egyptian mechanical toy

for which cannot lightly be set aside. That the dreamer has an inadequate understanding of the polarity is shown by the fact that the nuts have still to be cracked in reality, and also that they are all alike, i.e., not yet differentiated.

56. DREAM:

301   *Four children are carrying a large dark ring. They move in a circle. The dark unknown woman appears and says she will come again, for it is the festival of the solstice.*

302   In this dream the elements of dream 44 come together again: the children and the dark woman, who was a wicked witch before. The "solstice" indicates the turning-point. In alchemy the work is completed in the autumn (*Vindemia Hermetis*). Children (fig. 95), dwarf-gods, bring the ring—i.e., the symbol of wholeness is still under the sway of childlike creative powers. Note that children also play a part in the *opus alchymicum:* a certain portion of the work is called *ludus puerorum.* Save for the remark that the work is as easy as "child's play," I have found no explanation for this. Seeing that the work is, in the unanimous testimony of all the adepts, exceedingly difficult, it must be a euphemistic and probably also a symbolical definition. It would thus point to a co-operation on the part of "infantile" or unconscious forces represented as Cabiri and hobgoblins (homunculi: fig. 96).

273

97. The "Grand Peregrination" by ship. Two eagles fly round the earth in opposite directions, indicating that it is an odyssey in search of wholeness.—Maier,
Viatorium (1651)

98. The philosophical egg, whence the double eagle is hatched, wearing the spiritual and temporal crowns.—Codex Palatinus Latinus 412 (15th cent.)

57. VISUAL IMPRESSION:

303   *The dark ring, with an egg in the middle.*

58. VISUAL IMPRESSION:

304   *A black eagle comes out of the egg and seizes in its beak the ring, now turned to gold. Then the dreamer is on a ship and the bird flies ahead.*

305   The eagle signifies height. (Previously the stress was on depth: people descending to the water.) It seizes the whole mandala and, with it, control of the dreamer, who, carried along on a ship, sails after the bird (fig. 97). Birds are thoughts and the

flight of thought. Generally it is fantasies and intuitive ideas that are represented thus (the winged Mercurius, Morpheus, genii, angels). The ship is the vehicle that bears the dreamer over the sea and the depths of the unconscious. As a man-made thing it has the significance of a system or method (or a way: cf. Hinayana and Mahayana = the Lesser and Greater Vehicle, the two schools of Buddhism). The flight of thought goes ahead and methodical elaboration follows after. Man cannot walk the rainbow bridge like a god but must go underneath with whatever reflective afterthoughts he may have. The eagle—synonymous with phoenix, vulture, raven—is a well-known alchemical symbol. Even the *lapis,* the *rebis* (compounded of two parts and therefore frequently hermaphroditic as an amalgam of Sol and Luna), is often represented with wings (figs. 22, 54, 208), denoting intuition or spiritual (winged) potentiality. In the last resort all these symbols depict the consciousness-transcending fact we call the self. This visual impression is rather like a snapshot of an evolving process as it leads on to the next stage.

306   In alchemy the egg stands for the chaos apprehended by the artifex, the *prima materia* containing the captive world-soul. Out of the egg—symbolized by the round cooking-vessel—will rise the eagle or phoenix, the liberated soul, which is ultimately identical with the Anthropos who was imprisoned in the embrace of Physis (fig. 98).

99. Time-symbol of the *lapis:* the cross and the evangelical emblems mark its analogy with Christ.—Thomas Aquinas (pseud.), "De alchimia" (MS., 16th cent.)

III. THE VISION OF THE WORLD CLOCK

59. THE "GREAT VISION":[137]

307　*There is a vertical and a horizontal circle, having a common centre. This is the world clock. It is supported by the black bird.*

The vertical circle is a blue disc with a white border divided into $4 \times 8 = 32$ partitions. A pointer rotates upon it.

The horizontal circle consists of four colours. On it stand four little men with pendulums, and round about it is laid the

[137] This vision is treated in greater detail in Jung, "Psychology and Religion," pars. 112ff.

ring that was once dark and is now golden (formerly carried by the children).

The "clock" has three rhythms or pulses:

1. The small pulse: *the pointer on the blue vertical disc advances by 1/32.*

2. The middle pulse: *one complete revolution of the pointer. At the same time the horizontal circle advances by 1/32.*

3. The great pulse: *32 middle pulses are equal to one revolution of the golden ring.*

308   This remarkable vision made a deep and lasting impression on the dreamer, an impression of "the most sublime harmony," as he himself puts it. The world clock may well be the "severe image" which is identical with the Cabiri, i.e., the four children or four little men with the pendulums. It is a three-dimensional mandala—a mandala in bodily form signifying realization. (Unfortunately medical discretion prevents my giving the biographical details. It must suffice to say that this realization did actually take place.) Whatever a man does in reality he himself becomes.

309   Just why the vision of this curious figure should produce an impression of "the most sublime harmony" is, in one sense, very difficult to understand; but it becomes comprehensible enough as soon as we consider the comparative historical material. It is difficult to feel our way into the matter because the meaning of the image is exceedingly obscure. If the meaning is impenetrable and the form and colour take no account of aesthetic requirements, then neither our understanding nor our sense of beauty is satisfied, and we are at a loss to see why it should give rise to the impression of "the most sublime harmony." We can only venture the hypothesis that disparate and incongruous elements have combined here in the most fortunate way, simultaneously producing an image which realizes the "intentions" of the unconscious in the highest degree. We must therefore assume that the image is a singularly happy expression for an otherwise unknowable psychic fact which has so far only been able to manifest apparently disconnected aspects of itself.

310   The impression is indeed extremely abstract. One of the underlying ideas seems to be the intersection of two heterogeneous systems by the sharing of a common centre. Hence if we start as before from the assumption that the centre and its periphery

represent the totality of the psyche and consequently the self, then the figure tells us that two heterogeneous systems intersect in the self, standing to one another in a functional relationship that is governed by law and regulated by "three rhythms." The self is by definition the centre and the circumference of the conscious and unconscious systems. But the regulation of their functions by three rhythms is something that I cannot substantiate. I do not know what the three rhythms allude to. But I do not doubt for a moment that the allusion is amply justified. The only analogy I could adduce would be the three *regimina* mentioned in the Introduction (par. 31), by which the four elements are converted into one another or synthesized in the quintessence:

> 1st *regimen*: earth to water.
> 2nd   " : water to air.
> 3rd   " : air to fire.

311   We shall hardly be mistaken if we assume that our mandala aspires to the most complete union of opposites that is possible, including that of the masculine trinity and the feminine quaternity on the analogy of the alchemical hermaphrodite.

312   Since the figure has a cosmic aspect—world clock—we must suppose it to be a small-scale model or perhaps even a source of space-time, or at any rate an embodiment of it and therefore, mathematically speaking, four-dimensional in nature although only visible in a three-dimensional projection. I do not wish to labour this argument, for such an interpretation lies beyond my powers of proof.

313   The thirty-two pulses may conceivably derive from the multiplication of 4×8, as we know from experience that the quaternity found at the centre of a mandala often becomes 8, 16, 32, or more when extended to the periphery. The number 32 plays an important role in the Cabala. Thus we read in the *Sepher Yetsirah* (1 : 1): "Jehovah, the Lord of Hosts, the God of Israel, the living God and King of the world . . . has graven his name in thirty-two mysterious paths of wisdom." These consist of "ten self-contained numbers [*Sephiroth*] and twenty-two basic letters" (1 : 2). The meaning of the ten numbers is as follows: "1: the spirit of the Living God; 2: spirit from spirit; 3: water from spirit; 4: fire from water; 5-10: height, depth, East, West, South,

North." [138] Cornelius Agrippa mentions that "the learned Jews attribute the number 32 to Wisdom, for so many are the ways of Wisdom described by Abram." [139] Franck establishes a connection between 32 and the cabalistic trinity, Kether, Binah, and Hokhmah: "These three persons contain and unite in themselves everything that exists, and they in turn are united in the White Head, the Ancient of Days, for he is everything and everything is he. Sometimes he is represented with three heads which make but a single head, and sometimes he is likened to the brain which, without impairing its unity, divides into three parts and spreads through the whole body by means of thirty-two pairs of nerves, just as God spreads through the universe along thirty-two miraculous paths." [140] These thirty-two "canales occulti" are also mentioned by Knorr von Rosenroth,[141] who calls Hokhmah "the supreme path of all, embracing all," on the authority of Job 28 : 7 (A.V.): "There is a path which no fowl knoweth, and which the vulture's eye hath not seen." Allendy, in his very valuable account of number symbolism, writes: "32 . . . is the differentiation which appears in the organic world; not creative generation, but rather the plan and arrangement of the various forms of created things which the creator has modelled—as the product of 8×4. . . ." [142] Whether the cabalistic number 32 can be equated with the thirty-two fortunate signs (*mahavyanjana*) of the Buddha-child is doubtful.

314   As to the interpretation based on comparative historical material, we are in a more favourable position, at least as regards the general aspects of the figure. We have at our disposal, firstly, the whole mandala symbolism of three continents, and secondly, the specific time symbolism of the mandala as this developed under the influence of astrology, particularly in the West. The horoscope (fig. 100) is itself a mandala (a clock) with a dark centre, and a leftward *circumambulatio* with "houses" and planetary phases. The mandalas of ecclesiastical art, particularly those on the floor before the high altar or beneath the transept, make frequent use of the zodiacal beasts or the yearly seasons. A related idea is the identity of Christ with the Church calendar, of which

138 Bischoff, *Die Elemente der Kabbalah,* I, pp. 63ff. Further associations with "32" on pp. 175ff.   139 Agrippa, *De incertitudine,* II, ch. XV.
140 Franck, *Die Kabbala,* p. 137.
141 Knorr von Rosenroth, *Kabbala denudata,* I, p. 602.
142 Allendy, *Le Symbolisme des nombres,* p. 378.

100. Horoscope, showing the houses, zodiac, and planets.—Woodcut by Erhard
Schoen for the nativity calendar of Leonhard Reymann (1515)

101. Christ in the mandorla, surrounded by the symbols of the four evangelists.
—Mural painting, church of Saint-Jacques-des-Guérets, Loir-et-Cher, France

he is the fixed pole and the life. The Son of Man is an anticipation of the idea of the self (fig. 99): hence the Gnostic adultera-
tion of Christ with the other synonyms for the self among the
Naassenes, recorded by Hippolytus. There is also a connection
with the symbolism of Horus: on the one hand, Christ enthroned
with the four emblems of the evangelists—three animals and an
angel (fig. 101); on the other, Father Horus with his four sons,
or Osiris with the four sons of Horus[143] (fig. 102). Horus is also
the ἥλιος ἀνατολῆς (rising sun),[144] and Christ was still worshipped
as such by the early Christians.

[143] Bas-relief at Philae (Budge, *Osiris and the Egyptian Resurrection*, I, p. 3);
and *The Book of the Dead* (1899), Papyrus of Hunefer, pl. 5. Sometimes there
are three with animal heads and one with a human head, as in the Papyrus of
Kerasher (ibid.). In a 7th-century manuscript (Gellone) the evangelists actually
wear their animal heads, as in several other Romanesque monuments.

[144] So called by Melito of Sardis, *De baptismo*, in Pitra, *Analecta sacra*, II, p. 5.

102. Osiris, with the four sons of Horus on the lotus.—*The Book of the Dead*

315   We find a remarkable parallel in the writings of Guillaume de Digulleville, prior of the Cistercian monastery at Châlis, a Norman poet who, independently of Dante, composed three "pélerinages" between 1330 and 1355: *Les Pélerinages de la vie humaine, de l'âme,* and *de Jésus Christ.*[145] The last canto of the *Pélerinage de l'âme* contains a vision of Paradise, which consists of seven large spheres each containing seven smaller spheres.[146]

145 Delacotte, *Guillaume de Digulleville.*
146 An idea which corresponds to dream 21 (par. 198), of the large sphere containing many little spheres.

All the spheres rotate, and this movement is called a *siècle* (*saeculum*). The heavenly *siècles* are the prototypes of the earthly centuries. The angel who guides the poet explains: "When holy Church ends her prayers with *in saecula saeculorum* [for ever and ever], she has in mind, not earthly time, but eternity." At the same time the *siècles* are spherical spaces in which the blessed dwell. *Siècles* and *cieux* are identical. In the highest heaven of pure gold the King sits on a round throne which shines more brightly than the sun. A *couronne* of precious stones surrounds him. Beside him, on a circular throne that is made of brown crystal, sits the Queen, who intercedes for the sinners (fig. 103).

316   "Raising his eyes to the golden heaven, the pilgrim perceived a marvellous circle which appeared to be three feet across. It came out of the golden heaven at one point and re-entered it at another, and it made the whole tour of the golden heaven." This circle is sapphire-coloured. It is a small circle, three feet in diameter, and evidently it moves over a great horizontal circle like a rolling disc. This great circle intersects the golden circle of heaven.

317   While Guillaume is absorbed in this sight, three spirits suddenly appear clad in purple, with golden crowns and girdles, and enter the golden heaven. This moment, so the angel tells him, is *une fête,* like a church festival on earth:

> Ce cercle que tu vois est le calendrier
> Qui en faisant son tour entier,
> Montre des Saints les journées
> Quand elles doivent être fêtées.
> Chacun en fait le cercle un tour,
> Chacune étoile y est pour jour,
> Chacun soleil pour l'espace
> De jours trente ou zodiaque.

> (This circle is the calendar
> Which spinning round the course entire
> Shows the feast day of each saint
> And when it should be celebrate.
> Each saint goes once round all the way,
> Each star you see stands for a day,
> And every sun denotes a spell
> Of thirty days zodiacal.)

103. *Sponsus et sponsa.*—Detail from *Polittico con l'Incoronazione,* by Stefano da
Sant'Agnese (15th cent.)

104. God as Father and Logos creating the zodiac.—Peter Lombard, "De sacramentis" (MS., 14th cent.)

318   The three figures are saints whose feast day is even now being celebrated. The small circle that enters the golden heaven is *three* feet in width, and likewise there are *three* figures who make their sudden entry. They signify the moment of time in eternity, as does the circle of the calendar (fig. 104). But why this should be exactly three feet in diameter and why there are three figures remains a mystery. We naturally think of the three rhythms in our vision which are started off by the pointer moving over the blue disc, and which enter the system just as inexplicably as the calendar-circle enters the golden heaven.

319   The guide continues to instruct Guillaume on the significance of the signs of the zodiac with particular reference to sacred history, and ends with the remark that the feast of the twelve fishermen will be celebrated in the sign of Pisces, when the twelve will appear before the Trinity. Then it suddenly occurs to Guillaume that he has never really understood the nature of the Trinity, and he begs the angel for an explanation. The angel answers, "Now, there are three principal colours, namely green, red, and gold. These three colours are seen united in divers works of watered silk and in the feathers of many birds, such as the peacock. The almighty King who puts three colours in one, cannot he also make one substance to be three?" Gold, the royal colour, is attributed to God the Father; red to God the Son, because he shed his blood; and to the Holy Ghost

105. The Virgin, personifying the starry heaven.—"Speculum
humanae saluacionis" (MS., Vatican, 15th cent.)

green, "la couleur qui verdoye et qui réconforte." Thereupon
the angel warns Guillaume not to ask any more questions, and
disappears. The poet wakes up to find himself safely in his bed,
and so ends the *Pélerinage de l'âme*.

320   There is, however, one thing more to be asked: "Three there
are—but where is the fourth?" Why is blue missing? This colour
was also missing in the "disturbed" mandala of our dreamer (see
par. 287). Curiously enough, the *calendrier* that intersects the
golden circle is blue, and so is the vertical disc in the three-dimensional mandala. We would conjecture that blue, standing
for the vertical, means height and depth (the blue sky above, the
blue sea below), and that any shrinkage of the vertical reduces
the square to an oblong, thus producing something like an inflation of consciousness.[147] Hence the vertical would correspond to

147 Cf. my remarks on "inflation" in "The Relations between the Ego and the Unconscious," pars. 227ff.

287

the unconscious. But the unconscious in a man has feminine characteristics, and blue is the traditional colour of the Virgin's celestial cloak (fig. 105). Guillaume was so absorbed in the Trinity and in the threefold aspect of the *roy* that he quite forgot the *reyne*. Faust prays to her in these words: "Supreme Mistress of the world! Let me behold thy secret in the outstretched azure canopy of heaven."

321   It was inevitable that blue should be missing for Guillaume in the tetrad of rainbow colours, because of its feminine nature. But, like woman herself, the anima means the height and depth of a man. Without the blue vertical circle the golden mandala remains bodiless and two-dimensional, a mere abstraction. It is only the intervention of time and space here and now that makes reality. Wholeness is realized for a moment only—the moment that Faust was seeking all his life.

322   The poet in Guillaume must have had an inkling of the heretical truth when he gave the King a Queen sitting on a throne made of earth-brown crystal. For what is heaven without Mother Earth? And how can man reach fulfilment if the Queen does not intercede for his black soul? She understands the darkness, for she has taken her throne—the earth itself—to heaven with her, if only by the subtlest of suggestions. She adds the missing blue to the gold, red, and green, and thus completes the harmonious whole.

106. "Elixir of the moon."
—Codex Reginensis Latinus 1458
(17th cent.)

288

IV. THE SYMBOLS OF THE SELF

323   The vision of the "world clock" is neither the last nor the highest point in the development of the symbols of the objective psyche. But it brings to an end the first third of the material, consisting in all of some four hundred dreams and visions. This series is noteworthy because it gives an unusually complete description of a psychic fact that I had observed long before in many individual cases.[148] We have to thank not only the completeness of the objective material but the care and discernment of the dreamer for having placed us in a position to follow, step by step, the synthetic work of the unconscious. The troubled course of this synthesis would doubtless have been depicted in even greater completeness had I taken account of the 340 dreams interspersed among the 59 examined here. Unfortunately this was impossible, because the dreams touch to some extent on the intimacies of personal life and must therefore remain unpublished. So I had to confine myself to the impersonal material.

324   I hope I may have succeeded in throwing some light upon the development of the symbols of the self and in overcoming, partially at least, the serious difficulties inherent in all material drawn from actual experience. At the same time I am fully aware that the comparative material so necessary for a complete elucidation could have been greatly increased. But, so as not to burden the exposition unduly, I have exercised the greatest reserve in this respect. Consequently there is much that is only hinted at, though this should not be taken as a sign of superficiality. I believe myself to be in a position to offer ample evidence for my views, but I do not wish to give the impression that I imagine I have said anything final on this highly complicated subject. It is true that this is not the first time I have dealt with a series of spontaneous manifestations of the unconscious. I did so once before, in my book *Psychology of the Unconscious*,[149] but there it was more a problem of neurosis in puberty, whereas this is the broader problem of individuation.

148 Cf. my commentary on *The Secret of the Golden Flower*, pars. 31ff. Cf. also "Concerning Mandala Symbolism."
149 Revised edition: *Symbols of Transformation*.

107. Virgin carrying the Saviour.—"Speculum humanae saluacionis" (MS., Vatican, 15th cent.)

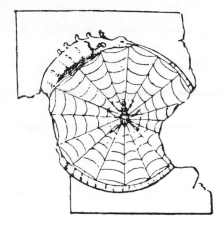

108. Maya, eternal weaver of the illusory world of the senses, encircled by the Uroboros.—Damaged vignette from a collection of Brahminic sayings

Moreover, there is a very considerable difference between the two personalities in question. The earlier case, which I never saw at first hand, ended in psychic catastrophe—a psychosis; but the present case shows a normal development such as I have often observed in highly intelligent persons.

325   What is particularly noteworthy here is the consistent development of the central symbol. We can hardly escape the feeling that the unconscious process moves spiral-wise round a centre, gradually getting closer, while the characteristics of the centre grow more and more distinct. Or perhaps we could put it the other way round and say that the centre—itself virtually unknowable—acts like a magnet on the disparate materials and processes of the unconscious and gradually captures them as in a crystal lattice. For this reason the centre is (in other cases) often pictured as a spider in its web (fig. 108), especially when the conscious attitude is still dominated by fear of unconscious processes. But if the process is allowed to take its course, as it was in our case, then the central symbol, constantly renewing itself, will steadily and consistently force its way through the apparent chaos of the personal psyche and its dramatic entanglements, just as the great Bernoulli's epitaph[150] says of the spiral: "Eadem mutata resurgo." Accordingly we often find spiral representations of the centre, as for instance the serpent coiled round the creative point, the egg.

326   Indeed, it seems as if all the personal entanglements and

150 In the cloisters of Basel Cathedral.

dramatic changes of fortune that make up the intensity of life were nothing but hesitations, timid shrinkings, almost like petty complications and meticulous excuses for not facing the finality of this strange and uncanny process of crystallization. Often one has the impression that the personal psyche is running round this central point like a shy animal, at once fascinated and frightened, always in flight, and yet steadily drawing nearer.

327   I trust I have given no cause for the misunderstanding that I know anything about the nature of the "centre"—for it is simply unknowable and can only be expressed symbolically through its own phenomenology, as is the case, incidentally, with every object of experience. Among the various characteristics of the centre the one that struck me from the beginning was the phenomenon of the quaternity (fig. 109). That it is not simply a question of, shall we say, the "four" points of the compass or something of that kind is proved by the fact that there is often a competition between four and three.[151] There is also, but more rarely, a competition between four and five, though five-rayed mandalas must be characterized as abnormal on account of their lack of symmetry.[152] It would seem, therefore, that there is normally a clear insistence on four, or as if there were a greater statistical probability of four. Now it is—as I can hardly refrain from remarking—a curious "sport of nature" that the chief chemical constituent of the physical organism is carbon, which is characterized by four valencies; also it is well known that the diamond is a carbon crystal. Carbon is black—coal, graphite—but the diamond is "purest water." To draw such an analogy would be a lamentable piece of intellectual bad taste were the phenomenon of four merely a poetic conceit on the part of the conscious mind and not a spontaneous product of the objective psyche. Even if we supposed that dreams could be influenced to any appreciable extent by auto-suggestion—in which case it would naturally be more a matter of their meaning than of their form—it would still have to be proved that the conscious mind of the dreamer had made a serious effort to impress the idea of the qua-

151 This was observed chiefly in men, but whether it was mere chance I am unable to say.
152 Observed mainly in women. But it occurs so rarely that it is impossible to draw any further conclusions.

109. The four evangelists with their symbols and the four rivers of paradise. Centre, the wheels of Ezekiel with the *spiritus vitae* that "was in the wheels" (Ezek. 1 : 21).—Miniature in an Evangeliary, Aschaffenburg (13th cent.)

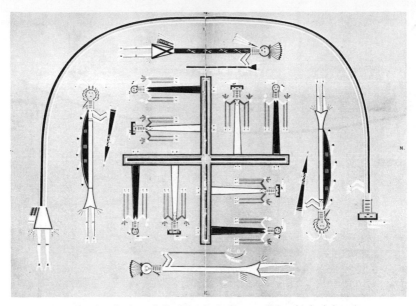

110. Sand-painting of the Navajo Indians.—Ethnological drawing

ternity on the unconscious. But in this case as in many other cases I have observed, such a possibility is absolutely out of the question, quite apart from the numerous historical and ethnological parallels[153] (fig. 110; cf. also figs. 50, 61–66, 82, 109). Surveying these facts as a whole, we come, at least in my opinion, to the inescapable conclusion that there is some psychic element present which expresses itself through the quaternity. No daring speculation or extravagant fancy is needed for this. If I have called the centre the "self," I did so after mature consideration and a careful appraisal of the empirical and historical data. A materialistic interpretation could easily maintain that the "centre" is "nothing but" the point at which the psyche ceases to be knowable because it there coalesces with the body. And a spiritualistic interpretation might retort that this "self" is nothing but "spirit," which animates both soul and body and irrupts into time and space at that creative point. I purposely refrain from all such physical and metaphysical speculations and content myself with establishing the empirical facts, and this seems to me infinitely more important for the advance of human knowledge

153 I have mentioned only a few of these parallels here.

than running after fashionable intellectual crazes or jumped-up "religious" creeds.

328   To the best of my experience we are dealing here with very important "nuclear processes" in the objective psyche—"images of the goal," as it were, which the psychic process, being goal-directed, apparently sets up of its own accord, without any external stimulus.[154] Externally, of course, there is always a certain condition of psychic need, a sort of hunger, but it seeks for familiar and favourite dishes and never imagines as its goal some outlandish food unknown to consciousness. The goal which beckons to this psychic need, the image which promises to heal, to make whole, is at first strange beyond all measure to the conscious mind, so that it can find entry only with the very greatest difficulty. Of course it is quite different for people who live in a time and environment when such images of the goal have dogmatic validity. These images are then *eo ipso* held up to consciousness, and the unconscious is thus shown its own secret reflection, in which it recognizes itself and so joins forces with the conscious mind.

329   As to the question of the origin of the mandala motif, from a superficial point of view it looks as if it had gradually come into being in the course of the dream-series. The fact is, however, that it only *appeared* more and more distinctly and in increasingly differentiated form; in reality it was always present and even occurred in the first dream—as the nymphs say later: "We were always there, only you did not notice us." It is therefore more probable that we are dealing with an *a priori* "type," an archetype which is inherent in the collective unconscious and thus beyond individual birth and death. The archetype is, so to speak, an "eternal" presence, and the only question is whether it is perceived by the conscious mind or not. I think we are forming a more probable hypothesis, and one that better explains the observed facts, if we assume that the increase in the clarity and frequency of the mandala motif is due to a more accurate perception of an already existing "type," rather

---

154 The image that presents itself in this material as a goal may also serve as the origin when viewed from the historical standpoint. By way of example I would cite the conception of paradise in the Old Testament, and especially the creation of Adam in the Slavonic Book of Enoch. Charles, *Apocrypha and Pseudepigrapha,* II, 425ff.; Förster, "Adams Erschaffung und Namengebung."

than that it is generated in the course of the dream-series.[155] The latter assumption is contradicted by the fact, for instance, that such fundamental ideas as the hat which epitomizes the personality, the encircling serpent, and the *perpetuum mobile* appear right at the beginning (first series: dream 1, par. 52, and vision 5, par. 62; second series: dream 9, par. 134).

330   If the motif of the mandala is an archetype it ought to be a collective phenomenon, i.e., theoretically it should appear in everyone. In practice, however, it is to be met with in distinct form in relatively few cases, though this does not prevent it from functioning as a concealed pole round which everything ultimately revolves. In the last analysis every life is the realization of a whole, that is, of a self, for which reason this realization can also be called "individuation." All life is bound to individual carriers who realize it, and it is simply inconceivable without them. But every carrier is charged with an individual destiny and destination, and the realization of these alone makes sense of life. True, the "sense" is often something that could just as well be called "nonsense," for there is a certain incommensurability between the mystery of existence and human understanding. "Sense" and "nonsense" are merely man-made labels which serve to give us a reasonably valid sense of direction.

331   As the historical parallels show, the symbolism of the mandala is not just a unique curiosity; we can well say that it is a regular occurrence. Were it not so there would be no comparative material, and it is precisely the possibility of comparing the mental products of all times from every quarter of the globe that shows us most clearly what immense importance the *consensus gentium* has always attached to the processes of the objective psyche. This is reason enough not to make light of them, and my medical experience has only confirmed this estimate. There are people, of course, who think it unscientific to take anything seriously; they do not want their intellectual play-

---

155 If we divide the four hundred dreams into eight groups of fifty each, we come to the following results:

I	.... 6 mandalas	V	.... 11 mandalas
II	.... 4 "	VI	.... 11 "
III	.... 2 "	VII	.... 11 "
IV	.... 9 "	VIII	.... 17 "

So a considerable increase in the occurrence of the mandala motif takes place in the course of the whole series.

ground disturbed by graver considerations. But the doctor who fails to take account of man's feelings for values commits a serious blunder, and if he tries to correct the mysterious and wellnigh inscrutable workings of nature with his so-called scientific attitude, he is merely putting his shallow sophistry in place of nature's healing processes. Let us take the wisdom of the old alchemists to heart: "Naturalissimum et perfectissimum opus est generare tale quale ipsum est." [156]

[156] "The most natural and perfect work is to generate its like."

111. The *cauda pavonis,* combination of all colours, symbolizing wholeness.—Boschius, *Symbolographia* (1702)

BIBLIOGRAPHY

A. VOLUMES CONTAINING COLLECTIONS OF ALCHEMICAL WORKS BY VARIOUS AUTHORS

ARS CHEMICA, quod sit licita recte exercentibus, probationes doctissimorum iurisconsultorum . . . Argentorati [Strasbourg], 1566.

Contents quoted in this volume:

ii   Tabula smaragdina [pp. 32–33]

ARTIS AURIFERAE quam chemiam vocant . . . Basileae [Basel], [1593]. 2 vols.

Contents quoted in this volume:

VOLUME I

  i   Turba philosophorum [two versions: pp. 1–64, 65–139]

vii   Maria Prophetissa: Practica . . . in artem alchemicam [pp. 319–24]

xii   Rosarium philosophorum [pp. 204–384; contains a second version of "Visio Arislei" at pp. 246ff.]

MANGETUS, JOANNES JACOBUS (ed.). *BIBLIOTHECA CHEMICA CURIOSA, seu Rerum ad alchemiam pertinentium thesaurus instructissimus* . . . Geneva, 1702. 2 vols.

Contents quoted in this volume:

VOLUME I

  ii   Hermes Trismegistus: Tractatus aureus de lapidis physici secreto [pp. 400–445]

iv   Allegoriae sapientum supra librum Turbae philosophorum XXIX distinctiones [pp. 467–79]

In hoc volumine DE ALCHEMIA continentur haec. Gebri Arabis . . . De investigatione perfectionis metallorum . . . Norimbergae [Nuremberg], 1541.

Contents quoted in this volume:

i   Rosarius minor [pp. 309–37]
ii Tabula smaragdina Hermetis Trismegisti [p. 363]
*MUSAEUM HERMETICUM reformatum et amplificatum . . .
continens tractatus chimicos XXI praestantissimos . . .* Franco-
furti [Frankfort], 1678. (For translation, see (B) WAITE, ARTHUR
EDWARD.) (Also an edn. of 1625. See fig. 240.)

Contents quoted in this volume:

xiv Philalethes: Introitus apertus . . . [pp. 647–700]
*THEATRUM CHEMICUM, praecipuos selectorum auctorum trac-
tatus . . . continens.* Ursellis [Ursel], 1602. 3 vols. (Vol. IV, Argentorati [Strasbourg], 1613; Vol. V, 1622; Vol. VI, 1661.)

Contents quoted in this volume:

VOLUME II

xi   Aegidius de Vadis: Dialogus inter naturam et filium philosophiae [pp. 95–123]
xxii Arnaldus de Villanova: Carmen [pp. 614–15]

VOLUME V

xxv Allegoriae sapientum . . . supra librum Turbae [pp. 64–
100]
xxvii Liber Platonis quartorum . . . [pp. 114–208]
xxviii Tractatus Aristotelis alchymistae ad Alexandrum Magnum de lapide philosophico [pp. 880–92]
xxix Epistola ad . . . Hermannum archiepiscopum Colonien-
sem de lapide philosophico [pp. 893–900]

B . GENERAL BIBLIOGRAPHY

AEGIDIUS DE VADIS. "Dialogus inter naturam. . . ." See (A) *Theatrum
chemicum*, xi.

ALLENDY, RENÉ FÉLIX. *Le Symbolisme des nombres*. Second edn.,
Paris, 1948.

APULEIUS, LUCIUS. *The Golden Ass. Being the Metamorphoses of
Lucius Apuleius*. With an English translation by W. Adlington.

ARISTOTLE, pseud. "Tractatus . . . alchymistae ad Alexandrum Magnum. . . ." See (A) *Theatrum chemicum*, xxviii.

ARNALDUS DE VILLANOVA. "Carmen." See (A) *Theatrum chemicum*, xxii.

ARNOBIUS. *Adversus gentes*. See MIGNE, *P.L.*, vol. 5, cols. 713–1290.

Aurea catena Homeri. Frankfort and Leipzig, 1723.

AVALON, ARTHUR (pseud. of Sir John George Woodroffe) (ed. and trans.). *The Serpent Power (Shat-cakra-nirūpana and Pādukāpanchaka)*. (Tantrik Texts.) London, 1919.

BACON, ROGER. *The Mirror of Alchimy . . . with Certaine Other Worthie Treatises of the Like Argument*. London, 1597.

BAYNES, CHARLOTTE AUGUSTA. *A Coptic Gnostic Treatise Contained in the Codex Brucianus—Bruce MS. 96, Bodleian Library, Oxford*. Cambridge, 1933.

BÉROALDE DE VERVILLE, FRANÇOIS (trans.). *Le Tableau des riches inventions couvertes du voile des feintes amoureuses, qui sont representees dans le Songe de Poliphile . . .* Paris, 1600. Contains the "Recueil stéganographique." For original, see COLONNA; for English paraphrase, see FIERZ-DAVID.

BERTHELOT, MARCELLIN. *Collection des anciens alchimistes grecs*. Paris, 1887–88. 3 vols.

———. *Les Origines de l'alchimie*. Paris, 1885.

BISCHOFF, ERICH (ed. and trans.). *Die Elemente der Kabbalah*. Berlin, 1913. 2 vols.

BÖHME, JAKOB. *De signatura rerum*. See "Schrifften"; for translation, see CLIFFORD BAX (ed.). *The Signature of All Things, with Other Writings by Jacob Boehme*. Translated by John Ellistone. (Everyman's Library.) London and New York, 1912.

———. *Gespräch einer erleuchteten und unerleuchteten Seele*. See "Schrifften." For translation, see BAX, as previous entry.

BONUS, PETRUS. *Pretiosa margarita novella de thesauro ac pretiosissimo philosophorum lapide . . .* Edited by Janus Lacinius. Venice, 1546. For translation see ARTHUR EDWARD WAITE (trans.). *The New Pearl of Great Price*. London, 1894. See also (A) *Bibliotheca chemica curiosa*, viii.

BOSCHIUS, JACOBUS. *Symbolographia, sive De arte symbolica sermones septem.* Augsburg, 1702.

BRUCHMANN, CARL FRIEDRICH HEINRICH (ed.). *Epitheta Deorum quae apud poetas Graecos leguntur.* (Ausführliches Lexikon der griechischen und römischen Mythologie. Supplement.) Leipzig, 1893.

BUDGE, SIR E. A. WALLIS (ed.). *The Book of the Dead. Facsimiles of the Papyri of Hunefer, Anhai, Kerasher* . . . London, 1899.

————. *The Gods of the Egyptians.* London, 1904. 2 vols.

CARTARI, VINCENZO. *Le imagini de i dei de gli antichi.* Lyons, 1581. For French translation, see: *Les Images des dieux des anciens.* [Translated and enlarged by Antoine du Verdier.] Lyons, 1581.

CHAMPOLLION, JEAN FRANÇOIS. *Panthéon égyptien.* Paris, 1823-35.

CHARLES, ROBERT HENRY (ed.). *The Apocrypha and Pseudepigrapha of the Old Testament in English.* Oxford, 1913. 2 vols.

Codices and Manuscripts.

vi   London. British Museum. MS. Additional 1316. Emblematical Figures in red chalk, of the process of the Philosophers' Stone, with Latin interpretations. 17th cent.

vii   ————. ————. MS. Additional 5025. Four rolls drawn in Lübeck. 1588. (The "Ripley Scrowle.")

xv   Milan. Biblioteca Ambrosiana. Codex I.

xvi   Modena. Biblioteca. Codex Estensis Latinus 209. "De Sphaera." 15th cent.

xxvii   ————. Bibliothèque nationale. Codex Latinus 511. "Speculum humanae salvationis." 14th cent.

xxxii   ————. ————. MS. Français 116. "Roman de Lancelot du Lac." 15th cent.

xxxviii   Rome. Biblioteca Angelica. Codex 1474. Alcadini. "De balneis Puteolanis." 14th cent.

xxxix   Tübingen. Universitätsbibliothek. MS. *c.* 1400.

xl   Vatican Biblioteca Vaticana. Codex Palatinus Latinus 412. Wynandi de Stega. "Adamas colluctancium aquilarum." 15th cent.

xl-a   ————. ————. Codex Palatinus Latinus 413. "Speculum humanae saluacionis." 15th cent.

xli ———. ———. Codex Palatinus Latinus 565. Peregrinus, "Speculum virginum seu Dialogus cum Theodora virgine." 13th cent.

xlii ———. ———. Codex Reginensis Latinus 1458. 17th cent.

xliii ———. ———. Codex Urbanus Latinus 365. Dante. "Inferno," "Purgatorio," "Paradiso." 15th cent.

xliv ———. ———. Codex Urbanus Latinus 899. 15th cent.

xlv ———. ———. Codex Vaticanus Latinus 681. Peter Lombard. "De sacramentis." 14th cent.

l Zwiefalten Abbey. Breviary no. 128. 12th cent. See also LÖFFLER.

DELACOTTE, JOSEPH. *Guillaume de Digulleville . . . Trois romans-poèmes du XIVe siècle.* Paris, 1932.

DELACROIX. See GOETHE.

DELATTE, LOUIS. *Textes latins et vieux français relatifs aux Cyranides.* (Bibliothèque de la faculté de philosophie et de lettres de l'Université de Liège, fasc. 93.) Liège and Paris, 1942.

DEUSSEN, PAUL. *Allgemeine Geschichte der Philosophie.* Leipzig, 1906. 2 vols.

DIETERICH, ALBRECHT. *Nekyia: Beiträge zur Erklärung der neuentdeckten Petrusapokalypse.* Leipzig and Berlin, 1913.

DREYFUSS, J. *Adam und Eva nach der Auffassung des Midrasch.* Strasbourg, 1894.

EISLER, ROBERT. *Orpheus—the Fisher.* London, 1921.

ELEAZAR, ABRAHAM. (Abraham le Juif). *Uraltes chymisches Werk,* Leipzig, 1760.

Enoch, Book of. See CHARLES, *Apocrypha and Pseudepigrapha,* II, pp. 163ff. For Slavonic Book of Enoch, see ibid., pp. 425ff.

Esdras, Second Book of. Included in Holy Bible, Apocrypha. See also CHARLES, *Apocrypha,* II, pp. 542–624, where it is called IV Ezra.

FICINO, MARSILIO. *Auctores Platonici.* Venice, 1497.

"Figurarum Aegyptiorum secretarum." See Codices and MSS., xiv, xxi, xxxiv.

FLAUBERT, GUSTAVE. *La Tentation de Saint Antoine.* Paris, 1874.

FLEISCHER, HEINRICH LIEBERECHT (ed.). *Hermes Trismegistus an die menschliche Seele.* Text in Arabic and German. Leipzig, 1870.

FLOURNOY, THÉODORE. "Automatisme téléologique antisuicide," *Archives de psychologie de la Suisse romande* (Geneva), VII (1908), 113–37.

———. *From India to the Planet Mars.* Translated by D. B. Vermilye. New York and London, 1900. (Orig.: *Des Indes à la Planète Mars; Étude sur un cas de somnambulisme avec glossolalie.* Paris and Geneva, 3rd edn., 1900.)

———. "Nouvelles observations sur un cas de somnambulisme avec glossolalie," *Archives de psychologie de la Suisse romande* (Geneva), I (1901, pub. 1902), 102–255.

FLUDD, ROBERT. . . . *summum bonum.* . . . Frankfort on the Main, 1629.

———. *Utriusque cosmi maioris scilicet et minoris metaphysica, physica atque technica historia.* Oppenheim, 1617.

FÖRSTER, MAX. "Adams Erschaffung und Namengebung. Ein lateinisches Fragment des s.g. slawischen Henoch," *Archiv für Religionswissenschaft* (Leipzig), XI (1908), 477–529.

FOUCART, PAUL FRANÇOIS. *Les Mystères d'Eleusis.* Paris, 1914.

FRANCK, ADOLPHE. *La Kabbale.* Paris, 1843. For German translation, see: *Die Kabbala* . . . Translated by Ad. Gelinek. Leipzig, 1844.

FREUD, SIGMUND. *The Psychopathology of Everyday Life.* Translated by A. A. Brill. New York and London, 1914.

FÜRST, EMMA. "Statistical Investigations on Word-Associations and on Familial Agreement in Reaction Type among Uneducated Persons." In JUNG, *Studies in Word-Association*, q.v. (Pp. 407–45.)

Geheime Figuren der Rosenkreuzer, aus dem 16ten und 17ten Jahrhundert. Altona, 1785–88. 2 vols.

GOETHE, JOHANN WOLFGANG VON. *Dichtung und Wahrheit.* See *Sämtliche Werke*, vols. 22–25. For translation, see: MINNA STEELE SMITH (trans.). *Poetry and Truth, from My Own Life.* London, 1908. 2 vols.

———. *Faust; A Tragedy.* In a modern translation by Alice Raphael. With plates after the lithographs of Eugène Delacroix. New York, 1939.

————. *Faust, Part Two.* Translated by Philip Wayne. (Penguin Classics.) Harmondsworth and Baltimore, 1959.

HAMMER-PURGSTALL, JOSEPH. *Mémoire sur deux coffrets gnostiques du moyen âge.* Paris, 1835.

HERMES TRISMEGISTUS. *An die menschliche Seele.* See FLEISCHER.

HERODOTUS. [*Histories.*] Translated by J. Enoch Powell. Oxford, 1949. 2 vols.

HERRAD OF LANDSBERG. *Hortus deliciarum.* See KELLER and STRAUB.

HERRLIBERGER, DAVID. *Heilige Ceremonien oder Religionsübungen der abgöttischen Völcker der Welt.* Zurich, 1748.

HONORIUS OF AUTUN. *Speculum de Mysteriis Ecclesiae.* See MIGNE, *P.L.*, vol. 172, cols. 313–1108.

[HORAPOLLO NILIACUS.] *Hori Apollinis Selecta hieroglyphica, sive Sacrae notae Aegyptiorum, et insculptae imagines.* Rome, 1597. For translation, see: GEORGE BOAS (trans. and ed.). *The Hieroglyphics of Horapollo.* (Bollingen Series XXIII.) New York, 1950.

IRENAEUS, SAINT. *Contra* [or *Adversus*] *haereses libri quinque.* See MIGNE, *P.G.*, vol. 7, cols. 433–1224. For translation, see JOHN KEBLE (trans.). *Five Books of S. Irenaeus . . . against Heresies.* Oxford, 1872.

JAMES, MONTAGUE RHODES (ed. and trans.). *The Apocryphal New Testament.* Oxford, 1924.

JUNG, CARL GUSTAV. *Aion. Collected Works,* 9, ii.

————. "The Archetypes of the Collective Unconscious." In *Collected Works,* 9, i.

————. "Basic Postulates of Analytical Psychology." In *Collected Works,* 8.

————. "Child Development and Education." In *Collected Works,* 17.

————. "Concerning Mandala Symbolism." In *Collected Works,* 9, i.

————. "Concerning Rebirth." In *Collected Works,* 9, i.

————. *Mysterium Coniunctionis. Collected Works,* 14.

————. "Paracelsus as a Spiritual Phenomenon." In *Collected Works,* 13.

————. "The Practical Use of Dream-Analysis." In *Collected Works,* 16.

————. *Psychological Types. Collected Works,* 6.

————. *Psychology and Alchemy. Collected Works,* 12.

————. "The Psychology of the Child Archetype." In *Collected Works,* 9, i.

————. "The Psychology of Dementia Praecox." In *Collected Works,* 3.

————. "Psychology and Religion." In *Collected Works,* 11.

————. "Psychology of the Transference." In *Collected Works,* 16.

————. "The Psychology of the Unconscious." In *Collected Works,* 7.

————. "The Relations between the Ego and the Unconscious." In *Collected Works,* 7.

————. "The Spirit Mercurius." In *Collected Works,* 13.

————. *Symbols of Transformation. Collected Works,* 5. (A translation of *Symbole der Wandlung,* Zurich, 1951. For the translation of the superseded version, *Wandlungen und Symbole der Libido,* see: *Psychology of the Unconscious.* Translated by Beatrice M. Hinkle. New York, 1916; London, 1917; new edn., 1921.)

————. "Transformation Symbolism in the Mass." In *Collected Works,* 11.

————. *Two Essays on Analytical Psychology. Collected Works,* 7.

————. "The Visions of Zosimos." In *Collected Works,* 13.

———— and KERÉNYI, C. *Essays on a Science of Mythology.* Translated by R.F.C. Hull. New York (Bollingen Series XXII), 1949; paperback edn., 1969. (British edn.: *Introduction to a Science of Mythology.* London, 1949.)

KANT, IMMANUEL. *Introduction to Logic.* Translated by Thomas Kingsmill Abbott. London, 1885.

KELLEY, EDWARD. *Tractatus duo egregii, de Lapide philosophorum.* Hamburg and Amsterdam, 1676.

KHUNRATH, HEINRICH CONRAD. *Von hylealischen, das ist, pri-materialischen catholischen, oder algemeinem natürlichen Chaos.* Magdeburg, 1597.

KNORR VON ROSENROTH, CHRISTIAN. *Kabbala denudata seu Doctrina Hebraeorum.* Sulzbach, 1677–84. 2 vols.

KNUCHEL, EDUARD FRITZ. *Die Umwandlung in Kult, Magie und Rechtsbrauch.* Basel, 1919.

KRANEFELDT, W. M. "Komplex und Mythos." In: C. G. JUNG and others, *Seelenprobleme der Gegenwart.* 4th edn., Zurich, 1950. (Orig., 1931.)

LACTANTIUS, FIRMIANUS. *Opera omnia.* Edited by Samuel Brandt and Georg Laubmann. (Corpus scriptorum ecclesiasticorum latinorum.) Vienna, 1890–97. 3 vols. For translation, see: WILLIAM FLETCHER (trans.). *The Works of Lactantius.* (Ante-Nicene Christian Library, 21–22.) Edinburgh, 1871. 2 vols.

LEISEGANG, HANS. *Die Gnosis.* Leipzig, 1924.

———. *Der heilige Geist.* Leipzig, 1919.

LÉVY-BRUHL, LUCIEN. *How Natives Think.* Translated by Lilian A. Clare. London, 1926. (Orig.: *Les Fonctions mentales dans les sociétés inférieures.* Paris, 1912.)

LIPPMANN, EDMUND O. VON. *Entstehung und Ausbreitung der Alchemie.* Berlin, 1919–54. 3 vols.

LÖFFLER, KARL. *Schwäbische Buchmalerei in romanischer Zeit.* Augsburg, 1928.

MAEDER, ALPHONSE. "Sur le mouvement psychanalytique: un point de vue nouveau en psychologie," *L'Année psychologique* (Paris), XVIII (1912), 389–418.

———. "Über die Funktion des Traumes," *Jahrbuch für psychoanalytische und psychopathologische Forschungen* (Leipzig and Vienna), IV (1912), 692–707.

———. *The Dream Problem.* Translated by Frank Mead Hallack and Smith Ely Jelliffe. (Nervous and Mental Disease Monograph Series, 20.) New York, 1916. (Orig.: "Über das Traumproblem," *Jahrbuch für psychoanalytische und psychopathologische Forschungen* (Leipzig and Vienna), V (1913), 647–86.)

MAIER, MICHAEL. *De circulo physico quadrato.* Oppenheim, 1616.

———. *Secretioris naturae secretorum scrutinium chymicum.* Frankfort on the Main, 1687. (Usually called *Scrutinium chymicum.*)

———. *Symbola aureae mensae duodecim nationum.* Frankfort on the Main, 1617.

———. *Viatorium, hoc est, De montibus planetarum septem seu metallorum.* Rouen, 1651.

MAIURI, AMEDEO. *La villa dei misteri.* Rome, 1931. 2 vols.

MANGET, JOANNES JACOBUS (ed.). *Bibliotheca chemica curiosa.* Geneva, 1702. 2 vols.

MASPERO, GASTON CAMILLE CHARLES. *Études de mythologie et d'archéologie égyptiennes.* Paris, 1893–1913. 7 vols.

MEIER, CARL ALFRED. *Antike Inkubation und moderne Psychotherapie.* Zurich, 1949.

MELITO OF SARDIS. *De baptismo.* See PITRA, *Analecta sacra,* II, pp. 3–5.

MICHELSPACHER, STEFFAN. *Cabala, speculum artis et naturae, in alchymia.* Augsburg, 1654.

MIGNE, JACQUES PAUL (ed.). *Patrologiae cursus completus.*
[*P.L.*] Latin series. Paris, 1844–64. 221 vols.
[*P.G.*] Greek series. Paris, 1857–66. 166 vols.
[These works are cited as "MIGNE, *P.L.*" and "MIGNE, *P.G.*" respectively. References are to columns, not to pages.]

MYLIUS, JOHANN DANIEL. *Philosophia reformata.* Frankfort on the Main, 1622.

ORIGEN. *Homiliae in Jeremiam.* See MIGNE, *P.G.,* vol. 13, cols. 255–544.

PARACELSUS (Theophrastus Bombast of Hohenheim). See: JOHANN HUSER (ed.). *Aureoli Philippi Theophrasti Bombasts von Hohenheim Paracelsi . . . Opera Bücher und Schrifften.* Strasbourg, 1589–91. 10 parts. Reprinted 1603, 1616. 2 vols. See also: KARL SUDHOFF and WILHELM MATTHIESSEN (ed.). *Theophrast von Hohenheim genannt Paracelsus Sämtliche Werke.* First section. *Medizinische Schriften.* Munich and Berlin, 1922–33, 14 vols.

PETRONIUS ARBITER. [*Works.*] With an English translation by Michael Heseltine. (Loeb Classical Library.) London and New York, 1913.

PETRUS LOMBARDUS (Peter Lombard). "De sacramentis." See Codices and MSS., xlv.

PHILALETHES, EIRENAEUS. *Ripley Reviv'd; or, An Exposition upon Sir George Ripley's Hermetico-Poetical Works.* London, 1678.

PICINELLI, PHILIPPUS. *Mundus symbolicus.* Cologne, 1680–81.

PITRA, JEAN BAPTISTE (ed.). *Analecta sacra* . . . Paris, 1876–91. 8 vols. (II, pp. 3–5, contains Melito of Sardis, *De baptismo.*)

PREISENDANZ, KARL (ed.). *Papyri Graecae magicae.* Leipzig and Berlin, 1928–31. 2 vols.

REITZENSTEIN, RICHARD. *Die hellenistischen Mysterienreligionen.* Leipzig, 1910.

———. *Poimandres: Studien zur griechisch-ägyptischen und frühchristlichen Literatur.* Leipzig, 1904.

REUSNER, HIERONYMUS. *Pandora: Das ist, die edelst Gab Gottes, oder der Werde und heilsame Stein der Weysen.* Basel, 1588.

REYMANN, LEONHARD. *Nativität-Kalender.* 1515. See STRAUSS.

RHENANUS, JOHANNES. *Solis e puteo emergentis sive dissertationis chymotechnicae libri tres.* Frankfort on the Main, 1613.

RHINE, J. B. *New Frontiers of the Mind.* New York and London, 1937.

Rosarium philosophorum. Secunda pars alchimiae de lapide philosophico vero modo praeparando. . . . Cum figuris rei perfectionem ostendentibus. (Vol. 2 of *De alchimia.*) Frankfort on the Main, 1550. See also *(A) Artis auriferae,* xii; *(A) Bibliotheca chemica curiosa,* ix.

RUSKA, JULIUS FERDINAND. *Tabula Smaragdina; ein Beitrag zur Geschichte der hermetischen Literatur.* Heidelberg, 1926.

———. *Turba Philosophorum: ein Beitrag zur Geschichte der Alchemie.* (Quellen und Studien zur Geschichte der Naturwissenschaften und der Medizin, 1.) Berlin, 1931.

"Sagesse des anciens, La." See Codices and MSS., xiii.

Saint-Graal. Edited by Eugène Hucher. Le Mans, 1878. 3 vols.

SALZER, ANSELM. *Die Sinnbilder und Beiworte Mariens in der deutschen Literatur und lateinischen Hymnen-Poesie des Mittelalters.* Linz, 1893.

SCHEDEL, HARTMANN, *Das Buch der Chroniken.* Nuremberg, 1493.

SCHMIDT, CARL (ed. and trans.). "Gnostische Schriften in koptischer Sprache aus dem Codex Brucianus herausgegeben," *Texte und Untersuchungen der altchristlichen Literatur* (Leipzig), VIII (1892), 1–692.

SENDIVOGIUS, MICHAEL (Michal Sendiwoj). "Dialogus Mercurii . . ." See (*A*) *Theatrum chemicum*, xxi.

SENIOR, ADOLPHUS. *Azoth, sive Aureliae occultae philosophorum . . .* Frankfort on the Main, 1613.

SILBERER, HERBERT. *Problems of Mysticism and Its Symbolism.* Translated by Smith Ely Jelliffe. New York, 1917.

———. "Über die Symbolbildung," *Jahrbuch für psychoanalytische und psychopathologische Forschungen* (Vienna and Leipzig), III (1911), 661–723; IV (1912), 607–83.

STEINSCHNEIDER, MORITZ. *Die europäischen Übersetzungen aus dem arabischen bis Mitte des 17. Jahrhunderts.* (Sitzungsberichte der kaiserlichen Akademie der Wissenschaften in Wien, Philosophisch-historische Klasse, 149, 151.) Vienna, 1904–5. 2 parts.

STOLCIUS DE STOLCENBERG, DANIEL. *Viridarium chymicum figuris cupro incisis adornatum et poeticis picturis illustratum . . .* Frankfort on the Main, 1624.

STRAUSS, HEINZ ARTUR. *Der astrologische Gedanke in der deutschen Vergangenheit.* Munich, 1926.

[SUDHOFF, KARL, ed.] *Historische Studien und Skizzen zur Natur- und Heilwissenschaft.* Memorial volume presented to Georg Sticker upon his seventieth birthday. Berlin, 1930.

"Tabula smaragdina" ("The Emerald Table of Hermes Trismegistus"). See (i) RUSKA; (ii) (*A*) *Ars chemica*, ii; (iii) (*A*) *De Alchemia*, ii; (iv) for translation, BACON, *The Mirror of Alchimy*, q.v.

THENAUD, JEAN. "Traité de la cabale." See Codices and MSS., xxiv.

THOMAS AQUINAS, pseud. "De alchimia." See Codices and MSS., v.

THURNEISSER ZUM THURN, LEONHART. *Quinta essentia, das ist die höchste Subtilitet, Krafft und Wirkung, beider der fürtrefflichen (und menschlichem Geschlecht den nutzlichsten) Künsten der Medicina, und Alchemia.* Leipzig, 1574.

TRISMOSIN, SALOMON. "Splendor solis." See Codices and MSS., x. See also: *Splendor solis: Alchemical Treatises of Solomon Trismosin.* With explanatory notes by J. K. London, 1920.

Upanishads. Translated by F. Max Müller. (Sacred Books of the East, 1, 15.) Oxford, 1879 and 1884. 2 vols.

VALLI, LUIGI. "Die Geheimsprache Dantes und der Fedeli d'Amore," *Europäische Revue* (Berlin), VI Jahrgang: 1 Halbband (January-June, 1930), 92–112.

VOLLERS, KARL. "Chidher," *Archiv für Religionswissenschaft* (Leipzig), XII (1909), 234–84.

VREESWYCK, GOOSEN VAN. *De Groene Leeuw.* Amsterdam, 1672.

WILHELM, RICHARD. *The Secret of the Golden Flower; a Chinese Book of Life.* Translated [into German] and explained . . . with a foreword and commentary by C. G. Jung. Translated into English by Cary F. Baynes. New and revised edn. London and New York, 1962.

WIRTH, ALBRECHT. *Aus orientalischen Chroniken.* Frankfort on the Main, 1894.

WOLFF, TONI. "Einführung in die Grundlagen der komplexen Psychologie." In: *Studien zu C. G. Jungs Psychologie.* Zurich, 1959. (Pp. 15–230.)

ZIMMER, HEINRICH. *Myths and Symbols in Indian Art and Civilization.* Edited by Joseph Campbell. (Bollingen Series VI.) New York, 1946.

Zwiefalten Abbey Breviary. See Codices and MSS., l. See also LÖFFLER.

INDEX

313

rope ladders, 267
rosa mystica, 260
Rosarium philosophorum, 152*f*&*nf*, 183,
    184*n*, 186, 192, 194*n*, 198*n*, 202, 222,
    233, 241*nf*, 243, 252*n*, 254*n*
Rosarius minor, 248*n*
rose(s), 150, 181, 246, 248*f*; Christ in,
    182*n*; garden of philosophers, 192,
    248
Rosicrucians, 150
"Rosie Crosse," 150
rota, see wheel
rotation/*rotatio*, 178, 198, 238*f*, 262,
    265*f*, 268, 284; see also *circulatio*;
    circumambulation
rotundum, 162; city as, 201*n*;
    head/skull as, 158*n*; production of,
    162; *see also* "round" motif
"round" motif, examples of:
    anima mundi, 158*n*, 162; circle,
    202; croquet ball, 189; gold, 158*n*,
    162; hat, 122; head, 161; Hermes,
    206; *lapis*, 202, 243; original man,
    158*n*; potter's wheel, 265; simple
    body, 243; soul, 157*f*; table, 249,
    251&*n*, 260; *vas*, 161, 202*n*;
    wholeness/self symbolized by, 189,
    191*n*, 265; see also *rotundum*
rubedo, see COLOURS
Rubicon, 194, 197*f*
running away, motif of, 123, 128, 188,
    217, 219*ff*, 228, 248, 263, 266
Ruska, J. G., 131*n*, 150*n*, 160, 227*n*;
    see also *Turba philosophorum*
rust, 233

S

Sabazius, 218
sacrifice: to the dead, 127*n*
sacrificium intellectus, 124
Saint Graal, 79*n*
salvation, 148, 153, 201, 228; *see also*
    redemption
Salzer, Anselm, 182*n*
satyr play, 155, 163, 205

savages, battle between, 248, 258
saviour, 259, 270*n*; *see also* redeemer
Scaiolae, 189
Schiller, J. F. C. von, 229
schizophrenia, 163
Schmidt, Carl, 234*n*
Schopenhauer, A., 189
sea, 122, 191, 262; symbol of
    (collective) unconscious, 122, 192,
    230, 262, 276
seasons, 206, 265, 280
secret, isolation by a, 123, 126, 128,
    163; of opus, 152; personal, 126
seed, golden, 256
self: Atman as, 181; attitude to, 256;
    borderline concept, 256; centre of
    personality, 115, 180, 279, 294;
    collective unconscious, 262; as
    conflict, 260; cosmic, 181; *Ding an
    sich*, 256; and ego, 115, 180, 191;
    entelechy of, 257; and integration,
    155, 270; as *lapis invisibilitatis*, 256;
    latent, 155*n*; mandala as, 255; as
    non-ego, 191; origin in instinct,
    194; as Pole, 262; quaternity of,
    292*ff*; realization of, 264, 296;
    roundness of, 189, 265; Son of Man,
    anticipation of, 282; as spirit, 296;
    as stranger's hat, 259; symbolized by
    Christ, 282; —garden with fountain,
    192; —El-Khidr, 192; —sun, 157;
    symbols of, 167, 262, 289*ff*; —of
    psyche, 115, 180, 256, 279;
    transcends consciousness, 256, 276;
    treasure hard to attain, 191*f*, 237;
    —of opposites, 260; as wholeness,
    189, 296
self-awareness, 56*f*, 61
self-fertilization, 235
self-realization, 268
self-redemption, 258
senarius, 236*n*
Sendivogius, Michael, 140*n*
Senior, Adolphus, *see* Adolphus
    Senior
Senior (Zadith), 233*n*
sense perception, *see* perception

THE COLLECTED WORKS OF

C. G. JUNG

THE PUBLICATION of the first complete edition, in English, of the works of C. G. Jung was undertaken by Routledge and Kegan Paul, Ltd., in England and by Bollingen Foundation in the United States. The American edition is number XX in Bollingen Series, which since 1967 has been published by Princeton University Press. The edition contains revised versions of works previously published, such as *Psychology of the Unconscious*, which is now entitled *Symbols of Transformation*; works originally written in English, such as *Psychology and Religion*; works not previously translated, such as *Aion*; and, in general, new translations of virtually all of Professor Jung's writings. Prior to his death, in 1961, the author supervised the textual revision, which in some cases is extensive. Sir Herbert Read (d. 1968), Dr. Michael Fordham, and Dr. Gerhard Adler compose the Editorial Committee; the translator is R. F. C. Hull (except for Volume 2) and William McGuire is executive editor.

The price of the volumes varies according to size; they are sold separately, and may also be obtained on standing order. Several of the volumes are extensively illustrated. Each volume contains an index and in most a bibliography; the final volume will contain a complete bibliography of Professor Jung's writings and a general index to the entire edition.

In the following list, dates of original publication are given in parentheses (of original composition, in brackets). Multiple dates indicate revisions.

* Published 1957; 2nd edn., 1970.

* Published 1960.   † Published 1961.
‡ Published 1956; 2nd edn., 1967. (65 plates, 43 text figures.)

* Published 1959; 2nd edn., 1968. (Part I: 79 plates, with 29 in colour.)

9. (*continued*)
   The Prophecies of Nostradamus
   The Historical Significance of the Fish
   The Ambivalence of the Fish Symbol
   The Fish in Alchemy
   The Alchemical Interpretation of the Fish
   Background to the Psychology of Christian Alchemical Symbolism
   Gnostic Symbols of the Self
   The Structure and Dynamics of the Self
   Conclusion

*10. CIVILIZATION IN TRANSITION
   The Role of the Unconscious (1918)
   Mind and Earth (1927/1931)
   Archaic Man (1931)
   The Spiritual Problem of Modern Man (1928/1931)
   The Love Problem of a Student (1928)
   Woman in Europe (1927)
   The Meaning of Psychology for Modern Man (1933/1934)
   The State of Psychotherapy Today (1934)
   Preface and Epilogue to "Essays on Contemporary Events" (1946)
   Wotan (1936)
   After the Catastrophe (1945)
   The Fight with the Shadow (1946)
   The Undiscovered Self (Present and Future) (1957)
   Flying Saucers: A Modern Myth (1958)
   A Psychological View of Conscience (1958)
   Good and Evil in Analytical Psychology (1959)
   Introduction to Wolff's "Studies in Jungian Psychology" (1959)
   The Swiss Line in the European Spectrum (1928)
   Reviews of Keyserling's "America Set Free" (1930) and "La Révo-
      lution Mondiale" (1934)
   The Complications of American Psychology (1930)
   The Dreamlike World of India (1939)
   What India Can Teach Us (1939)
   Appendix: Documents (1933–1938)

†11. PSYCHOLOGY AND RELIGION: WEST AND EAST
   WESTERN RELIGION
   Psychology and Religion (The Terry Lectures) (1938/1940)

* Published 1964; 2nd edn., 1970. (8 plates.)
† Published 1958; 2nd edn., 1969.

* Published 1953; 2nd edn., completely revised, 1968. (270 illustrations.)
† Published 1968. (50 plates, 4 text figures.)
‡ Published 1963; 2nd edn., 1970. (10 plates.)

* Published 1966.
† Published 1954; 2nd edn., revised and augmented, 1966. (13 illustrations.)
‡ Published 1954.

The Development of Personality (1934)
Marriage as a Psychological Relationship (1925)

18. MISCELLANY
Posthumous and Other Miscellaneous Works

19. BIBLIOGRAPHY AND INDEX
Complete Bibliography of C. G. Jung's Writings
General Index to the Collected Works

See also:

C. G. JUNG: LETTERS
Selected and edited by Gerhard Adler, in collaboration with Aniela Jaffé.
Translations from the German by R.F.C. Hull.
   VOL. 1: 1906–1950*
   VOL. 2: 1951–1961

*Published 1973. In the Princeton edition, the *Letters* constitute Bollingen Series XCV.

†THE FREUD/JUNG LETTERS
The Correspondence between Sigmund Freud and C. G. Jung
Translated by Ralph Manheim and R.F.C. Hull
Edited by William McGuire

†Published 1974. In the Princeton edition, *The Freud/Jung Letters* constitutes Bollingen Series XCIV.

Also available in Princeton/Bollingen Paperbacks

ON THE NATURE OF THE PSYCHE by C. G. Jung, trans. by R.F.C. Hull, Extracted from *The Structure and Dynamics of the Psyche*, Vol. 8, Collected Works (P/B #157)

The PSYCHOLOGY OF THE TRANSFERENCE by C. G. Jung, trans. by R.F.C. Hull, Extracted from *The Practice of Psychotherapy*, Vol. 16, Collected Works (P/B #158)

PSYCHOLOGY AND EDUCATION by C. G. Jung, trans. by R.F.C. Hull, Extracted from *The Development of Personality*, Vol. 17, Collected Works (P/B #159)

ESSAYS ON A SCIENCE OF MYTHOLOGY by C. G. Jung and C. Kerényi, trans. by R.F.C. Hull (P/B #180)

THE ORIGINS AND HISTORY OF CONSCIOUSNESS by Erich Neumann, trans. by R.F.C. Hull (P/B Paperback #204)

FOUR ARCHETYPES: MOTHER/REBIRTH/SPIRIT/TRICKSTER by C. G. Jung, trans. by R.F.C. Hull, Extracted from *The Archetypes and the Collective Unconscious*, Vol. 9, part I, Collected Works (P/B #215)

AMOR AND PSYCHE: THE PSYCHIC DEVELOPMENT OF THE FEMININE by Erich Neumann, trans. by Ralph Manheim (P/B #239)

ART AND THE CREATIVE UNCONSCIOUS by Erich Neumann, trans. by R.F.C. Hull (P/B #240)

COMPLEX/ARCHETYPE/SYMBOL IN THE PSYCHOLOGY OF C. G. JUNG by Jolande Jacobi, trans. by Ralph Manheim (P/B #241)

THE SPIRIT IN MAN, ART, AND LITERATURE by C. G. Jung, trans. by R.F.C. Hull, Vol. 15, Collected Works (P/B #252)

THE GREAT MOTHER by Erich Neumann, trans. by Ralph Manheim (P/B #265)

MANDALA SYMBOLISM by C. G. Jung, trans. by R.F.C. Hull, Extracted from *The Archetypes and the Collective Unconscious*, Vol. 9, part I, Collected Works (P/B #266)

TWO ESSAYS ON ANALYTICAL PSYCHOLOGY by C. G. Jung, trans. by R.F.C. Hull, Vol. 7, Collected Works (P/B #268)

ANSWER TO JOB by C. G. Jung, trans. by R.F.C. Hull, Extracted from *Psychology and Religion: West and East*, Vol. 11, Collected Works (P/B #283)

PSYCHOLOGICAL REFLECTIONS: A NEW ANTHOLOGY OF HIS WRITINGS, 1905–1961 by C. G. Jung, ed. by Jolande Jacobi and R.F.C. Hull (P/B #284)

PSYCHIC ENERGY: ITS SOURCE AND ITS TRANSFORMATION by M. Esther Harding (P/B #296)

SYNCHRONICITY: AN ACAUSAL CONNECTING PRINCIPLE by C. G. Jung, trans. by R.F.C. Hull, Extracted from *The Structure and Dynamics of the Psyche*, Vol. 8, Collected Works (P/B #297)

DREAMS by C. G. Jung, trans. by R.F.C. Hull, Extracted from *Freud and Psychoanalysis*, Vol. 4; *The Structure and Dynamics of the Psyche*, Vol. 8; *Psychology and Alchemy*, Vol. 12; and *The Practice of Psychotherapy*, Vol. 16; all in the Collected Works (P/B #298)

THE 'I' AND THE 'NOT-I': A STUDY IN THE DEVELOPMENT OF CONSCIOUSNESS by M. Esther Harding (P/B #307)

THE PSYCHOANALYTICAL YEARS by C. G. Jung, trans. by R.F.C. Hull and Leopold Stein, Extracted from *Experimental Researches*, Vol. 2; *Freud and Psychoanalysis*, Vol. 4; and *The Development of Personality*, Vol. 17; all in the Collected Works (P/B #314)

THE PSYCHOLOGY OF DEMENTIA PRAECOX by C. G. Jung, trans. by R.F.C. Hull, Extracted from *The Psychogenesis of Mental Disease*, Vol. 3 in the Collected Works (P/B #315)